WHOSE COMMON FUTURE?

Reclaiming the Commons

The Ecologist

EARTHSCAN

Earthscan Publications Ltd, London

First published 1993 by
Earthscan Publications Limited
120 Pentonville Road, London N1 9JN

British Library Cataloguing-in-Publication Data
A catalogue record for this book is available from the British Library

ISBN 1 85383 149 2

Typeset by Saxon Graphics Ltd, Derby

Printed by Clays Ltd, St Ives plc

Earthscan Publications Limited is an editorially independent subsidiary of Kogan Page Limited and publishes in association with the International Institute for Environment and Development and the World Wide Fund for Nature.

CONTENTS

PREFACE

In early June 1992, 3,500 diplomats and advisors, 700 UN officials, and 120 heads of states converged on Rio de Janeiro for a self-styled "Earth Summit", more correctly known as the United Nations Conference on Environment and Development or UNCED. For over a week, they debated and voted upon a package of measures ostensibly intended "to elaborate strategies and measures for promoting sustainable development and reversing environmental degradation". The meeting climaxed with the heads of state agreeing to a series of international agreements, including two "framework conventions" (one on climate and the other on biodiversity); an "Earth Charter", setting out "the principles of sustainable development"; and an "action programme" laying down an "Agenda for the 21st Century".

Few international gatherings have been so heavily hyped as UNCED. Gus Speth, president of the World Resources Institute, a leading US environmental consultancy group, pronounced it "a once-in-a-generation opportunity for the world community". The World Bank described it as "offering the world the chance to move beyond rhetoric to real action", whilst The Other Economic Summit (TOES) looked to UNCED "to open the way to a new era of sustainable development for the one-world human community of the 21st century". Others spoke of UNCED as "the first time ever that the heads of states of almost all the countries in the world have come together to discuss a common goal" and "a unique opportunity to show that the UN system can be pulled together to deal effectively with complex, interrelated transnational issues."

Rock stars and sports personalities were vocal in their enthusiasm for the process, as were politicians — even if, in the end, political circumstances ruled out their attending. Before the collapse of the Soviet Union and his removal from power, President Gorbachev, for example, extolled the Summit as evidence of "a readiness on the part of the world community in the person of its top repre- sentatives to construct life in the 21st century to new laws", whilst Pele, the Brazilian soccer star, was enlisted in the role of a "green ambassador", visiting some 35 countries in the run up to the conference to explain "why the Earth Summit will be so important, especially to the young". Anyone who was anyone in the envi- ronment and development industry was expected to "be there" — from the representatives of global corporations to the activists who oppose them — all supposedly united in a common goal of "protecting the future of planet earth and to secure for all inhab- itants a more sustainable and more equitable future".

But, as the limousines took the heads of state from their embassies to the massive conference centre on the outskirts of Rio, many of those going about their daily lives outside the conference hall — in effect, the many millions whose fate and livelihoods were under discussion — no doubt asked: what lies behind the razzamatazz? Were the world's political leaders attending the meeting out of a genuine concern for the "environment" or for "equity"? Or were the anonymous but high-ranking "representatives" of Gorbachev's "world community" simply repositioning themselves so as to minimize the changes that "constructing life in the 21st century" will inevitably entail? And if, as Maurice Strong, Secretary- General of UNCED, claimed, there was "a groundswell of support from the grassroots for the objectives of the Earth Summit", why were the issues which have been central to the work of grassroots groups — in particular the right of local communities to determine their own future — excluded from the agenda?

Such scepticism would have been well-placed. For the top- down, technocratic policies that have increasingly come to charac- terize the "greening" of development are depressingly similar to those that have characterized the development process from the moment the idea of "development" was born. Indeed, sustainable development — now the "buzzword" of environmentalists, politi- cians, business leaders and strategic planners alike — would appear to cloak an agenda that is just as destructive, just as undermining of peoples' rights and livelihoods as the development agenda of old. In 1990, *The Ecologist* embarked on a two year project to bring together some of the critiques that have emerged of the concept. *Whose Common Future?* is the result.

The report was not the product of any one person but rather arose out of the work of many: hence, its lack of named authors. Four of us — Simon Fairlie, Nicholas Hildyard, Larry Lohmann and Sarah Sexton — were directly responsible for the final text, with numerous others from many different organizations, South and North, contributing passages, comments, critiques, information and views. Through letters and meetings, scores of groups and individuals gave their input: their contributions were invaluable and, though too many to name, we would like to thank them all. Of those who were involved more directly throughout the two year project, we should like to thank in particular Tracey Clunies-Ross, Marcus Colchester, Patrick McCully and Pam Simmons.

We would also like to thank FINNIDA, NOVIB and HIVOS for generously supporting the project.

INTRODUCTION
The Earth Summit Débâcle

The United Nations Conference on Environment and Development, the self-styled Earth Summit, finished where it began. After ten days of press conferences, tree-planting ceremonies and behind-the-scenes wheeling and dealing, the diplomats went home to their various other assignments and the politicians to their next round of international talks. Rio gave way to the Munich conference and the more familiar territory of GATT, G-7 power politics and interest rates.

For the major players, the Summit was a phenomenal success. The World Bank emerged in control of an expanded Global Environmental Facility, a prize that it had worked for two years to achieve. The US got the biodiversity convention it sought simply by not signing the convention on offer. The corporate sector, which throughout the UNCED process enjoyed special access to the secretariat, was confirmed as the key actor in the "battle to save the planet". Free-market environmentalism — the philosophy that transnational corporations brought to Rio through the Business Council on Sustainable Development — has become the order of the day, uniting Southern and Northern leaders alike. For many environmental groups, too, the Summit was a success: credibility has been achieved (some even having seats on government delegations) and their concerns are no longer marginalized. They are now recognized as major players themselves.

The Summit, in fact, went according to plan: indeed the outcome was inevitable from the start. Unwilling to question the desirability of economic growth, the market economy or the development process itself, UNCED never had a chance of addressing the real problems of "environment and development". Its secretariat provided delegates with materials for a convention on biodiversity

1

but not on free trade; on forests but not on logging; on climate but not on automobiles. Agenda 21 — the Summit's "action plan" — featured clauses on "enabling the poor to achieve sustainable livelihoods" but none on enabling the rich to do so; a section on women but none on men. By such deliberate evasion of the central issues which economic expansion poses for human societies, UNCED condemned itself to irrelevance even before the first preparatory meeting got under way.

The best that can be said for the Earth Summit is that it made visible the vested interests standing in the way of the moral economies which local people, who daily face the consequences of environmental degradation, are seeking to re-establish. The spectacle of the great and the good at UNCED casting about for "solutions" that will keep their power and standards of living intact has confirmed the scepticism of those whose fate and livelihoods were being determined. The demands from many grassroots groups around the world are not for more "management" — a fashionable word at Rio — but for agrarian reform, local control over local resources, and power to veto developments and to run their own affairs. For them, the question is not *how* their environment should be managed — they have the experience of the past as their guide — but *who* will manage it and in *whose* interest. They reject UNCED's rhetoric of a world where all humanity is united by a common interest in survival, and in which conflicts of race, class, gender and culture are characterized as of secondary importance to humanity's supposedly common goal. Although they acknowledge that a peasant in Bihar shares the same planet as a corporate executive, they view the suggestion that the two share a common future as farcical. Instead, they ask, "Whose common future is to be sustained?" Their struggle is not to win greater power for the market or the state, but to reinstate their communities as sources of social and political authority. *Whose Common Future?* is an attempt to describe the background to that struggle.

1 THE COMMONS

Where the Community has Authority

To Western eyes, the streets and lanes of Bangkok, like those of many cities in the South, may seem a strange mixture of order and chaos. In the shadow of shining high-rise hotels, apartment and office blocks, slum dwellers squat in dark, seemingly random collections of shacks near railway lines, on construction sites, and over swamps. In front of rows of concrete shophouses and air-conditioned banks, carts and stalls selling noodles, dried squid, curries and iced drinks jostle for kerb-space with amulet-sellers, fruit-vendors and beggars. Souvenir merchants block pedestrian traffic by jamming their tables up against those of purveyors of cheap baby clothes, leather-goods, sweets and dubious track shoes. Streetcorner vendors show open contempt for the solemnities of intellectual property by loudly inviting passers by to invest in fake Rolex watches, pirated rock music cassettes and bogus Lacoste shirts. Under the eyes of bored policemen, pedestrians jaywalk across roads congested with roaring, grinding, smoke-belching trucks, buses and motorcycles.

The hints of anarchy in these scenes may trouble the Western mind. Who are all these people raising pigs and drying clothes next to the railroad tracks? Why don't the police do something about the jaywalkers, the hawkers and the polluting vehicles? What is the law here? *Is* there a law here? Why doesn't anybody seem to know what it is? A Westerner setting up a food stall on the kerb of a busy street might have an uneasy sense of encroaching on public space, enforced by a worry about bureaucrats and police. Not the Bangkok vendors! Like the slum dwellers, they seem ready to take all the space they can get. Of course, now and then the police clear them off. But this hardly seems to be out of a real concern for public order. More likely the World Bank or a foreign dignitary is arriving for a meeting and some high official, fearful of losing face, has sent

3

out an order to spruce up the streets. In any case, as soon as the police are gone the vendors trickle back. In a week things are back to normal.

A HIDDEN STRUCTURE

Longer acquaintance with Bangkok may shift the Westerner's view. Beneath the seeming vacuum of public order and responsibility, the outlines of a different kind of moral and environmental order begin to appear. It becomes clear that while public space may not always be respected, informal boundaries are well-marked within communities of people who know each other. In the slum or along the row of street vendors, anyone who takes up too much space, or the wrong space, or leaves too much of a mess, is brought back into line by neighbours. The community may not possess much space, and has little opportunity to make it clean and attractive, but it makes the most of what it has. And because no one group is powerful enough to usurp too much space for itself, everybody has a share.

External borders are defended as well. When the police undertake a sweep of sidewalk vendors, furious mutterings spread down the lines of stalls. "This is our turf! We've been here for years! What right do the authorities have to evict us?" Elsewhere, outrage may lead to more organized resistance. In an area of orchards nestled in a bend of the Chao Phraya River near the city centre, landowners and squatters join together to protest the proposed conversion of their land into a "public park", pointing out that they and their ancestors have kept the place green for over a century. In a slum, when lines of policemen step forward to begin dismantling squatters' homes, children rush forward to grasp their legs. Shaking them off, the police advance a few steps further only to come up against a phalanx of angry, taunting women, baring their breasts to shame them into retreat. Behind them, in reserve, wait the men of the community. People may recognize the city's law as a fact rather than as a social norm, and value customs more than contracts, but their sense of rights and justice is sharp.

The order people seek is seldom a public one. Few are overly concerned about obligations toward unseen strangers. Few set much store by anonymous and formal words typed or printed on headed paper, or on proclamations that this or that area is "public property". Rather, people try to establish personal, face-to-face connections. Strangers feel each other out to find out where they stand. Who is the most powerful person here? Who the most senior? Do I know any of their relatives? Where can I carve out a space for my family? How much can I enlarge it by cultivating the right people and making the right alliances? How much can my family and friends get away with before we offend our neighbours? As new acquaintances jockey for position on the pavements, in the alleys, in the communities and restaurants and meeting rooms, invisible grid-lines are drawn, connections made, and unspoken rules laid down. As relationships become established and power is balanced, interdependence grows and benevolence is exchanged for respect. Insiders are distinguished from outsiders, and consideration and love flourish among familiars. Indulgences quickly become rights which cannot be violated without denying the growing personal ties themselves. It is in these rights and ties, more than in the formal machinery of the law or an inculcated sense of "the public", that ordinary people, and even police and businesses, place their faith.

ORIGINS, CHANGE, REVIVAL

This order does not emerge from nowhere. It recreates in broken form a long tradition visible more clearly in the countryside: a tradition of the commons.[1] There, until recently, the category of "the public" barely existed. In day-to-day practice, it was above all the community which exercised dominion over time, space, agriculture and language. Woods and streams feeding local irrigation systems remained intact because anyone degrading them had to brave the wrath of neighbours deprived of their livelihood, and no one was powerful enough to do so. Everybody was subject to everybody else's personal scrutiny and sanctions.

Bangkok twists this tradition. Benefiting from the growth of the state and "economic development", élites have gained the power to usurp larger and larger domains of common space — streets, clean air, green space — without having to concern themselves with the reaction of others. Webs of personal relationships have been stretched or frayed, losing their anchorage to a particular locality, reducing people's ability to defend their space and make it liveable. People whose livelihoods have been taken away by this process fall into increasingly abject dependency on those who have taken it away. At the same time, new webs of personal relationships ramify across the upper levels of society. Dynastic, commercial and military alliances concentrate and reconcentrate power largely beyond the ability of ordinary people to place checks upon it.

In this sense, disorder in Bangkok originates less in the huddled shacks of the slums or the haphazard rows of street vendors than in the forces — partly foreign — that lie behind the modern public and private high-rise buildings, fast-food outlets and brightly-coloured billboards which look so reassuring and orderly to the Western visitor. Indeed, it is in *commons* such as those found in slums and on street vendors' turf that the order which can safeguard the interests of ordinary Bangkokians and their environment is largely found. When subsistence is at stake, they often improvise or reconstruct rough-and-ready new commons regimes rather than pin their hopes on either the market economy or public institutions. For better or worse, the commons is the social and political space where things get done and where people derive a sense of belonging and have an element of control over their lives. In Bangkok, as in many places throughout the South, when the commons is gone, there is little that can take its place.

AN EVERYDAY REALITY

The tale of Bangkok and its broken commons may seem remote from Western experience. For many people in the West, the word "commons" carries an archaic flavour: that of the medieval village pasture which villagers did not own but where they had rights to graze their livestock. Yet, for the vast majority of humanity, the commons is an everyday reality. Ninety per cent of the world's fishers rely on small inshore marine commons, catching over half the fish eaten in the world today.[2] In the Philippines, Java and Laos, irrigation systems are devised and run by villagers themselves, the water rights being distributed through rules laid down by the community.[3] Even in the North, there are communities which still manage their forests and fisheries jointly (lobster harvesters in Maine, for example, or forest communities in many areas of Finland), bestowing on themselves the power to divide up what they regard as "their" patches of sea or soil among their own communities and kin.[4] Moreover, new commons are constantly being born, even among what might seem the most fragmented communities. In the inner cities of the US, black communities' dialects express concepts that the language taught in state schools cannot touch. At toxic dump sites and around proposed nuclear plants in France, Switzerland, and elsewhere, people have insisted on their "rights" to keep the earth and air around their communities free from the threat of poisonous and radioactive substances, damning the economic and "public" rationality which dictates that their homes are "objectively" the best locations for waste sinks. For them, the sentiments expressed by an elder of a Brazilian tribe, despite the religious language in which they are couched, cannot be completely unrecognizable:

> "The only possible place for the Krenak people to live and to re-establish our existence, to speak to our Gods, to speak to our nature, to weave our lives, is where God created us. We can no longer see the planet that we live upon as if it were a chess-board where people just move things around."[5]

THE COMMONS: NEITHER PUBLIC NOR PRIVATE

Despite its ubiquity, the commons is hard to define. It provides sustenance, security and independence, yet (in what many Westerners feel to be a paradox) typically does not produce commodities. Unlike most things in modern industrial society, moreover, it is neither private nor public: neither commercial farm nor communist collective, neither business firm nor state utility, neither jealously-guarded private plot nor national or city park. Nor is it usually open to all. The relevant local community typically decides who uses it and how.[6]

The unlimited diversity of commons also makes the concept elusive. While all commons regimes involve joint use, what they define access to is bewilderingly varied: for example, trees, forests, land, minerals, water, fish, animals, language, time, radio wavelengths, silence, seeds, milk, contraception and streets.

Trying to find some order in this field, some theorists claim that the commons are "resources for which exclusion is difficult" and boundary-setting not worthwhile, or which "are needed by all but whose productivity is diffuse rather than concentrated, low or unpredictable in yield, and low in unit value": for example, seasonally inundated swamplands in Borneo, moorland in England, semi-arid rangeland in Botswana or Ethiopia, and scrubby *maquis* or *garrigues* in France and Spain.[7] Yet smaller, more easily divisible, and more highly productive and defensible arable lands are often also treated as communal property. In traditional Malaysia and Laos as well as Ethiopia and much of the rest of contemporary Africa, plots have been traditionally allocated to individuals by the community, which nevertheless reserve the authority to redistribute them if they are not used for subsistence. In such cases of usufruct, common rights can be defined as the right not to the land or the soil, which rests with the community, but the right to what the soil brings forth over a particular period.

Other theorists suggest that the commons are jointly-used resources whose use by one person may subtract from the welfare of the next, and which are thus potentially subject to crowding, depletion and degradation. Yet while this may be true of a great range of cases, genetic diversity or knowledge of contraception (to cite just two examples of "resources" often maintained by commons regimes) are not "subtractible" in this way.

SOCIAL ORGANIZATION IS THE KEY

More fruitful than such attempts to define commons regimes through their domains are attempts to define them through their social and cultural organization: for example, local or group power, distinctions between members and non-members, rough parity among members, a concern with common safety rather than accumulation, and an absence of the constraints which lead to economic scarcity. Even here, however, it would be a mistake to demand too much precision. For example, what does the "local" in "local power" mean? In Shanxi province in China, communal forests were owned by villages, several villages together, or clans. In India the relevant bodies may be caste groups, while for Switzerland's city forests, it is "citizenship" (election to a given community) that counts.[8]

Similarly, what does the "power" in "local power" consist in? Sometimes it is the power to exclude outsiders or to punish them if they abuse the commons. Often this power lays the foundation for an additional structure of internal rules, rights, duties and beliefs which mediates and shapes the community's own relationship with its natural surroundings. In Maine, for example, it is only in strongly defended territories that lobster harvesters have successfully enacted informal and formal regulations on the numbers of traps used, and elsewhere in North America there have been clear "post-fur-trade linkages between the existence of viable hunting territories and intentional conservation measures."[9] Sometimes the meshes of power internal to commons regimes give rise to notions of "property" or "possession", but in many cases the relevant group does not regard itself as owning, but rather as owned by, or as stewards of, water or land.

PERCEPTIONS OF SCARCITY

A further characteristic often ascribed to the commons is that, unlike resources in the modern economy, it is "not perceived as scarce". This is not only because many things available as commons, such as silence, air or genetic diversity, will renew themselves continually until deliberately made scarce by the encroachment of outside political actors. More importantly, the needs which many commons satisfy are not infinitely expanding. They are not determined by a growth-oriented external system producing goods and services, but rather are constantly adjusted and limited by the specific commons regime itself, whose physical characteristics remain in everyone's view. Without the race between growth and the scarcity which growth creates, there can thus be a sense of "enoughness". Even where produce from the commons is sold, the "needs" defined by consumerism and external market demand for goods and services will be subject to internal revision.

THE WORLDLY COMMONS

Despite their resolutely local orientation and resistance to being swallowed up by larger systems, commons regimes have never been isolated in either space or time. Nor have their social organizations ever been static. Commons regimes welcome, feed upon and are fertilized by contact, and evolve just like any other social institution.[10] Communities maintaining commons often work out arrangements over larger geographical areas with other groups. For example, inter-village commons boundaries are acknowledged by villagers in the Munglori area of Tehri Garhwal: each village has a recognized "turf" and encroachment by other villages for fodder-collection is likely to provoke objections.[11] In the Philippines, competing claims to water rights among different *zanjaras*, or communal irrigation societies, have customarily been decided by inter-village councils composed of *zanjara* officers and family elders in the community.[12]

Systems of common rights, in fact, far from evolving in isolation, often owe their very existence to interaction and struggle between communities and the outside world. It is arguably only in reaction to invasion, dispossession or other threats to accustomed security of access that the concept of common rights emerges.

10

Today, such rights are evolving where access to seeds, air and other resources which were previously taken for granted are being challenged through commoditization, legal enclosure or pollution.

Existing commons regimes, too, vary continuously with changes in their natural or social environment. Property-rights systems can shift back and forth in long, short or even seasonal cycles from communal to private and back again, depending on struggles among prospective beneficiaries, ecological change, and shifts in social relationships. For example, common-field systems are instituted in some new or revived villages in Ethiopia to attract labour and people; where this succeeds the tenure system may be switched to one based on inheritance. Later on, villages may revive communal tenure.[13]

DEFINING ONESELF

Each commons regime may be as different culturally from the next as all are from, say, a factory. But it is not only their cultural diversity that makes such regimes difficult to "capture" in technical or universal terms. Ivan Illich makes this point when he says that the "law establishing the commons was unwritten, not only because people did not care to write it down, but because what it protected was a reality much too complex to fit into paragraphs."[14] This is somewhat inexact; commons rules are sometimes written down; and where they are not, this is not so much because what they protect is complex as because the commons requires an open-endedness, receptiveness and adaptability to the vagaries of local climate, personalities, consciousness, crafts and materials which written records cannot fully express. But Illich's point is important. What makes the commons work, like the skills of wheelwrights, surgeons or machinists, cannot easily be encoded in written or other fixed or "replicable" forms useful to cultural outsiders. These forms can make some of the workings of commons regimes "visible" to moderns but have generally functioned to transfer local power outside the community.

In this and other respects, the concept of the commons flies in the face of the modern wisdom that each spot on the globe consists merely of coordinates on a global grid laid out by state and market: a uniform field which determines everyone's and everything's rights and roles. "Commons" implies the right of local people to define their own grid, their own forms of community respect for watercourses, meadows or paths; to resolve conflicts their own way; to translate what enters their ken into the personal terms of their own dialect; to be "biased" against the "rights" of outsiders to local "resources" in ways usually unrecognized in modern laws; to treat their home not simply as a location housing transferrable goods and chunks of population but as irreplaceable and even to be defended at all costs.

NO FREE-FOR-ALL

For many years, governments, international planning agencies (and many conservationists) have viewed commons regimes with deep hostility. Nothing enrages the World Bank more, for example, than the "Not-In-My-Back-Yard" or "NIMBY" mentality which so many communities display in defending their commons against dams, toxic waste dumps, polluting factories and the like.[15] Many UNCED delegates and conservationists, similarly, view local control over land, forests, streams and rivers as a recipe for environmental destruction. The only way to secure the environment, they say, is to put a fence around it, police it and give it economic value through development.

In defence of such views, development agencies have played upon two related confusions. The first, promulgated most famously in the 1960s by Garrett Hardin and others, is the myth of the "tragedy of the commons". According to Hardin, any commons (the example he used was a hypothetical rangeland) "remorselessly generates tragedy" since the individual gain to each user from overusing the commons will always outweigh the individual losses he or she has to bear due to its resulting degradation.[16] As

12

many critics have pointed out, however, and as Hardin himself later acknowledged, what he is describing is not a commons regime, in which authority over the use of forests, water and land rests with a community, but rather an *open access* regime, in which authority rests nowhere; in which there is no property at all; in which production for an external market takes social precedence over subsistence; in which production is not limited by considerations of long-term local abundance; in which people "do not seem to talk to one another";[17] and in which profit for harvesters is the only operating social value.

TENDING THE COMMONS

The difference is critical. Far from being a "free-for-all", use of the commons is closely regulated through communal rules and practices.

In Canada, for example, the peoples of the Wabigoon Lake Ojibway Nation of Ontario still harvest wild rice as a commons, despite efforts by the state government to impose modern management methods. The rice grows in Rice Lake and until the 1950s was harvested entirely by hand from canoes, but recently machine harvesting has also been introduced. Both machine harvests and canoe harvests are regulated through community meetings in which harvesting rights are allocated. Depending on the will of the meeting, certain areas (generally those which have been recently seeded or which are more remote) may be set aside for machine harvesters, or else machines are allowed to enter into certain areas for a limited period "only after the customary canoe harvesters have been allowed to exercise their rights to the extent decided upon at the community meeting."[18] Violations of harvest allocations by machine harvesters are dealt with at community meetings: a recent case resulted in one machine harvester being denied harvest rights for the rest of one season. For each canoe harvest area, the community agrees upon a "field boss" whose responsibilities are to regulate the harvest cycle according to custom, and to arbitrate in any disputes. Where harvesting rules are breached, the offender may be "grounded", one person in a recent harvest being told to "relearn the Indian way by sitting on the shore and watching."[19]

Amongst the Barabaig, a semi-nomadic pastoralist group in Tanzania, rights of use and access to land are variously invested in the community, the clan and individual households. As Charles Lane explains, "the Barabaig recognize that, to make efficient use of resources, access to grazing needs to be controlled to prevent exploitation beyond the capacity to recover. Although surface water is universally accessible to everyone, its use is controlled by rules . . . water sources must not be diverted or contaminated . . . A well becomes the property of the clan of the man who digs it. Although anyone may draw water for domestic purposes from any well, only clan members may water their stock there."[20] Whether land is privately or collectively owned, there are rules ensuring that the use made of it is not detrimental to the community as a whole, while certain species of tree are regarded as sacred for the same reason. Disputes, which are rare, are resolved by a public assembly of all adult males, though sometimes in the case of a particularly difficult issue a special committee is formed. There is a parallel council of women, who also have property rights over land and animals, and occasionally may be the head of a family. Women have jurisdiction in matters concerning offences by men against women and in matters concerning spiritual life. Lane describes how recently a women's council upbraided the men for ploughing sacred land. At a regional level, a similar council oversees the movement of herds and people to ensure that there is no overgrazing.

A third example comes from Torbel in Switzerland, a village of some 600 people, where grazing lands, forests, "waste" lands, irrigation systems and paths and roads connecting privately and communally-owned property are all managed as commons. Rights to these commons are not open to all but are conferred by existing commoners who have the power to decide whether or not an outsider should be admitted as "citizens" in the community. Under a regulation which dates back to 1517, which applies to many other Swiss mountain villages, no one can send more cows to the communal grazing area than they can feed during the winter, a rule that is still enforced with a system of fines. As Elinor Ostrom reports, "This and other forms of 'cow rights' are relatively easy to monitor and enforce. The cows are all sent to the mountain to be cared for by the herdsmen. They must be counted immediately, as the number of cows each family sends is the basis for determining the amount of cheese the family will receive at the annual distribution."[21] Once again, the commons are administered by a council, in this case consisting of all local cattle-owners. Besides grazing rights, it assigns timber for construction and fuel, arranges the distribution of manure, and is responsible for the upkeep of fences, huts and so on.

THE TRAGEDY OF ENCLOSURE

A second confusion that muddies the debate over the commons is between environmental degradation which can be attributed to commons regimes themselves and that which typically results from their breakdown at the hands of more global regimes. As many authors have pointed out, "tragedies of the commons" generally turn out on closer examination to be "tragedies of enclosure".[22] Once they have taken over land, enclosers, unlike families with ties and commitments to the soil, can mine, log, degrade and abandon their holdings, and then sell them on the global market without suffering any personal losses. It is generally enclosers rather than commoners who benefit from bringing ruin to the commons.

In the mid-North region of Brazil, for example, poverty has sometimes been blamed on dependence on babaçu palm in secondary forest, but can be more accurately attributed to the displacement of the babaçu commons by commercial forces. The palm has long been revered by local forest dwellers as a "tree of life" and was used to furnish leaves for shelter, husks for fuel and fodder for animals.[23] Following a period of open access when the region was first colonized, common property rights to the palms were established informally, and many peasants depend partly on sales of babaçu products harvested from trees growing on agri-cultural land. When large-scale investors moved into the area to produce sugar, alcohol and cellulose, much land previously cov-ered with babaçu stands was cleared. Ranchers have also cleared large areas for pasture. Peasants who gather babaçu fruits from this pastureland are castigated as trespassers and blamed for "starting wild fires, cutting fences and leaving behind fragments of fruit husks that can cause injury to the hooves of cattle," justifying further cuttings which lead to deeper impoverishment.

COMMONS REGIMES AND THEIR NATURAL SURROUNDINGS

None of this is to suggest that all commons regimes are always capable of preventing degradation of forests, fisheries or land indefinitely. But as Martin Khor of Third World Network puts it, "local control, while not necessarily sufficient for environmental protection, is necessary, while under state control the environment necessarily suffers."[24]

One reason why local control is essential is that, as Richard O'Connor has argued, "the environment itself is local; nature diversifies to make niches, enmeshing each locale in its own intricate web. Insofar as this holds, enduring human adaptations must also ultimately be quite local."[25] Biological diversity, for example, is related to the degree to which one locale is distinct from the next in its topography and natural and human history. It is best preserved by societies which nourish those local differences — in which the traditions and natural history of each area interact to create distinctive systems of cultivation and water and forest use.

This local orientation is displayed par excellence in small commons regimes. As Elinor Ostrom notes:

"Small-scale communities are more likely to have the formal

conditions required for successful and enduring collective management of the commons. Among these are the visibility of common resources and behaviour toward them; feedback on the effects of regulations; widespread understanding and acceptance of the rules and their rationales; the values expressed in these rules (that is, equitable treatment of all and protection of the environment); and the backing of values by socialization, standards, and strict enforcement."[26]

A second reason why local control is important is that where people rely directly on their natural surroundings for their livelihood, they develop an intimate knowledge of those surroundings which informs their actions. The Barabaig, for example, fully understand that if cattle were to be kept permanently on pastures near local water sources, the land would quickly become degraded. "As herds of livestock are brought to the river margins every day, whatever the season, they know that the forage there is needed by those who are watering their stock. If others are allowed to permanently graze it, this forage would soon be depleted and not available to those who go there to draw water. This would ultimately result in destruction of the land through over-grazing and damage from concentration of hoof traffic. The Barabaig, therefore, have a customary rule that bans settlement at the river margins and denies herders the right to graze the forage if they are not there to water their stock."[27]

Similarly, the many diverse systems of agriculture evolved by peasant farmers around the world have not evolved randomly but reflect a "thorough understanding of the elements and interactions between vegetations and soils, animals and climate."[28] They are both dynamic and innovative, evolving out of a continuing dialogue with the land. Because each technique used is evaluated above all for its long-term local impact, the lore which governs commons regimes, unlike modern science, tends not to split itself into rigid disciplines which pretend to have application in all circumstances. Instead, it tends to focus on a "set of restraints which [help] conserve the social and physical environment for generations."[29] Indeed, the notion that present generations are merely stewards who hold the land of the ancestors in trust for future generations is one held by many local communities, particularly in the South.

That notion is not simply an ideal but, where commons regimes still hold sway, informs and influences day-to-day behaviour. Some commons, for example, are totally protected against even subsistence harvesting: for example, the *iiri* groves of the Mbeere of East Africa, where even fallen timber could not be gathered. In Nigeria around Yoruba villages, and around Akha villages in Yunnan, Burma and Thailand, traditional rings of thick forest used for defence, where cultivation was not permitted, were also sites of shrines to village deities. In the Himalayas, too, it is through a mix of religion, folklore and tradition that peasants draw a "protective ring around the forests";[30] and in British Columbia, conscious management and ceremonial life alike "dictated periods of abstention from fishing so that adequate escapement of salmon to their spawning grounds up the rivers and to other upriver groups was ensured."[31]

CHECKS AND BALANCES

The remarkable success of local commons in safeguarding their environments is well documented. A detailed study of Japanese common land (*iriaichi*) by M. A. McKean, for example, was unable to find a single example of a "commons that suffered ecological destruction while it was still a commons."[32] In Pakistan, even the official National Report to UNCED ranks traditionally-managed *shamilaat* communal forests as more effective in environmental protection than forests owned and managed by the state.[33]

But that success depends on more than local knowledge of the environment, respect for nature or indigenous technologies. The extent to which sanctions against environmental degradation are observed depends greatly on the extent to which members of a community rely on their natural surroundings for their long-term livelihood and thus have a direct interest in protecting it. Once that direct interest is removed — once members of the community look outside the commons for their sustenance and social standing —

the cultural checks and balances that limit potential abuses of the environment are rendered increasingly ineffective. The authority of commons regimes declines.

In that respect, the key to the success of commons regimes lies in the limits that its culture of shared responsibilities place upon the power of any one group or individual. The equality which generally prevails in the commons, for example, does not grow out of any ideal or romantic preconceived notion of *communitas* any more than out of allegiance to the modern notion that people have "equal rights". Rather, it emerges as a by-product of the inability of a small community's élite to eliminate entirely the bargaining-power of any one of its members, the limited amount of goods any one group can make away with under the others' gaze, and the calculated jockeying for position of many individuals who know each other and share an interest both in minimizing their own risks and in not letting any one of their number become too powerful. In contemporary Laos, for example:

> "relations among the villagers may seem strikingly egalitarian, but this is not due to explicit ideology . . . For the Lao, no one's survival should be put at risk by someone else in the community: instability could endanger the survival of the entire village. In a natural economy barely providing sustenance, everyone knows this primary rule, so no one pushes. Older families can sometimes gain influence in a village, but only if the villagers see it as enhancing their chance of survival. Clientage of this sort does not last for long since the environment is not stable. Influence eventually disappears as a family's branches fade, move elsewhere, or experience bad weather . . . No one is in charge — although sometimes there is a village elder who helps make decisions, and who must work just as hard as everyone else . . . Everyone works hard, eats adequately, and gets along well together."[34]

Where everyone has some degree of bargaining power, no one is likely to starve while others are comfortable. As in Indonesian or medieval European village society, any hardship must be shared. (This helps to explain why exclusion from the group is still regarded as tantamount to a death sentence in many societies in which the commons plays a central role.) In many such societies, commoditization of food is often perceived as a threat, since it takes power over subsistence out of the hands of the less well-off.

Changes in the power base of a local élite or increases in effective community size entailed by integration into a global social fabric can rapidly undermine the authority of the commons. The sense of shame or transgression so important to community controls, as well as the monitoring of violations themselves, is diluted or denatured by increase in numbers, while envy of outsiders unconstrained by those controls flourishes. At some point, "the breakdown of a community with the associated collapse in concepts of joint ownership and responsibility can set the path for the degradation of common resources in spite of abundance."[35]

It is precisely this process that development fuels. The expansion of modern state, international and market institutions entails a shrinking space for the commons. Today, virtually all "human communities are encapsulated within or fully integrated into larger sociopolitical systems" as are their "local systems of resource use and property rights",[36] making enclosure an ever-present threat. As political, social and ecological boundaries are erased, control is centralized or privatized, skills are made obsolete, people put at the service of industry or made redundant, and land is commercialized or placed under management. As their environments are destroyed or degraded, their power eroded or denied, and their communities threatened, millions are now demanding a halt to the development process. As the social activist Gustavo Esteva writes, "if you live in Rio or Mexico City, you need to be very rich or very stupid not to notice that development stinks . . . We need to say 'no' to development, to all and every form of development. And that is precisely what the social majorities — for whom development was always a threat — are asking for."[37] For them, the struggle is to reclaim, defend or create their commons and with it the rough sense of equity that flows from sharing a truly common future.

2 DEVELOPMENT AS ENCLOSURE

The Establishment of the Global Economy

The creation of empires and states, business conglomerates and civic dictatorships — whether in pre-colonial times or in the modern era — has only been possible through dismantling the commons and harnessing the fragments, deprived of their old significance, to build up new economic and social patterns that are responsive to the interests of a dominant minority. The modern nation state has been built only by stripping power and control from commons regimes and creating structures of governance from which the great mass of humanity (particularly women) are excluded. Likewise, the market economy has expanded primarily by enabling state and commercial interests to gain control of territory that has traditionally been used and cherished by others, and by transforming that territory— together with the people themselves — into expendable "resources" for exploitation. By enclosing forests, the state and private enterprise have torn them out of fabrics of peasant subsistence; by providing local leaders with an outside power base, unaccountable to local people, they have undermined village checks and balances; by stimulating demand for cash goods, they have impelled villagers to seek an ever wider range of things to sell. Such a policy was as determinedly pursued by the courts of Aztec Mexico, the feudal lords of West Africa, by the factory-owners of Lancashire and the British Raj, as it is today by the International Monetary Fund or the Coca-Cola Corporation.

Only in this way has it been possible to convert peasants into labour for a global economy, replace traditional with modern agriculture, and free up the commons for the industrial economy. Similarly, only by atomizing tasks and separating workers from the moral authority, crafts and natural surroundings created by their communities has it been possible to transform them into modern, universal individuals susceptible to "management". In short, only by *deliberately* taking apart local cultures and reassembling them in new forms, has it been possible to open them up to global trade.[1] As one advocate of development argued in the early 1960s:

> "Economic development of an underdeveloped people by themselves is not compatible with the maintenance of their traditional customs and mores. A break with the latter is prerequisite to economic progress. What is needed is a revolution in the totality of social, cultural and religious institutions and habits, and thus in their psychological attitude, their philosophy and way of life. What is, therefore, required amounts in reality to social disorganization. Unhappiness and discontentment in the sense of wanting more than is obtainable at any moment is to be generated. The suffering and dislocation that may be caused in the process may be objectionable, but it appears to be the price that has to be paid for economic development: the condition of economic progress."[2]

To achieve that "condition of economic progress", millions have been thrown onto the human scrapheap as a calculated act of policy, their commons dismantled and degraded, their cultures denigrated and devalued and their own worth reduced to their value as labour. Seen from this perspective, the processes that now go under the rubric of "nation-building", "economic growth" and "progress" are first and foremost processes of expropriation, exclusion, denial and dispossession. In a word, of enclosure.

ENCLOSURE IN BRITAIN

They hang the man and flog the woman
That steal the goose from off the common,
But let the greater villain loose
That steals the common from the goose.
(Traditional Rhyme)

Although enclosure of commons has taken place at many isolated moments throughout world history, it was in Britain between the 15th and the 19th centuries that the phenomenon became identifiable as a historical process. It is no coincidence that the country which gave birth to the expression "inclosure", should also be the country that spearheaded the drive towards an industrialized market economy, for the one was essential to the other.

Enclosure in Britain can be distinguished from earlier forms of expropriation and enclosure in that it did not merely involve a transfer of power from the commons to an expropriating élite, but also signalled a more profound change in the social order in two related respects. Firstly, enclosure, by redefining land as "property", gave it the status of a commodity, tradeable within a rapidly expanding market system; and as a corollary, since the majority of people were denied access to the land and forced to become wage-labourers, labour also became a tradeable commodity. Secondly, enclosure in Britain has consistently been justified by its perpetrators and apologists as "improvement". The first legal act to enforce enclosures, the Statute of Merton of 1235, spoke of the need to "approve" (ie., improve) the land in order to extract greater rent.[3] "Improvement" was seen as linked, if not completely synonymous, with profit in the same way that the later term "development" has come to be associated with "economic growth".

The system of "open-field" — unfenced and communally managed strips of arable land — that predominated in England throughout the Middle Ages had several advantages for the peasantry as well as disadvantages. Most importantly, it guaranteed access to the land for the bulk of the population. Although the poorer villagers were obliged to work for stipulated periods on the local Lord's land, for the rest of the time they were free to work their own plots. At the time of the *Domesday Book* census in 1086, more than half the arable land belonged to the villagers. This unfenced land was worked with varying degrees of collectivization, which allowed a certain elasticity both to the size of peasants' holdings and to the level of their labour contribution, as the size of their families changed over the years. After the harvest, the arable land became a collective pasture for villagers' stock and remained fallow during the following year. The greater part of the land consisted of meadow, heath, moorland or woodland, all of which were managed communally, and where peasants held many rights, such as *estovers* (fuelwood), *turbary* (peat cutting) and *pannage* (turning pigs into the woods).

However, the system was not easily adaptable to change. There was no place in it for the ambitious farmer who wished to specialize in breeding sheep, or who in later centuries wished to apply more complex rotations including crops such as turnips or clover. But after the Black Death plague of 1348, which wiped out over a third of the population, the scarcity of labour and the abundance of land prompted a change in land-tenure from the bottom levels of society upward, whereby individual holdings existed alongside the open-field system, while the common pastures and woodlands remained substantially intact.

The rate of change, however, was not fast or lucrative enough for ambitious landowners who found that they could extract more value from the land by turning it over to sheep to supply the booming wool export market. Between the 14th and the 16th centuries, thousands of peasants were evicted from their holdings, while many more saw the common lands that were the basis of their independence fenced off for sheep. Other commoners found that their small plots of arable land were harder to maintain when deprived of the common pasture for cattle and were forced to sell up.

While newer tenants could be summarily evicted, those with traditional rights had recourse to the law. But the courts were invariably biased against the poor, as Bishop Latimer in 1552, testified:

> "Be the poor man's cause never so manifest, the rich shall, for money, find six or seven counsellors that shall stand with subtleties and sophisms to cloak an evil matter and hide a known truth . . . Such boldness have these covetous cormorants that now their robberies, extortion and oppression have no end or limits, no banks can keep in their violence. As for turning the poor out of their holdings, they take it for no offence, but say their land is their own and they turn them out of their shrouds like mice. Thousands in England, through such, beg now from door to door which have kept honest houses."[4]

By Latimer's day, enclosure was seen to be causing a severe law-and-order problem. It had created a dispossessed proletariat of potential wage-earners, without providing any industry to employ them. Recurrent peasant revolts and the menacing presence of large bands of beggars upon the highways persuaded the 16th century Tudor monarchs to apply legal brakes to the enclosure process, which they did with partial success.

However, the English revolution of 1649–1660 brought to power the very class of landowners that benefited from enclosure and the process recommenced in earnest. "Early in the 18th century there begins the great series of Private Acts of Enclosure, of which 4,000 in all, covering some 7,000,000 acres were passed before the General Enclosure Act of 1845. During the same period it is probable that about the same area was enclosed without application to Parliament."[5] By 1876, the "New Domesday Book" calculated that about 2,250 people owned half the agricultural land in England and Wales, and that 0.6 per cent of the population owned 98.5 per cent of it.[6]

Of these 4,000 Acts of Enclosure, two-thirds involved open fields belonging to cottagers, while one-third involved commons such as woodland and heath. Initially the impetus for enclosure was the still expanding sheep industry. But by the 19th century, as cotton began to be imported, the relative importance of wool declined, although the sheep industry continued to expand to poorer lands in Scotland, where many thousands of peasants were evicted from their homes by the most brutal means and either left to fend for themselves, or else transported to America.[7] In England, newer agricultural methods and more complex crop rotations, which had been developed anonymously over the previous two centuries, were now being vigorously championed by men such as "Turnip" Townshend and Arthur Young; ambitious landlords found that by enclosing and amalgamating several farms and applying these methods they could raise the rents of their lands by phenomenal amounts. The government was happy to sanction this process, since it could derive increased taxes from these higher rents, much of which went towards the costs of war against France, which in turn benefited the farmers by raising the price of food.

But although the farming methods looked good on paper, there were a number of "externalities" that the improvers had failed to anticipate, as Arthur Young in his later life came to acknowledge.[8] The environmental effects, though by no means as severe as those caused by the chemical agriculture of today, were nonetheless considerable. Valuable ancient meadows were ploughed up to take short-term advantage of artificially high corn prices, and then, when prices dropped, allowed to relapse to degraded pasture,[9] and large amounts of heathland and forest were destroyed.[10] Forest land was regarded by the new breed of agriculturalists as "the nest and conservatory of sloth, idleness and misery" and many forests such as Enfield Chase in 1777, Windsor Forest in 1817 and Hainault Forest in 1851 were destroyed by parliamentary Acts of Enclosure.[11]

But the principal "externality" was the creation of a massive proletariat of dispossessed labourers, who could no longer feed themselves, nor afford to pay the high price of corn associated with the high land rents. This, as William Cobbett observed, was an effect that the advocates of enclosure had preferred to ignore:

> "Those who are so eager for new inclosure seem to argue as if the wasteland in its present state produced nothing at all. But is this the fact? Can anyone point out a single inch of it which does not produce something and the produce of which is made use of? It goes to the feeding of sheep, of cows, of cattle of all descriptions, and . . . it helps to rear, in health and vigour, numerous families of the children of the labourers, which children, were it not for these wastes, must be crammed into the stinking suburbs of towns amidst filth of all sorts, and congregating together in the practice of every species of idleness and vice."[12]

The responsibility for the upkeep of dispossessed commoners fell upon taxpayers and for a time was a considerable drain upon the economy. The eventual solution proved to lie in further liberalization of trade at home and intervention abroad. The repeal of the Corn Laws in 1846 allowed free importation of cheap American wheat, while the enforced destruction of local textile industries in India and other colonies (*see* Box: King Cotton) provided work for the dispossessed multitudes at home. By 1900, British agriculture, despite the "improvements" of the previous century, was in a state of decline, whereas the industrial workers were beginning to share the rewards of development. This rise in the standard of living has been taken by apologists as a vindication of enclosure, which, even

King Cotton and the Enclosure of Markets

The enclosure of diverse local industries and markets into a single global system was achieved largely through the medium of a handful of luxury commodities — in particular gold, sugar, tea, cotton and opium. Of these, cotton had perhaps the most far-reaching effects.

The growth of the British cotton industry was phenomenal. Before the invention of Arkwright's spinning frame in 1769, cotton was a luxury material imported in small quantities to Europe from the Orient. By 1912, Britain was importing nearly 900,000 tons of raw cotton, and exporting nearly seven billion yards of woven material each year — almost enough to provide a suit of clothes for every man, woman and child alive in the world at the time. The absurdity of shipping such a staggering quantity of material from all over the world to one island and then shipping it all out again was of no concern to the protagonists of an economic system whose only priority was profit.

The rise to dominance of cotton as a textile in the early 19th century was not due to any inherent superiority of the fibre as a textile, but to two characteristics which made it competitive in a global market. Firstly, being "a plant fibre, tough and relatively homogenous . . . where wool is organic, fickle and subtly varied in its behaviour", it adapted more readily to mechanization and the factory system. This made it more attractive to industrialists who found the disciplining of a reluctant workforce considerably easier in the centralized factory environment than in a system where outworkers worked under their own speed at home. Secondly, it grew in the tropics, where labour was cheap and land for the taking. The importation of cotton spared land in England for food production, and labour to work in the new factories.

Enclosure of Land

The repercussions of the cotton trade were catastrophic and affected people of almost every hue and clime. In the US, about 90,000 Cherokee Indians were evicted from their lands to make way for cotton plantations, 30,000 of them dying on the march west. The period 1784–1860 saw an eightfold increase in the number of slaves in the Southern states, specifically for the cotton planta-tions, an increase which came to a climax in the most bloody conflict of the 19th century, the American Civil War.

In Egypt, the ruler Mehemet Ali:

> "initiated in the 1820s a program to decrease the production of grain for domestic subsistence and to increase production of the one crop that could be exported, long staple cotton . . . Peasants were also drafted in large numbers to build irrigation works and canals in order to create the hydraulic infrastructure required for cotton cultivation . . . Between 1818 and 1844, the land in the hands of the peasantry diminished from 85–90 per cent of the total land area to 56 per cent . . . In 1882, the British took over Egypt. They reinforced the pattern of cotton growing on large estates, thus laying the basis for the problems that were to plague Egypt in the 20th century".

The process has continued into modern times. Under Ethiopia's Third Five-Year Plan, 60 per cent of the lands brought under cultivation in the fertile Awash Valley were devoted to cotton production. The local Afar pastoralists were evicted from their traditional pastures and pushed into fragile uplands, contributing to the deforestation that has been partly responsible for Ethiopia's ecological crisis.

The Enclosure of Markets

It was not only the cultivation of cotton that destroyed communities, but also the marketing of the finished product. In England, handloom weavers were put out of business, and driven to find work in the factories, where the conditions were appalling. The Irish linen industry was progressively forced out of existence after the manufacture of lawn and cambric was prohibited there in 1767. In India, the British set about the deliberate destruction of the indigenous industry. By building up its own network of cotton and cloth dealers, the British-owned East India Company was able to exert coercive control over India's handloom weavers, who rapidly lost their independence as producers and in many instances became waged workers employed on terms and conditions over which they had no control. Over 10,000 Bengali weavers were obliged by the terms of their contract to work entirely for the Company. When the East India Company's monopoly was abolished in 1813, the Indian weaving industry was too debilitated to resist the flooding of the market with inferior products from the Lancashire mills. India found the cash to pay for this imported cloth partly by growing opium to be sold to China as a means of breaking down its closed markets, a trade which resulted in the Opium Wars of the second half of the 19th century.

By the end of the century, India was taking nearly half of Britain's cotton exports, even though it was now producing cotton cloth itself in factories based around Bombay. Most of the rest went to other colonies where much the same inroads had been made into local markets. In 1886 the British consul of Lourenço Marques (Maputo) reported that native weaving and indigenous textile skills had completely disappeared from the area. Within the space of less than a hundred years, the Lancashire cotton industry had consigned to extinction countless native textile industries, whose techniques and designs had evolved over centuries.

In the early 20th century, Mahatma Gandhi organized a boycott of British-made cloth and championed the spinning wheel as a means of reviving the local economy. In public meetings he "would ask the people to take off their foreign clothing and put it on a heap. When all the hats, coats, shirts, trousers, underwear, socks and shoes had been heaped high, Gandhi set a match to them". After Gandhi's death his influence persisted in the large numbers of *khadi* workshops producing handspun material, although the Indian government under Nehru and Indira Gandhi pursued a policy of increasing centralization and industrialization. The *charkha*, the spinning wheel, remains upon the Indian flag as a reminder of the traditional industries and markets that were consumed by the cotton industry.

though it "made some terrible mistakes", "blazed a trail for the whole world."[13] In reality, the social and environmental "externalities" of enclosure were simply transferred to the colonies —

the process of enclosure went on to blaze its trail *across* the whole world. It gave added impetus to the process of expropriation that was already underway in some areas of the South and extended the process to others.

THE COLONIAL PERIOD

The European colonial powers perceived their "mission" as one of overt transformation, their primary objectives being: to secure new sources of raw materials for their expanding economies; to exploit the peoples of the colonies for cheap labour; to provide living space for Europe's "surplus population" — in effect, those who had been dispossessed of their lands and livelihoods by the encroachment of market capitalism; and to create markets for European (and later North American) goods by denying markets to local artisans and by forcing local people into the colonial market economy.

In the long term, this last objective was to prove to be the most important, because control of an expanding market became critical for the survival of capitalism. As one French official wrote of the colonization of North Africa:

> "Apart from the civilizing mission she is pursuing in her colonies, France has created a colonial empire to develop her external commerce. Indeed, we only occupied the region of Niger to Chad to find an outlet for our products and a source of raw materials for our industry."[14]

Britain's colonial motives were made equally plain by Cecil Rhodes, the "founder" of Rhodesia:

> "We must find new lands from which we can easily obtain raw materials and at the same time exploit the cheap slave labour that is available from the natives of the colonies. The colonies would also provide a dumping ground for the surplus goods produced in our factories."[15]

DISPOSSESSION

But in order to create an international constituency of eager consumers, the colonialists first had to build up a labour force with access to cash — and to achieve this they first had to commandeer land. This they did by dispossessing indigenous communities of the greater part of their traditional territories: in effect, by enclosing the commons. Throughout the colonies, it became standard practice to declare all "uncultivated" land to be the property of the colonial administration. At a stroke, local communities were denied legal title to lands they had traditionally set aside as fallow and to the forests, grazing lands and streams they relied upon for hunting, gathering, fishing and herding.

Where, as was frequently the case, the colonial authorities found that the lands they sought to exploit were already "cultivated", the problem was remedied by restricting the indigenous population to tracts of low quality land deemed unsuitable for European settlement. In Kenya, such "reserves" were "structured to allow the Europeans, who accounted for less than one per cent of the population, to have full access to the agriculturally rich uplands that constituted 20 per cent of the country."[16] In Southern Rhodesia, white colonists, who constituted just five per cent of the population, became the new owners of two-thirds of the land.[17] In Northern Rhodesia, the policy of reserving the best land for European agriculture was explicit, the 1932 *Agricultural Survey Commission* stating:

> "Any land that had poor soils, inadequate water supplies, low nutrition grasses unsuitable for European cattle or [was] overgrown with impenetrable bush, was not suitable for Europeans and should be allocated to Africans."[18]

Once secured, the commons appropriated by the colonial administration were typically leased out to commercial concerns for plantations, mining and logging, or sold to white settlers. In India, the British designated vast tracts of forest as "reserve forests". The rights of access which villagers had traditionally enjoyed were curtailed and large areas were logged to supply timber for shipbuilding and sleepers for the expanding railway system. In French Equatorial Africa, the granting of commercial concessions proceeded at such a pace that by 1899, 70 per cent of the country had been leased to just 40 such companies, with one company receiving 140,000 square kilometres.[19]

Afforded little protection under the law, local peoples found themselves liable to eviction even from the "cultivated" land that was, in theory, theirs. Boer settlers in South Africa regularly drove local farmers off their tribal lands on the grounds that the "natives were merely subsistence farmers and deserved to be treated as squatters since they were not engaged in any systematic forms of agriculture."[20] Even where "reserves" had been set up, the indigenous population were without legal security of tenure. In Kenya, the Crown Lands Ordinance of 1915, which supposedly "guaranteed" tribal land rights, made explicit provisions for any part of a reserve to be cancelled if it were decided that the land was "needed" for railroads and highways or any public purpose.[21]

Not content with dispossessing the indigenous population of vast areas of land, the colonial authorities also sought to break up communal systems of tenure and to substitute private ownership. In the Philippines, Malaysia, India and parts of Africa, land laws were passed actively encouraging individuals to register their plots as private holdings. In North Africa, the French deliberately set about breaking up the collectively owned lands of local nomadic herders by decreeing in 1873 that families would not enjoy any land rights under French law unless they established and registered their own individual holdings. Under the new law, "individualization" of the entire group holding was mandatory if any one individual in the group desired registration, regardless of the wishes of the other collective owners. The new laws were exploited by both French colonists and indigenous urban élites to acquire large tracts of the best land, the number of French landholdings in Algeria alone doubling between 1870 and 1890.[22]

FORCED LABOUR

If dispossession was the favoured means of securing land for the colonial economy, finding labour presented a more intractable problem. Where elements of the commons remained, local peoples were still largely self-reliant and had little incentive to grow crops for export to London, Paris or Amsterdam, nor any incentive to indulge in backbreaking labour down mines, on plantations or building roads and government offices. As an editorial in the *Rabaul Times* noted of New Guinea in the mid-1930s:

> "One of the greatest contributing factors to the unsatisfactory services rendered by native labourers in this country is their economic independence. For it must not be forgotten that every native is a landed proprietor, and nature has endowed New Guinea with a prolific soil, which provides adequate sustenance for a minimum of labour. Dismissal from employment, if he fails to carry out his duties, holds no terrors for the New Guinean native ... Unless and until our natives reach such a stage of development that they must work to obtain sustenance or a livelihood, they will never make suitable indentured labour for the average white resident."[23]

Typically, in the early years of colonial rule, indigenous labour could only be recruited by force. Throughout the Americas, for example, the violent subjugation of the Indians was integral to the imposition of the export-orientated economy that the Spanish colonists required. Resistance to enforced assimilation has been continuous. In Guatemala alone there has been an average of one Indian rebellion every sixteen years since the Conquest in 1524.[24]

In West Africa, the French and British also responded to labour shortages by imposing forced labour, even though both powers were nominally committed to the abolition of slavery. The colonial mind "resolved" this potential moral dilemma by "declaring slavery to be uncivilized and forced labour to be a necessary way of instructing primitive people about the advantages of modernity."[25] The French Minister of Commerce stated in 1901:

> "The black does not like work and is totally unaccustomed to the idea of saving; he does not realise that idleness keeps him in a state of absolute economic inferiority. It is therefore necessary to use ... slavery to improve his circumstances and afterwards lead him into an apprenticeship of freedom."[26]

In Senegal alone, the corvée provided an estimated five million person-days of free labour every year in the early 1920s. Even in the 1930s, nine-tenths of the public work in French West Africa was undertaken through corvée labour, until it was finally abolished in 1946.[27] The conditions were so bad that, according to one observer, "the Society for the Prevention of Cruelty to Animals would have prosecuted me if I had given a dog the same quantity and quality of food and shelter."[28] The death toll in some work gangs was as high as 60 per cent.[29]

TAXED INTO THE MARKET

But the colonial "mission" went beyond simply the expropriation of land and the coercion of local people into the labour force. Central to colonial enterprise was the drive to build up a cash economy and, with it, a market for goods from the industrial North. To achieve that task, the colonial authorities set about the systematic dismantling of those elements of the commons that stood in the way of market penetration. To that end, widespread use was made of such economic instruments as taxation, a strategy that not only introduced the need to earn cash but which also (by requiring village elders to collect it) undermined the balance of power that is central to the maintenance of the commons.[30]

Taxes were levied on whatever the colonial authorities deemed most vital to villagers. In Vietnam, a poll-tax was imposed, followed by a tax on salt, opium and alcohol, with a minimum consumption level being set for each region and village leaders rewarded for exceeding the quota.[31] In the Sudan, crops, animals, houses and households were singled out for taxation.[32] To meet their tax obligations, rural people throughout the colonies had little option but to sell their labour or to grow crops for sale. In French colonial West Africa, punishments for "tax evasion" included "holding women and children hostage until the dues had been paid, burning huts, whipping and tying up people and leaving them without food for several days."[33]

Similarly, a combination of force and taxation was used to destroy indigenous craft industries, particularly textiles, and to harness traditional trading patterns to the needs and interests of Western Europe. In South Asia, elaborate regional trading patterns, developed over at least two millennia, were ruthlessly commandeered as the Portuguese, Spanish, Dutch and British carved out their own areas of control through military force and, subsequently, by imposing a system of monopolies. Thousands of native traders and seafarers, deprived of their livelihoods, resisted by turning to piracy, giving the imperial powers an excuse for further intervention.[34] In French West Africa, the authorities deliberately set out to dismantle traditional inter-regional trading patterns by imposing, in 1905, special levies on all goods which did not come from France or a region under French control, thus forcing up the price of local products, to the ruin of local artisans and traders. Within five years, nearly half of the goods imported into France's West African colonies came from France.

In the Sudan, the British used similar tactics.

"Along the middle reaches of the Rahad River, for example, peasants preferred the cloth produced by their traditional methods from cotton they grew themselves to the more expensive Manchester cloth. As a result, the British banned private cotton cultivation in Blue Nile Province (and others nearby) and when the peasants persisted by moving their cotton plants inside their fenced compounds, the police searched them out and burned them. In either case, the result was the substitution of a regular cash need for a key indigenous handicraft industry."[35] (*See* Box: King Cotton)

NEW ELITES

Stripped of much of their land, reduced to labouring for another's benefit and increasingly dependent on world markets, local peoples throughout the colonies found themselves caught up in political and social changes that divided their communities and imposed new structures of oppression on society at large.

Critically, the colonial system of administration undermined the moral authority of commons regimes by co-opting traditional leadership of the communities it sought to control. Local leaders slowly became distanced from their fellow villagers with each colonial edict they enforced, and gradually transferred their allegiance to the colonial regime. In the Dutch East Indies, for example, village leaders were made responsible for ensuring that "their" villages produced specific quotas of crops under the so-called "Culture System."[36] Increasingly regarded "as a source of governmental oppression rather than as a source of village solidarity and protection,"[37] village leaders inevitably came to rely on the colonial regime to legitimize their authority. In turn, the villagers — reduced to mere "administered producers"[38] — found their own power eroded as consensus gave way to dictat in decision making.

Likewise, the checks and balances that had helped to curtail the abuse of power and privilege in many pre-colonial societies were eaten away by the encroachment of the market economy and the imposition of European systems of jurisprudence and land tenure. In India, for example, the introduction of British contract law profoundly altered the traditional relationship between moneylenders and their clients, stripping villagers of the protection they had customarily enjoyed against dispossession through indebtedness. Before the arrival of the British the power of the moneylender was circumscribed:

> "The money-lender could assure himself a portion of the harvest, but could not seize the debtor's land or contest hereditary rights to his land. The village would not allow the transfer of land to outsiders, and according to Hindu law, the debt could not build up to more than twice the original principal. With the coming of British tax law and land policy, however, mortgaging became possible and with that, a shift in favour of the money-lender in cases of flagrant insolvency on the part of the debtor. Protection of the village community and customary law largely ceased, since the lender could bring action in a British court. The latter, basing its judgement on the common law of contracts, would protect him. In contrast to Indian law, the entire property of the debtor could be seized in service of the debt. Without the protection of the village, moreover, the peasants were often swindled. They signed contracts containing obligations they had not agreed to; false bookkeeping entries were attested to as correct; and oral agreements were no longer, as formerly, valid . . . Because the local money-lender was very often the local merchant as well, he could easily collect his interest payments at harvest time. Later in the year, however, when the peasant's supplies were used up, he had to buy foodstuffs from the same merchant at higher prices."[39]

A similar process took place in many other cultures throughout the colonies as individuals took advantage of the shattering of customary law to accrue power and influence for themselves at the expense of the commons. Cash-cropping, for example, created or widened differences in wealth. In themselves, such differences need not have resulted in divisive social change: on the contrary, it was customary in many pre-colonial communities for wealth to be redistributed through a variety of channels — feasting, for example — to the benefit of the community as a whole. Equally, where land tenure was still held communally, opportunities to accumulate land at the expense of other members of the community were circumscribed. But where private property had been legitimized through the imposition of European law, the way was cleared for the accumulation of wealth, creating a new élite that was able to buy into the colonial system, albeit at a rank lower than that of their white rulers. Authority within the commons thus began to pass to those who shared the values and outward trappings of the colonist: those who had been to school or university or who had a profession and so on.

MALE DOMINANCE

Enclosure did not affect women and men in the same way. Underpinning all the enclosures essential to industrialism and colonialism is the enclosure of women.[40]

From at least the 12th century onwards in Europe, women were persecuted, tortured and burnt as witches. A main objective of the witch-hunts was to remove women's control over their bodies, in particular their knowledge of contraception, abortion and childbirth. There was also an economic motivation: the rising class of merchant traders felt threatened by independent women involved in trade and commerce, while entrepreneurs, landowners and the emerging nation-state benefited from confiscated witch property. By the 19th century, many women had little option but to depend on a male breadwinner, a position reinforced by marriage and property laws. They were confined to the home to bear children, be sexually available and consume industrial products and imports from the colonies.

Although the workplace was separated from the home, women

did not stop working. Housewives' work became work to be done at any time, at any place, unpaid or poorly paid, and, in a cash economy, hardly valued. Like nature, women's work was considered free, but like nature, the system could not exist without it.

This transformation was paralleled in the colonies by the overturning of women's substantial influence in trade, agriculture and crafts. Like the European witches before them:

> "women of the colonized peoples [were] progressively brought down from a former position of relative power and independence to that of 'beastly' and degraded 'nature'. This 'naturalization' of colonized women is the counterpart of the 'civilizing' of the European women into housewives . . . The rise and generalization of the decent . . . marriage and family as protected insititutions are *causally* linked to the disruption of clan and family relations of the 'natives'".[41]

Writing in Burma at the close of the 19th century, Fielding Hall described how local industries in the hands of women were destroyed by the import of commodities from England. "In Rangoon, the large English stores are undermining the Bazaars where the women used to earn an independent livelihood." The next step, according to Hall, was to change marriage and inheritance laws so that Burma could become a "progressive" country:

> "with [the Burmese woman's] power of independence will disappear her free will and her influence. When she is dependent on her husband, she can no longer dictate to him. When he feeds her, she is no longer able to make her voice as loud as his. . . The nations who succeed are not feminine nations but the masculine . . . It has never been good for women to be too independent, it has robbed them of many virtues. It improves a man to have to work for his wife and family, it makes a man of him. It is demoralising for both if the woman can keep herself and, if necessary, her husband too."[42]

The transition from a female traditional agricultural system to a white Christian settlers' agriculture disempowered Native American Iroquois women, not only in agricultural and economic fields but in family, social, political and religious spheres as well. Prior to the 19th century, Iroquois women worked communally in the fields for hours at a time. Men's work centred on hunting, diplomacy and trading. The people of the matrilineal Iroquois culture lived in multi-family longhouses. But after the American Revolution, Quaker missionaries introduced private ownership of land and intensive farming methods, using iron ploughs and horses driven by men rather than the hand-held hoes used by women. Gradually the husband became the sole farmer and sole head of the family: his wife was relegated to keeping house, small-scale gardening, chores around the farm and child-raising within the nuclear family.[43]

The enclosure of women is clearly linked to the rise of modern medicine, science and the market economy as women have been classed as "nature" and thus considered as a vast reservoir of resources — future human resources. Francis Bacon asserted that much as "woman's womb had . . . yielded to the forceps, so nature's womb harboured secrets that through technology could be wrestled from her grasp for use in the improvement of the human condition."[44] Enclosure has given rise to an almost universal male dominated and hierachical system which is more intense, extreme and absolute than any form of patriarchy before.[45]

FROM COLONIALISM TO COLONIALISM

The élites who came to dominate the independence movements in many colonies showed themselves to be as committed to the extractivist economy of the colonial regime as the colonists they helped unseat. For them, the argument was not over what type of economy to run, but over who should run it and who should reap the greatest rewards. In India, for example, what had most irked the middle-class members of Congress was not that village commons had been enclosed, nor that land was being used for cash-crops, nor that industrial development was undermining local livelihoods, but that they — "the natural rulers" — were excluded from power. In their minds, there was never any doubt that the future lay in further industrialization, in "catching up" with the West. Their fear was that the opportunity to transform India into a modern industrial state would be denied them by colonialism.[46]

Indeed, it was precisely the commitment of Congress to industrialization that led Mahatma Gandhi to warn, "God forbid that India should ever take to industrialism after the manner of the West. The economic imperialism of a single tiny island kingdom is today keeping the world in chains. If an entire nation of 300 million took to similar economic exploitation, it would strip the world bare like locusts."[47]

But Gandhi's views, rooted in the aspirations of village India rather than the back-room politics of Delhi, did not prevail. Prime Minister Nehru rejected the Gandhian vision of an India consisting of numerous village republics — a vision that reflected the struggles of popular movements throughout the sub-continent to reclaim the commons — and instead set out to industrialize India through export-led growth, a path that would be broadly followed by other colonies once they had achieved independence.

A process of internal colonization, as devastating to the commons as anything that had gone before it, was thus set in motion. Using the slogans of "nation-building" and "development" to justify their actions, Third World governments have employed the full panoply of powers established under colonial rule to further dismantle the commons. Millions have lost their homelands — or the lands they had made their home — to make way for dams, industrial plants, mines, military security zones, waste dumps, plantations, tourist resorts, motorways, urban redevelopment and other schemes intended to transform the South into an appendage of the North. Deals have been made with Northern interests in return for aid and military protection; debts incurred to build projects that line the pockets of local commercial interests but which drive millions into poverty; multinational companies offered land, cheap labour and tax breaks at the expense of workers, peasants and the environment; subsidies handed out to richer farmers; industries allowed to pollute; and national economies tied more tightly than ever to the interests of global capital. Moreover, where popular movements have threatened to break the alliances that now exist between Southern élites and Northern interests, such movements have been suppressed or, where they have come to power, toppled by local élites operating in consort with Northern powers.

ENCLOSURE AND THE PEASANTRY

The continual enclosure of farming communities illustrates this general process. With the backing of international development agencies, commons have been vilified and destroyed; peasants have been corralled into the market and taxed into growing cash crops; prime agricultural lands have been expropriated for plantations and ranches; and once independent farmers have been reduced to landless labourers or agricultural workers for domestic and international corporations.

Even after the demise of colonialism, dispossession still remains the most visible means of enclosure. In the Philippines, where agribusiness interests were given a virtually free hand under the Marcos regime to take over land for export agriculture, thousands were dispossessed during the 1970s and early 1980s. Thirty per cent of the total cultivated land area is now given over to cash-crop production for export, mainly bananas, pineapples and sugar-cane. The island of Negros is now little more than a vast sugar estate, producing 68 per cent of the Philippines' sugar crop. The most fertile area of the island of Mindanao, Davao del Norte, is almost entirely under cash crops, with 25,000 hectares of banana plantations alone. The plantations are run principally by foreign multinationals: Dole Philippines acquired over 30,000 hectares in South Cotabato, NDC-Guthrie gobbled up 8,000 hectares in Agusan, and Provident Tree Farms Inc. laid claim to 23,000 hectares for an industrial tree plantation to supply matchsticks.[48]

Human rights abuses are common. As Memong Patayan, a Filipino activist, told the 1986 International Solidarity Conference for the Filipino Peasantry, "the use of force to terrorize the people and to make them accept relocation and resettlement is a necessary component of corporate landgrabbing."[49] From January 1981 to May 1982 alone, over 75 cases of military abuses were reported in areas of North and South Agusan province, targeted for plantation by the Manila Paper Mills Inc. The use of arbitrary detention and physical harassment created "such a climate of fear that widespread evacuations occurred . . . The abandoned lands have reportedly been planted to *ipil-ipil* trees by Manila Paper Mills."[50]

The overthrow of the Marcos regime and the coming to power of the Aquino government brought little relief for peasants. In the case of Provident Tree Farms:

> "Coercive measures have been instituted to edge out peasants stubbornly clinging to precious parcels of land. These range from hamletting to burning of homes to strafing and even salvaging [executing] local residents who actively oppose the entry of agribusiness corporations. Goons, private armies, religious cults and, more often than not, the military are employed to conduct these operations under the guise of counter-insurgency drives."[51]

Moreover, although Aquino ordered the sequestration of all "crony property", the government is committed to the same "Balanced Agro-Industrial Development Strategy" (BAIDS) first developed by the Marcos regime. Under BAIDS, the planting of export crops is to be further widened to include non-traditional crops such as rubber, cocoa, sorghum, yellow corn and beans. The strategy aims to encourage private and foreign firms to invest in agribusiness management over agricultural lands devoted to these non-traditional crops. The International Solidarity Conference for the Filipino Peasantry concludes: "To the poor farmers, BAIDS could only mean more landgrabbing and military harassment."[52]

Africa has also experienced an invasion of corporate agribusiness interests as post-colonial regimes have opened up their countries to foreign investment in the pursuit of export-led growth. In Nigeria, for example, Fiat, through its subsidiary Impresit Nigeria Ltd, capitalized on grants for large-scale irrigation schemes to set up the Talata–Mafara project on 10,000 acres near the Sokoto River. Some 60,000 peasants were forcibly removed from their land, without compensation.[53] When they protested, the state sent in armed police, brutally repressing the resistance.[54]

However, transnational companies (TNCs) are now moving away from direct control of land and are operating instead through direct contracts with peasants, whereby a company agrees to buy

Dispossessed for Development: Mining

During the colonial period, mining interests were quick to establish themselves in the colonies, especially where there were rare and expensive minerals such as gold, silver and copper. Baser minerals such as iron and coal were mined mainly in Europe. But recently, as labour costs in the North have risen, and as the public has become increasingly unwilling to tolerate the pollution caused by mining, the production of iron and coal is being phased out in Western Europe, and supplies imported from Eastern Europe and the ex-colonies.

In Brazil, the Grande Carajas project, funded in part by the EC, is intended to open up an area the size of Nigeria in the north-east of the country to industry and industrialized agriculture. The centrepiece of the project is the Serra dos Carajas open-cast iron ore mine, which already supplies iron to Europe, USA and Japan, but there are many subsidiary mines and smelters, both for iron and aluminium.The project as a whole will affect the homelands of 23 tribal groups. Already 20,000 people have been evicted to make way for the giant Alumar aluminium smelter, and others are threatened as the smelter works expand. The smelters are fuelled by charcoal, made from local timber — if all the projects become operational they will require the chopping down of about 250,000 hectares of forest every year. The project is also likely to cause severe water and air pollution problems. The livelihoods of eighty thousand people in the State of Maranhão who make their living from fishing will be severely disrupted .

In Indonesia, where mining contracts are agreed by the government in Jakarta, rather than local landowners, indigenous peoples are regularly dispossessed of their lands to make way for mines. In Kalimantan, more than 100 mining contracts, many for gold and coal, were signed in the three years between 1985 and 1988, leading to an invasion of multinational mining interests. Recently, Conzinc Rio Tinto of Australia (CRA) — an associate company of the British mining giant Rio Tinto Zinc — opened the Kelian gold mine, the biggest in the country. CRA also operate, together with BP, the Kaltim Prima coal mine, one of the biggest in South-East Asia. At both sites CRA have been accused of engineering the forcible removal of indigenous people and their families.

In the Philippines, CRA operate a mining operation in the northern Cordillera region, together with Lepanto Mining, a domestic Filipino company which built its wealth on exploiting gold deposits on land claimed by the Igorot peoples. The Igorot workforce is dragooned into the company's own union. "Attempts by workers in 1982 to form a branch of the National Federation of Labour Unions resulted in arbitrary dismissals. In 1989, Lepanto recruited members of Kadre, a notorious vigilante group, in order to ensure that Union elections proceeded without disturbing their control over the workforce . . . The farmers around the mine, in the Illocos Sur and Abra area, have constantly reported pollution of their crops and major problems created by Lepanto's ore drying plant."

Minewatch, in its exhaustive study, *The Gulliver File*, lists nearly 4,000 mining companies, operating in over 120 countries, extracting metals and fuels mainly for the North and for the emerging economies of South-East Asia. Precious little of the profits ever finds its way to the people whose lands and communities have been torn apart. One Australian aborigine described his feelings thus:

"One time I sat in our Church, I looked around. It was sunset after the rain. I saw the beautiful sea and the creeks rippling, and thought how wonderful God has created the earth. And I looked out over my land, ripped up by human hands and machines. I thought — what will I get out of that dust? What will I get out of that bauxite? *Nothing.*"

The Gulliver File, by Roger Moody, is available from Minewatch, 218, Liverpool Road, London, N1 1LE, UK.

given quantities of crops with particular specifications at a fixed price in return for supplying inputs and advice. Under this arrangement, the peasants retain ownership of their land, but have to abide by the conditions set by the company regarding cultivation, marketing and pricing, if they are to sell their crop.[55] The risks of production, which have been heightened both by unstable global markets and increasingly unpredictable climates, are thus transferred to the peasant, who becomes a virtual tied-labourer for the company. Alternatively, companies are opting for "outgrower schemes", whereby independent producers are used to supplement output from company plantations. Either way, peasants become increasingly dependent for their livelihoods on corporations, their ability to hold onto their land being determined to a great extent by their preparedness to work to the company's specifications and accept its prices.

In many African countries, the state plays much the same role as TNCs elsewhere. In Zambia, for example, the setting up of large-scale state farms has been the favoured route to agricultural modernization, with peasants being dispossessed of their lands to make way for state-run plantations. In Senegal and Mali, peasants have been forced to grow specified crops under contract to the government. Peasants are subject to draconian constraints, with supervision by project officers frequently "taking on the shape of a police operation."[56] At San in Mali, for example, "the least lack of respect for the new techniques being disseminated and the time-table for crops leads to the peasant's expulsion from the project zone and repossession of the plot [the farmer] was occupying."[57]

In South America, the same pattern of land-grabbing and dispossession prevails as in Asia and Africa. In Brazil, land conflicts and rural violence have escalated dramatically in the last 20 years as more and more of the prime land is taken over by companies (many of them multinationals) and large estate owners. The Catholic Church's Pastoral Land Commission estimates that in the whole of Brazil in 1971, land conflicts resulted in 20 deaths.[58] Twenty years later, the death rate was running at over 100 deaths a year. Yet, as Oxfam points out:

> "The tragic figures for deaths fail to give the whole picture. Over the period 1985 to 1989, there were 2,973 land conflicts. The extent of land under dispute totalled over three-quarters of a million square kilometres. And over two million people were involved. To put this another way, during those five years, some 16 Brazilians in every 1,000 were disputing ownership of almost nine per cent of the national territory (an area almost equal to Britain and France together)."[59]

In the North-East of Brazil, thousands of small farmers have been squeezed off their land to make way for cattle ranches or for plantations of sugar cane to be made into alcohol for fuel. Terror tactics are common. In the Amazon region, "where smallholders refuse to be bought out, the ranchers in many cases take the land by outright robbery, known as *grilagem*: they simply fence the land and declare it to be theirs. Anyone on the land is violently expelled. Some large landowners are said to have created private militias to clear the land."[60]

Land grabs, escalating land prices, mechanization and rural violence have pushed millions of farmers and labourers off the land and created "an unprecedented exodus" to the cities.[61] "Since the mid-1960s, the number of people living solely off the land has halved; the rural population now constitutes only 30 per cent of Brazil's 135 million people ... The shift has been most marked in the fertile southern region, but the same economic policies and priorities have affected the entire country."[62]

LAND SPECULATION

As the "winners" of the development process use their increasing amounts of disposable income to buy up land held by people with low and diminishing bargaining power, so land speculation is now becoming an increasingly important force driving enclosure. Tax breaks, development projects, and a boom in industrial estates, golf courses and garden resorts have helped transform rural land into a valuable commodity and make it an increasingly attractive form of investment in many Third World countries — particularly where inflation levels are high and paper money is virtually worthless.

In Brazil, land values have soared as Amazonia has been opened up for ranching and mining, with big ranching interests following the settlers to the new frontier, displacing them once the forest has been cleared.[63] The profit from such ranches comes not from the beef raised (indeed, several of the largest ranches have never sent a single cow to market)[64] but from the subsidies, tax breaks and subsidized credit that could, until recently, be "captured" through ranching. Although many of the subsidies have recently been removed, ranching is still an attractive proposition. As Susannah Hecht remarks:

> "A recognized land claim permits the holder to assert royalty rights on subsurface minerals that are technically owned by the Brazilian state. Thus areas adjacent to gold strikes frequently experience vigorous clearing. Cattle claim what is under their feet. The other main way in which extraction is linked to pasture expansion is through the use of valuable timber to subsidize pasture development costs. This is a more recent phenomenon due to improved infra-structure, expanding timber markets."[65]

Moreover, because land in "effective" use cannot be expropriated for the purposes of land reform, the title to it is relatively secure.

In South-East Asia, too, land speculation is rife. Thailand saw a sevenfold increase in the value of land transactions between 1986 and 1990, with the number of transactions rising by 250 per cent. Tourist development has become a major force for expropriation.[66] In Indonesia, "developers are snatching away prime agricultural land to develop luxury resorts. Land-greedy golf courses are appearing, even in overcrowded Java and Bali, while transmigrants are shipped out to less fertile sites outside Java."[67]

DEBT AND DISPOSSESSION

The vulnerability of local peoples to enclosure is compounded by growing personal indebtedness. Using some of the same taxes, threats and strong-arm tactics as the colonial powers before them, post-colonial regimes have dragooned peasants not only into growing cash crops but also into adopting intensive methods of agriculture. In many countries, it is standard practice for credit to be extended only to farmers who use pesticides. In Costa Rica, the main bank, the Banco Central de Costa Rica, requires tobacco farmers to spray their crop with ten pesticides if they are to receive assistance; for cucumbers, the bank stipulates the use of seven different pesticides and for peppers, eight.[68] Other strategies to promote intensive agriculture include: "national promotion campaigns through the media, literature distribution, agricultural extension programs, business advertising, tax discounts or exemptions for imports, subsidies, price controls to keep prices artificially low, tax shelters for distributors and agricultural credit policies."

With the control of markets firmly in their hands, multinational corporations and state-controlled enterprises have driven down farm prices while driving up the cost of the inputs on which farmers are increasingly dependent. The result is a cost-price squeeze that sends many farmers spiralling into debt, and eventually into bankruptcy. In the Indian Punjab, small farmers — who make up nearly half of the farming population — have been particularly badly hit. A survey carried out between 1976 and 1978 indicated that small farmers' households were running into an annual deficit of around 1,500 rupees. Between 1970 and 1980, the number of smallholdings in the Punjab declined by nearly a quarter due to their "economic non-viability."[69]

Burdened in addition with heavy taxation, farmers have become trapped in a cycle of debt. To pay for inputs and taxes, they borrow money, often at exorbitant rates. To service their loans, they frequently have to sell their crop immediately it is harvested at a time when prices are lowest. They are then forced to buy in food

Dispossessed for Development: Timber Plantations

The enclosure of forests for timber extraction, agriculture or mining has been taking place for centuries, but since World War II, the pace has increased greatly. As more communities become enclosed into the global market, the demand for timber, paper, agricultural land and minerals increases, and the world's forests are now under an unprecedented threat.

Forced to admit the environmental consequences of deforestation, corporations, governments and development banks are stretched to find a way of continuing to plunder, expropriate and enclose further forest areas, whilst maintaining environmental credibility. Their solution has been to blur the distinction between a highly variegated natural forest (an environment propitious to the commons) — and a monocultural plantation (the ultimate in arboreal enclosure). Thus the *Forest Principles* section of Agenda 21, declares "these principles should apply to all types of forests, both natural and planted, in all geographic regions" and makes no attempt to discriminate between the two.

Thailand: Forest Reserves Before Community Forest

The rising demand for paper, together with the overlogging of natural forests, have prompted many governments to embark on ambitious plantation programmes. In Thailand, following the 1989 logging ban, forest reserves are being turned over to eucalyptus. As much as 4,000,000 hectares of so-called "degraded" forest (consisting mainly of farmland, pasture and community woodlands) will be leased to commercial planters to provide pulp and woodchips for both the domestic and the export markets. Under the recently-begun *khor chor kor* programme, villagers will lose almost 1,600,000 hectares of farmland, over 90 per cent of which will be given over to commercial plantations. They will be compensated with 768,000 hectares of Forest Reserve land of inferior quality (and often already-occupied) . There is little doubt that an influx of uprooted peasants will put pressure on the forest in other areas. Altogether, 80 per cent of the occupants of National Reserve Forests, up to 970,000 families, are to be resettled.

The evictions have already started. In December 1991, troops marched into the villages of *Baan* Dong Sakran and *Baan* Tad Faa in the north-east of Thailand, "tossed out the residents' furniture and other belongings and tore down their houses as children and the elderly watched in despair." Both villages were founded over 100 years ago, whereas the land was made a forest reserve in 1964. "The villagers", says the Bangkok newspaper, *The Nation*, "had marked out their own community forest which they called *kok orn sorn*. They made and enforced their own rules to protect the forest."

The plans to plant eucalyptus have received funding from the Asian Development Bank, the United Nations Development Programme, and Japanese, Australian, Canadian and Finnish aid agencies. If fully implemented, the plans are by themselves enough to doom most of Thailand's remaining forests through their potential to displace peasants. But in December 1991 the government approved a similar resettlement and reforestation scheme for the North of Thailand, called *ror for tor*, or "Accelerated Watershed Rehabilitation", which will cover the watersheds of four major tributaries of the Chao Phaya river, an area inhabited by minority hill peoples.

at the beginning of the planting season to feed their families, at prices which have doubled or tripled in the meantime. For many, the only option is to take up waged labour, placing an intolerable work load on the remaining members of the household, mainly women and children, who are burdened with the task of maintaining an uneconomical holding. As individual farmers carry out more and more tasks in the production cycle by themselves, traditional systems of mutual support, such as communal planting and harvesting, begin to atrophy.[70]

New inequalities have thus been created, widening the gap between rich and poor villagers and increasing the power and influence of those (principally men) who have access to credit, new machinery, irrigation water and other inputs. Mechanization has exacerbated the problem, not least by increasing rural unemployment and underemployment. As the poorest farmers go to the wall, their land holdings are bought up by richer farmers, leading to the concentration of land into fewer and fewer hands; money, rather than the fulfilment of communal obligations, becomes the currency of power.

CHAIN REACTION

As the numbers of landless multiply, so one dispossession leads to another; farmers move from one area to enclose someone else's land elsewhere, often encouraged to do so by government-sponsored migration schemes or by patron-client networks. In Thailand, for example, merchants, millers, traders in forest products, timber companies and speculators have financed settlers who have cleared forests to plant maize, sugar-cane, cassava, rubber and eucalyptus. These new rural patrons have provided settlers with seeds, marketing and money to buy food or hire labour or tools at exorbitant interest rates of five per cent a month, or more. In some areas, peasants have been bought out after a few years, or otherwise pushed on to occupy new land and dislodge any isolated subsistence cultivators they may encounter there. After an interval, the peasants are again displaced by their corporate patrons, and the cycle is repeated. As the frontier has advanced and the forest has disappeared, the government has begun to crack down on peasant colonizers, who are now increasingly being forced into a marginal existence as casual agricultural labourers.

Elsewhere, government-sponsored migration programmes have persuaded the landless to clear forest land. In Brazil, such colonization schemes were promoted under the slogan of "land without men for men without land". In Indonesia, the "transmigration" of "surplus people" from the inner islands has led to the massive destruction of forests and the takeover of forest dwellers' lands in Kalimantan and West Papua. Planned land settlement in tropical forests has also been promoted in Paraguay, Bolivia, Peru, Ecuador, and Colombia.

Planned colonization, however, has been far outstripped by unplanned settlement. In Indonesia, for example, the World Bank estimates that for every colonist resettled under the official transmigration programme, two more moved into the forest due to its "draw effect". Yet there is little to offer settlers in these places. The land is frequently unsuited to the farming they have traditionally practised, and it is quite common to see settlers give up their clearings after the first meagre harvest. They have to make new clearings every year, until eventually the whole area is cleared and they move on again. Many have returned home to an uncertain future in Java.

Ultimately, large numbers of those dispossessed through development drift towards the major cities of the Third World. Even here, however, the threat of eviction is ever present. To make way for commercial buildings and new roads or to smarten up the city for sporting occasions and visiting heads of state, the slums and shanty towns that they have made their homes are regularly cleared. In India, at least 500,000 citizens of Calcutta were thrown out of their homes between 1983 and 1985,[71] whilst 900,000 people were violently evicted in a drive to beautify Seoul for the 1988 Olympic Games.[72] Moreover, as Miloon Kothari of India's National Campaign for Housing Rights, notes, the incidence of

Reneging on Land Reform

A call to reclaim the commons is often reflected, in political terms, in a demand for land reform. Many Third World governments have come to power on the promise of agrarian reforms only to renege on their promise once in power.

In Kenya, where dispossessed farmers formed the backbone of the Mau Mau nationalist movement in the 1950s, President Kenyatta rapidly sidelined land reform as a political priority; the skewed land distribution inherited from the colonial regime remained as firmly entrenched as ever. Although it was agreed, under the terms of independence, that one million acres of land previously "owned" by Europeans would be transferred to some 25,000 landless and unemployed African families, the "beneficiaries came in fact from a small élite group, often comprising absentee civil servants rather than the landless." No attempt was made to redress the loss of women's traditional rights to land: on the contrary, the colonial system of investing land titles in men — the presumed "head of the household" — was continued.

In Egypt, independence brought minimal long-term change to the pattern of land ownership. Prior to a series of land reform programmes introduced by President Nasser from 1952 to 1969, 94.3 per cent of farmers were squeezed onto just 35 per cent of the country's farmland, living on small-holdings of under five acres. By contrast, the richest 0.4 per cent of farmers controlled 35 per cent of the land, usually that of the highest quality, their estates covering a minimum of 50 acres. Although the reforms initially reduced the concentration of landholdings, large estates began to re-emerge as those wealthier farmers bought out poorer farmers, the percentage of land holdings with 50 acres or more rising from six per cent in 1965 to 16 per cent by 1974. The greatest beneficiaries, however, were middle-sized farmers with holdings of between 10 and 50 acres. Their share of land more than doubled from its pre-reform days, primarily because they received the lion's share of credit under agricultural modernization programmes. Today, there are more landless farmers in Egypt than ever before.

In South Korea, land has been redistributed — but the imposition of modern intensive agriculture has left many crippled with debt: the number of rural households in debt rose "from 76 per cent in 1971 to 90 per cent in 1983 and to an astounding 98 per cent in 1985." The result is that farmers are leaving the land, the rural population dropping by three per cent between 1985 and 1988. As poorer families sell out, land is once again becoming concentrated in fewer and fewer hands.

Reviewing the record of land reform since the break up of the colonies, the UN Food and Agriculture Organization (FAO) admits, "the history of land reform . . . is largely one of failures." Indeed, land reform measures on their own are unlikely to achieve a permanent reversal of poverty and insecurity unless some attempt is made to eliminate the forces that led to inequities of land tenure in the first place. In a world where market forces, government regulations, vested interests and military conflicts conspire to undermine the stability of the commons, simply redistributing land provides no guarantee that the beneficiaries will be able to hold onto it for long.

forced evictions is growing :

"Forced evictions take place almost daily somewhere in the world

... The total number of people forcibly uprooted from their homes annually is in the millions. This staggering figure is all the more alarming given the fact that, according to UN figures, over one billion people throughout the world are already either homeless or inadequately housed."[73]

THE EXTENSION OF ENCLOSURE
IN THE NORTH

Neither evictions nor enclosure in the name of modernization and "improvement" are problems confined to the South, nor are they confined to rural areas. The forces that have shaped colonial and post-colonial history in the Third World have been at work either blatantly or insidiously in the Northern industrialized countries, and are still very much operative today, reactivating old forms of enclosures and initiating new ones. The intricate nature of this process is clearly visible in the evolution of agriculture in Europe and the US.

The expression "from seedling to supermarket", employed to describe the vertical penetration of the food industry by multinational companies, indicates the extent to which the human food chain has been enclosed. Indeed the phrase does not go far enough, for every aspect of food production, from seed nursery to the dining table, has been wrenched out of its vernacular context and drawn into a new web of reciprocating influences. It is no longer merely land and labour that are subject to enclosure, but also the agricultural input, in the form of seeds, chemicals, drugs and machinery; and the agricultural output, that is, the food itself, processed and distributed through a variety of sophisticated marketing strategies. The person who would challenge the logic or justice of any one aspect of the chain must eventually confront the logic and the justice of the entire system.

For example, any British smallholder applying for permission to start an agricultural enterprise risks receiving the refusal given in 1991 to a prospective free-range chicken farmer. "We must try and put a stop to these quasi-agricultural activities which are springing up all over the country," stated a member of the Salisbury District Council Planning Committee, who went on to explain: "What I mean by 'quasi-agricultural' is a mess of peasant farming . . . which prevents the Common Agricultural Policy from working efficiently in Europe."[74] His use of the word "agricultural" is revealing. Although in its origins the word means "growing in fields", in the councillor's book only large factory units merit the expression, while smallholdings where the birds are actually allowed to feed in the fields are merely "quasi-agricultural". "Agriculture", in effect, has been redefined to mean "economically competitive food production".

In such a regime, the elimination of supposedly inefficient farmers is viewed not as a social and cultural loss, but as an economic necessity. With the advent of the agro-chemical age, thousands of farmers have been bankrupted, and hundreds of thousands of farm-hands have been made redundant by the increasing use of machinery and chemicals. Between 1946 and 1989, the total number of people working on farms in Britain (full-time and part-time) declined from 976,000 to 285,000.[75] In 1990 alone, 6,000 farmers sold up and 4,000 full-time workers lost their jobs.[76] In the United States, in the six years between 1980 and 1986, 235,000 farms went out of business, and 650,000 people were lost from the farm workforce.

The disappearance of so many farms — and the personal tragedies that these figures conceal — should not be dismissed simply as the overdue streamlining of a pampered and inefficient industry. The majority of these farmers have not chosen to leave their land: they have been forced to do so by circumstances over which they have no control. Their ability to make a living has been undermined as a direct result of policies that favour large farmers over small, agribusiness over local control and intensive use of chemicals over sound husbandry. Governments, abetted by commercial interests, have applied a system of price mechanisms and subsidies which forces farmers to cover rising production costs by increasing production, and consequently to borrow heavily to invest in the most up-to-date machinery and in increasing quantities of chemical fertilizers and pesticides. Since subsidies are allotted according to gross output, farmers with less land, however sound their farming methods, have found themselves unable to pay off their debts in the face of stagnating food prices.

The decline in the number of farms in Europe and the US, and hence of the established rural population, results in a decline in rural services. Inexorably, the rural fabric is enclosed within an urban framework of distribution and consumption, which in turn serves to undermine the viability of the remaining farms. As the rural population falls, local schools and hospitals close down, and shops, public transport services and other facilities decline through lack of support At the same time, the cost of goods on sale in local shops tends to be considerably higher than in the cities (even for produce that is grown or reared locally). This decline in infra-structure prompts still more people, especially young families with children, to move to urban areas. Half-empty villages become "gentrified" as urban commuters and second-home-owners move into rural communities, bringing with them urban patterns of consumption which only hasten the decline of local structures.[77]

Small retailers are among the principal victims of this latest round of enclosures. Ninety-five thousand food shops closed down between 1961 and 1983 in Britain alone, a decline which continued during the 1980s, so that there are now less than 45,000 outlets remaining.[78] Grocers, greengrocers, fishmongers and butchers have been squeezed out by a centralized supermarket network which in Britain now accounts for 83 per cent of all food sold. The trend has been much the same in France, Germany and Benelux.

This enclosure of retailing has enabled a small number of giant companies to increase their control of the food chain. Most food-processing in Britain is in the hands of a handful of conglomerates such as Nestlé (whose subsidiaries include Carnation, Crosse and Blackwell, Rowntree, Chambourcy and Findus) or Philip Morris (who control Marlboro, Kraft, Suchard and General Foods). These companies operate hand-in-glove with large commodity mer-chants such as Cargill, Continental Grain, Luis Dreyfus, Bunge, Andre and Co. and Mitsui/Cook, who between them exported 85 per cent of all US wheat, 95 per cent of its corn and 80 per cent of its sorghum.[79]

The influence of these companies now stretches right back to the farm. Once markets are enclosed, outright ownership of land or livestock units is no longer a pre-condition for controlling production, nor is it a guarantee that control can be maintained. As in Southern countries, many companies adopt a system of contract farming, in which farmers, often for want of any secure alternative outlet, are induced to sell exclusively to one retailing company, growing crops or rearing livestock to its specifications. Within the last 15 to 20 years, contract farming in Britain has increased to such an extent that most of the poultry, eggs, pork and bacon, and over 90 per cent of vegetables such as peas and beans are grown to the order and specification of the food industry.[80] Supermarket chains such as Sainsbury already control each stage in the production of meat for their stores, from the animal feed through to the slaughterhouse, through a series of commercial ties with other companies. Corporate enclosure of the livestock industry is gaining pace so rapidly within the US that four companies now control 41 per cent of all poultry production, and three companies control three-quarters of all intensive beef production.[81]

Products grown under contract have to be produced to the right specifications at the right time. To help farmers with this process, specialist advice is given on what variety to plant, and the timing and application of chemical treatments. Farmers are transformed into outworkers for corporations over which they have no control. In some cases, they have been reduced to virtual peons for food companies, their costs exceeding the money they receive in sales. Christopher Turton, a British poultry producer, puts it in this way: "It distresses me. I would prefer to be seen as a craftsman, not as a commercial exploiter of animals, but I feel I am being turned from one to the other . . . I am just a small cog in a big industry . . . Today poultry management is dictated by the company accountant rather than the stockman."[82]

The enclosure of the entire food chain — from growing through processing, marketing and retailing, to consumption — thus has a dynamic that is self-reinforcing. The enclosure of small farms and the consequent decline of the farming community weakens local markets and leaves them open to enclosure by a centralized retailing system. These supermarkets in turn steadily increase their hold over the production process, resulting in further enclosure of the farming sector. Significantly, the whole system is based on the heavy use of oil: to manufacture the chemicals and provide fuel for the machines that boost production; to power the transcontinental transport of commodities; and to get consumers from their homes to the hypermarket and back.

THE SEED ENCLOSED

It might seem that the transnational corporations already have the agricultural market well under their control. However there are still more forms of enclosure on the horizon, in particular those linked to the burgeoning genetic-engineering industry.

As part of the process of extending their control of inputs, agrochemical corporations have come to dominate the seed industry. Thousands of independent seed companies have already fallen prey to corporate take-overs.[83]

By the late 1980s, three firms controlled nearly 80 per cent of the garden seed market in Britain. In The Netherlands, three companies held 70 per cent of the agricultural seed market, and four companies controlled 90 per cent of the market for horticultural seeds. In the US, one firm — Pioneer Hi-Bred — had tied up 38 per cent of the corn seed market.[84] Transnational seed houses now control about a quarter of seed sales in the North, and five to ten per cent of sales in the Third World.[85] In India, the pharmaceutical giant, Sandoz India, has entered into an agreement with Northrup King of the US and the Dutch conglomerate Zaaduine.[86] Two other US companies, Seedtec International and Dehlgien, have entered into agreements with Maharastra Hybrid and Nath Seed Company respectively. Pioneer Hi-Bred has formed an Indian subsidiary and Hindustan Lever is negotiating with a Belgian firm, whilst Hoechst and Ciba-Geigy are reportedly negotiating other tie-ups.[87]

The enclosure of seeds threatens to complete the enclosure of agricultural production. The adoption of agrochemicals has already put the majority of Western farmers in a position where they no longer have control over their key inputs but instead must purchase them from farm suppliers. Yet whether farmers use agrochemicals or not, they are reliant on hybridized seeds which, because they fail to breed true, require the purchase of new seeds every year. Seeds which used to be saved from the previous harvest must now be purchased on the market, shifting control over biological diversity from farmers to transnational corporations and changing a self-reproducing resource into a mere input.[88]

With the advent of biotechnology, the domination exercised by corporations over the farmer is likely to become a stranglehold. Agrochemical companies are working to identify plant genes that will impart resistance to certain herbicides — usually their own brands — in order to sell seeds as part of a package deal designed to increase chemical sales. Worldwide, there are now at least 65 research programmes focusing on breeding herbicide tolerance into agricultural crops, with corporations like Monsanto, Du Pont, Ciba-Geigy and Bayer leading the pack.[89]

To tighten their control over seeds, agrochemical companies are forging new tools for enclosure and reworking old ones. Companies such as Ciba-Geigy, which a hundred years ago argued vigorously against patents, on the grounds that they were a "paradise for parasites" and "a playground for plundering patent agents and lawyers",[90] are now lobbying, cajoling and threatening national legislatures into adopting patents for every new innovation, including new seeds. To oppose patents, they argue, is to put national interests above "internationally accepted principles of fair trade."[91] Since the early 1970s, seed varieties developed by companies have been patentable, making it illegal for farmers to trade in such seeds. In the US, the Patents Office has extended patents to any genetically-engineered organism, from micro-organisms to plants and animals — only genetically-engineered humans are excluded — thereby enclosing the entire non-human gene pool in one regulatory stroke.

The move to protect patents and other forms of "intellectual property" is a significant part of the current trade negotiations within the GATT Uruguay Round. Curiously, while the thrust of the proposals made by GATT economists has been to promote international free trade, their approach as regards patents is, in its effect, protectionist: there should be no free circulation of knowledge. The difference lies in the fact that information is an inexhaustible and intangible bequest, rather than a "subtractible" finite resource. In a capitalist system, free trade in exhaustible commodities leads, apparently inevitably, to the enclosure of the market by powerful oligopolies. But to achieve a parallel enclosure of human knowledge, an artificial structure of patents and property rights must first be introduced and enforced. As Jeremy Rifkin comments:

> "The granting of patents represents the culmination of a five-hundred-year movement to enclose the planetary commons that began inauspiciously on the village green in small rural hamlets scattered throughout England and the European continent. Now even the building blocks of life itself have been enclosed, privatized, and reduced to a marketable product."[92]

Urban Enclosure

While the commons in the rural South is threatened by development, in the urban North it is threatened by redevelopment. As the commercial hub of the city expands and the radial road system broadens, poorer neighbourhoods and communities are characterized as slums or run-down inner-city areas and targeted for urban renewal. Of the innumerable conflicts and tensions that fill the pages of daily newspapers, a sizeable proportion are rooted in the resistance of an urban community to the forces of enclosure.

City Centres

Like the "improvement" of agricultural land, the redevelopment of urban space is driven by the need to extract an ever higher rent from a given area. The centres of our cities and towns have been the arena of a battle between powerful interests who wish to enclose public space and the communities who will be thereby displaced. City blocks — long-established communities of homes, shops and workplaces — are systematically bought up by syndicates of wealthy redevelopers, razed to the ground and replaced by spectacular tower-blocks and sprawling "complexes" of superhuman dimensions. Millions of square metres of office space are constructed, not to answer any human need, but to generate profit. Sometimes, as in the case of Centrepoint Tower in London, they remain empty for years, or even decades, since they gain more value as enclosed land than they could do by being rented. In other cases, developers miscalculate the market and have to be bailed out: to salvage London's showpiece Canary Wharf scheme, the British government is planning to demolish another massive office block in Marsham Street, built only 25 years ago, so that office workers can be decanted to fill unrented offices in the new complex. The communities displaced by these developments, though they put up a fight, are no match for the steamroller of commerce, and are frequently dispersed to soulless housing estates or to dormitory suburbs of enclosed rural land, leaving only a rump of marginalized squatters prepared to resist to the end.

Shops

In tandem with the redevelopment of town centres, there has been a progressive enclosure of what is now known as the retail sector. As high-streets are transformed into malls, pedestrian precincts and shopping centres, rents rise to a height only affordable by national and international chains of shops, often masquerading under two or three different names, but selling the same restricted range of internationally distributed products. The small outlets which supply local, fresh, handmade, secondhand or unusual products — in fact anything that does not benefit from economies of scale — are unable to afford the rents. The hitherto public forum of the market-place is transformed into a privately owned precinct, managed by a business syndicate or a corporation such as British Telecom. Often these places are locked up in the evening or placed out of bounds to "undesirable" individuals, who are thus, in effect, barred from their own city centre.

Streets

The most ubiquitous enclosure of the public domain has been in the street, where the principal agent of enclosure has not been a capitalist élite, but a technology with "democratic" pretensions, namely the motor car. Whereas the street until early this century was an arena for social intercourse, for commercial exchange, for idle dalliance and for banter and play, it has now become mainly a thoroughfare for expensive, pollutant and dangerous automobiles transporting busy citizens from A to B and then back to A again. Without doubt, those who have suffered most from this enclosure have been children, many of whom are virtually held prisoner in their own house; and by association their exasperated parents.

Although the motor car has been effective, in the main, at clearing human activity off the streets and enclosing it in pedestrian precincts, hypermarkets and leisure centres, people still strive to recreate urban commons. An army of officials — police, social workers, planning officers — are therefore employed to "keep people off the streets": to clamp down on unlicensed street dealing, unofficial advertising (bill-sticking and graffiti), open air festivities and games, disorderly assembly, begging and loitering. It is in the so-called deprived inner-city areas that the commons is often the most resilient; and it is these deprived areas that are most frequently targeted for enclosure and redevelopment.

3 THE ENCOMPASSING WEB

The Ramifications of Enclosure

Because history's best known examples of enclosure involved the fencing in of common pasture, enclosure is often reduced to a synonym for "expropriation." But enclosure involves more than land and fences, and implies more than simply privatization or takeover by the state. It is a compound process which affects nature and culture, home and market, production and consumption, germination and harvest, birth, sickness and death. It is a process to which no aspect of life or culture is immune.

The *Oxford English Dictionary* offers a general definition of enclosure — to "insert within a frame". Enclosure tears people and their lands, forests, crafts, technologies and cosmologies out of the cultural framework in which they are embedded and forces them into a new framework which reflects and reinforces the values and interests of newly-dominant groups. Any pieces which will not fit into the new framework are devalued and discarded. In the modern age, the architecture of this new framework is determined by market forces, science, state and corporate bureaucracies, patriarchal forms of social organization, and ideologies of environmental and social management.

Land, for example, once it is integrated into a framework of fences, roads and property laws, is "disembedded" from local fabrics of self-reliance and redefined as "property" or "real estate". Forests are divided into rigidly defined precincts — mining concessions, logging concessions, wildlife corridors and national parks — and transformed from providers of water, game, wood and vegetables into scarce exploitable economic resources. Today they are on the point of being enclosed still further as the dominant industrial culture seeks to convert them into yet another set of components of the industrial system, redefining them as "sinks" to absorb industrial carbon dioxide and as pools of "biodiversity". Air is being enclosed as economists seek to transform it into a marketable "waste sink"; and genetic material by subjecting it to laws which convert it into the "intellectual property" of private interests.

People too are enclosed as they are fitted into a new society where they must sell their labour, learn clock-time, and accustom themselves to a life of production and consumption; groups of people are redefined as "populations", quantifiable entities whose size must be adjusted to take pressure off resources required for the global economy. Women are enclosed by consigning them to the "unproductive" periphery of a framework of industrial work, which they can only enter by adopting "masculine" values and ways of being, thinking and operating. Skills, too, are enclosed, as are systems of knowledge associated with local stewardship of nature.

NEW VALUES

Enclosure inaugurates what Ivan Illich has called "a new ecological order."[1] It upsets the local power balance which ensured that survival was "the supreme rule of common behaviour, not the isolated right of the individual."[2] It scoffs at the notion that there can be "specific forms of community respect" for parts of the environment which are "neither the home nor wilderness", but lie "beyond a person's threshold and outside his possession"[3] — the woods or fields, for example, that secure a community's subsistence, protect it from flood and drought, and provide spiritual and aesthetic meaning.

Instead enclosure transforms the environment into a "resource" for national or global production — into so many chips that can be cashed in as commodities, handed out as political favours and otherwise used to accrue power. The sanctions on exploitation imposed by commons regimes in order to ensure a reliable local subsistence from local nature are now viewed "simply as constraints to be removed".[4]

Control over those resources is assigned to actors outside the community. Most obviously, land — and in particular, the best-quality land — is concentrated in proportionately fewer and fewer hands. Enclosure of water and other resources has also generated scarcity and conflict. Large-scale irrigated plantations, for example, deny water to local farmers who work outside the plantation system.[5] In central India "whilst staple crops in the drought stricken areas . . . are denied water, the sugar-cane fields and grape vines are irrigated with scarce groundwater. A soil water drought has been created not by an absolute scarcity of water but by the preferential diversion of a limited water supply."[6]

In cities, meanwhile, as Ivan Illich explains, people without motor cars are progressively shut out from access to the street:

> "What a difference there was between the new and the old parts of Mexico City only 20 years ago. In the old parts of the city, the streets were still true commons. Some people sat on the road to sell vegetables and charcoal. Others put their chairs on the road to drink tequila. Others held their meetings on the road to decide on the new headman for the neighbourhood or to determine the price of a donkey. Others drove their donkeys through the crowd, walking next to the heavily-loaded beast of burden; others sat in the saddle. Children played in the gutter, and still people walking could use the road to get from one place to another.

> "Such roads were not built for people. Like any true commons, the street itself was the result of people living there and making that space liveable. The dwellings that lined the roads were not private homes in the modern sense — garages for the overnight deposit of workers. The threshold still separated two living spaces, one intimate and one common. But neither homes in this intimate sense nor streets as commons survived economic development. In the new sections of Mexico City, streets are no more for people. They are nowadays for automobiles, for buses, for taxis, cars and trucks. People are barely tolerated on the streets unless they are on the way to a bus stop. If people now sat down or stopped on the street they would become obstacles for the traffic, and traffic would be dangerous to them. The road has been degraded from a commons to a simple resource for the circulation of vehicles."[7]

Enclosure thus cordons off those aspects of the environment that are deemed "useful" to the encloser — whether grass for sheep in 16th century England or stands of timber for logging in modern-day Sarawak — and defines them, and them alone, as valuable. A street becomes a conduit for vehicles; a wetland, a field to be drained; flowing water, a wasted asset to be harnessed for energy or agriculture. Instead of being a source of multiple benefits, the environment becomes a one-dimensional asset to be exploited for a single purpose — that purpose reflecting the interests of the encloser, and the priorities of the wider political economy in which the encloser operates.

NEW FORMS OF EXCHANGE

Enclosure reorganizes society to meet the overriding demands of the market. It demands that production and exchange conform to rules that reflect the exigencies of supply and demand, of competition and maximization of output, of accumulation and economic efficiency.

In the commons, activities we now call "economic" are embedded in other activities. The planting of fields or the harvesting of crops cannot be reduced to acts of production: they are also religious events, occasions for celebration, for fulfilling communal obligations and for strengthening networks of mutual support. Farming, for example, is carried out not to maximize production — though a healthy crop is always welcome — but to feed the gods, enable cultural practices to continue with dignity, or minimize risk to the community as a whole, not least by strengthening networks of mutual support. Thus when enclosure begins, people feel threatened not only by material expropriation but by the cultural and personal humiliations that inevitably accompany it. Unsurprisingly, their resistance against enclosure is also developed and codified in non-economic forms; gossip, songs, jokes, rumours, drama and festivals.[8]

Rules of exchange in the commons are also often local and idiosyncratic, bringing them into conflict with those of the world market. In local bazaars, no one feels guilty about bilking strangers: after all, if they can't take care of themselves, why did they venture out of their own community? Even haggling may be less a sign of desperate profit-seeking than a way of sizing people up, teasing them, or just passing time.

Because economic relations need not be crucial to survival in commons regimes, they generally take a back seat to other social relationships. *Homo economicus* — the obsessively rent-maximizing archetype around whose supposed universality modern economic theory has been constructed — might in fact be unable to scratch together a living in many commons regimes. Unwilling to share with neighbours in times of dearth or to "waste time" in "unprofitable" labour-sharing, rituals of reciprocity, craft acquisition, gossip and the like, he or she could well be cut off from the community support needed to make ends meet.

As production and exchange are enclosed by the market, economic activity is cordoned off from other spheres of social life, bounded by rules that actively undermine previous networks of mutual aid. As Gerald Berthoud observes:

> "The market tends to become the only mode of social communication, even between those who are intimately connected. Within this universe of generalized commodities, it becomes logical that individuals increasingly become strangers to one another. Even for those who are culturally and socially close, the market mentality maintains a distance between them, almost as if close and distant relationships had become indistinguishable."[9]

In an undiluted market economy, access to food, for example, is no longer dependent on being part of — and contributing to — a social network: instead, food goes to those who have the money to buy it. Only those who, in the economists' jargon, have the income to translate their biological needs into "effective demand" get to eat. In the global supermarket, people earning perhaps 100 dollars a year — if they are lucky — must compete for the same food with people earning 100 dollars a week, 100 dollars an hour, or even 100 dollars a minute.

As the market eats into the fabric of local self-reliance, commons regimes begin to atrophy. Their members can no longer rely on family, friends, neighbours, community, elders and children for support, but increasingly must go to the market, not only for food, clothing and shelter, but also for recreation, amusement and care of the young, the old, the sick and the handicapped.[10] In time, not only material and service needs but even emotional needs are channelled through the market. The commons is transformed from a community that feeds itself into one which is fed by, or feeds others; from a community that amuses itself into one that is amused by others, and so on. Community gives way to state, personal credibility to "rational standards", craft to profession, respect for people to using them as tools. The Thai temple which used to be built by local craftspeople to a local design using local funds is now built according to a set of blueprints issued by the Department of Religious Affairs with collections from urban benefactors. The locally-supported village school, where monks taught the arts and morals necessary for community life, is supplanted by the tax-supported state school with a set curriculum and city-trained teachers whose effect is to lure a small stratum of talented and ambitious pupils out of the village and make those who remain feel that they are "failures". The self-help group gives way to the state benefits office, and the communal work party to solo tractor drivers and casual wage labour. Debts and dependency increase, and how many acres are farmed or fishing nets set begins to depend not on what the land or sea can bear but on external market demands, the investment of outside entrepreneurs and people's need to measure their status against the standards of the capital.

NEW ROLES

Enclosure redefines community. It shifts the reference points by which people are valued. Individuals become "units" whose "value" to society is defined by their relationship to the new political entity that emerges from enclosure. Increasing numbers of people do not have access to the environment, the political process, the market or the knowledge they need.

Thus women, who in a vernacular setting were generally accorded respect *as women*, who had their own spheres of influence and areas of life, both within the household and outside, and hence a political space in which they and they alone operated, have seen their domain encroached upon, devalued and restricted. In many pre-colonial African societies, for example, it was women who assumed responsibility for sowing and choosing which crop to plant and when. Tasks such as taking goods to market and trading them were also considered women's work, not men's. Men by contrast were responsible for clearing the fields, for preparing the land for planting, whilst both men and women shared the weeding and harvesting.[11] Tasks were divided between the genders, but responsibility was shared: complementarity, rather than hierarchy, was the underlying principle for regulating relationships. Women also had their own areas of land over which they alone had rights as women.

Enclosure denies the possibility of such balance. The need to earn wages has forced men out of the household, diminishing the possibility for them to share household tasks or the raising of children, while women have been enclosed within the household. As women's work becomes unpaid "shadow work"— and hence deemed to have no value within a society that divides labour into "productive" work (work that earns a wage) and "unproductive" work (work that does not) — women see their status downgraded and their contribution to society, including child-bearing and rearing, devalued.[12] As waged work has become a necessary part of life, so power within the household has become concentrated in the hands of the male "head of the household" — the presumed wage earner.

In addition, the lands to which women in many societies once had exclusive access have increasingly been assigned to the men of the village, not only enclosing part of the women's domain but, in the process, stripping them of the independence and bargaining power within village politics that access to land previously accorded them. Yet when the men are forced to migrate away from their villages in search of work, women in Third World countries have been burdened with responsibility for the entire agricultural cycle.

A NEW POLITICAL ORDER

Enclosure ushers in a new political order. When the environment is turned over to new uses, a new set of rules and new forms of organization are required. Enclosure redefines how the environment is managed, by whom and for whose benefit. Old forms of environmental management are forced into redundancy or vilified, derided or outlawed.

Hence, as state and commercial enterprises have sought to impose "scientific forestry" regimes with the objective of maintaining a constant annual yield of timber for industrial purposes, so traditional methods of forest management have been denigrated as "inefficient", "irrational", "untidy", "unruly" and "destructive of the environment", their practitioners decried as "squatters" or worse.[13] By contrast, "scientific forestry" is lauded for "putting the forest to work", for "bringing order to chaos", for its efficiency and for its progressive use of science and technology in the public good — thus justifying further encroachment by the state or private interests. Decisions cease to be made by consensus — by the community listening to the community — but are pushed on the community by enclosers or their delegated officials.

Compare the allocation of water rights in a vernacular setting and in a modern irrigation scheme. In the *muang faai* irrigation system of Northern Thailand, for example, water rights are allocated so that everyone gets enough to survive.[14] Keeping a *muang faai* system going demands co-operation and collective management, sometimes within a single village, sometimes across three or four sub-districts including many villages. On the whole, the systems also rest on the assumption that local water is a common property. No one can assume control of irrigation water, and it must be used in accordance with communal agreements reached at the beginning of every agricultural year. These agreements govern how water is to be distributed, how flow is to be controlled according to seasonal schedules, how barriers are to be maintained and channels dredged, how conflicts over water use are to be settled, and how the forest around the reservoir is to be preserved as a guarantee of a steady water supply and a source of materials to repair the system. Despite this variety of tasks, management systems are generally simple, unbureaucratic and independent (sometimes defiantly so) of government authority.

By contrast, farmers in modern intensive irrigation systems have no real say in how water is distributed — that decision is left to "management", to irrigation staff acting under orders from government or corporate bureaucrats sitting in distant offices and with minimal knowledge of or responsiveness to local conditions or concerns. The concern of irrigation staff is with the technicalities of water delivery rather than equity, output rather than agricultural realities. The rules imposed are crude and inflexible and often run counter to what farmers themselves know will work. In the Sudan's Gezira scheme, for example, water is allocated according to "the average principle". The result, as Carl Widstrand notes, is that:

> "the 'average' farmer gets an 'average' amount of water for an 'average' crop over the year. Everyone gets water over the year but not necessarily at the precise or necessary moments. This concept is closely related to the idea of 'normal rainfall' and other peculiarities of the 'folklore of the normal' that simplifies administrative thought."[15]

Irrigation staff are not accountable to local people. This, continues Widstrand, "leads to what we, in our Calvinistic approach to life, call corrupt practices." Things get done not within the transparent setting of communal and individual rights, but because the right money changes hands "under the counter". "The gate keeper may be persuaded to open the gate to let more water through; the gauge reader may under-report the amount of water taken; the overseer may install large watercourse outlets."[16] In such a regime, decision-making has been wrested from the community and a semblance of order is only achieved through authoritarian rule.

NEW FORMS OF EXPERTISE

Enclosure not only redefines the forum in which decisions are made but also redefines whose voice counts in that forum. In order to place management in the hands of "others", whose allegiances and sources of power lie outside the community, it cuts knowledge off from local ethics. As Tariq Banuri and Frédérique Apffel-Marglin note:

> "Local knowledge is bound by time and space, by contextual and moral factors. More importantly, it cannot be separated from larger moral or normative ends . . . Once knowledge is meant to be universally applicable, it begins to gravitate into the hands of experts or professionals, those 'conspiracies against the laity', as George Bernard Shaw once called them, whose interests in acquiring, creating, promoting, or acting upon the basis of such knowledge begins more and more to be motivated by internal professional considerations, rather than by normative social implications. In fact under these circumstances, the activity can often become an end in itself and become unmoored from its narrow technical objectives."[17]

Enclosure opens the way for the bureaucratization and enclosure of knowledge itself. It accords power to those who master the language of the new professionals and who are versed in its etiquette and its social nuances. It creates a new language of power, inaccessible to those who have not been to school or to university, who do not have professional qualifications, who cannot operate computers, who cannot fathom the apparent mysteries of a cost-benefit analysis, or who refuse to adopt the forceful tones of an increasingly "masculine" world.

In that respect, as Illich notes, "enclosure . . . is as much in the interest of professionals and of state bureaucrats as it is in the interests of capitalists." For as local ways of knowing and doing are devalued or appropriated, and as vernacular forms of governance are eroded, so state and professional bodies are able to insert themselves within the commons, taking over areas of life that were previously under the control of individuals, households and the community. Enclosure "allows the bureaucrat to define the local community as impotent to provide for its own survival."[18] It invites the professional to come to the "rescue" of those whose own knowledge is deemed inferior to that of the encloser. It provides a tool for control.

Even conception, pregnancy, childbirth and the care of children, the sick and the old are all areas that are now increasingly dominated by the rule of professionals. As Vandana Shiva notes of modern childbirth:

> "Women's labour and knowledge are ignored: their only part in pregnancy and birth is to follow the instructions of the doctor. The direct organic bond with the foetus is substituted by machines and the knowledge of professionals. Even the mother's love for her baby has to be demonstrated by doctors and technicians."[19]

Traditional means of contraception, such as rhythm methods, herbal potions and prolonged breast-feeding — means over which women or couples had control and which gave them the possibility of determining their family size for themselves — have been ridiculed and denied in favour of chemical implants, the pill and other contraceptives distributed by corporations. Contraception has been transformed from a means of spacing births to a means of controlling populations — corporations and the state now think they have the tools to decide who should be permitted to have children and who should not. New reproductive technologies, such as *in vitro* fertilization, which potentially enable specialists to decide "both the quantity and quality of children born", will shift power still further away from women and into the hands of professionals and the state:

> "Medical personnel are increasingly viewed as the 'active' creators, arranging the union of the egg and the sperm, or transferring the embryo from test tube to womb. Women are the passive vessel, the vacant waiting womb . . . The ownership of the woman's body is eroded by the presence of a group of people who reputedly have superior knowledge of it."[20]

ENCLOSURE AS CONTROL

Enclosure is thus a change in the networks of power which enmesh the environment, production, distribution, the political process, knowledge, research and the law. It reduces the control of local people over community affairs. Whether female or male, a person's influence and ability to make a living depends increasingly on becoming absorbed into the new polity created by enclosure, on accepting — willingly or unwillingly — a new role as a consumer, a worker, a client or an administrator, on playing the game according to new rules. The way is thus cleared for cajoling people into the mainstream, be it through programmes to bring women "into development", to entice smallholders "into the market" or to foster paid employment.[21]

Those who remain on the margins of the new mainstream, either by choice or because that is where society has pushed them, are not only deemed to have little value: they are perceived as a threat. Thus it is the landless, the poor, the dispossessed who are blamed for forest destruction; their poverty which is held responsible for "overpopulation"; their protests which are classed as subversive and a threat to political stability. And because they are perceived as a threat, they become objects to be controlled, the legitimate subjects of yet further enclosure. Witness the measures taken by the Tanzanian authorities to curb street-traders. After the Human Resources Deployment Act in 1983:

> "Those who could not produce proper identification were to be resettled in the countryside. In the Dar es Salaam region, all unlicensed, self-employed people, including fish sellers, shoe repairmen, tailors, etc., were to be considered 'idle and disorderly' and treated as 'loiterers'. President Nyerere ordered the Prime Minister to be 'bold' in implementing the Act, saying: 'If we don't disturb loiterers, they will disturb us.' The loiterers were compared with economic saboteurs and racketeers 'whom the nation has declared war on.'"[22]

From the dispossessed beggars of Tudor England to the slum-dwellers of Sao Paolo, people have been defined as too poor, too dependent, too inarticulate, too marginal to be of "use" to mainstream society. They are shunted from one place to another as further areas are enclosed, or, as in the case of the street children of Brazil, they are simply murdered. Enclosure creates, as one New Guinea villager has put it, "rubbish people" — in the North no less than in the South.

CONCEPTUAL TRAPPING: THE ENCLOSURE OF
LANGUAGE AND CULTURE

Enclosure defines power. But it involves more than the taking over of public office, natural resources or markets by one group at the expense of another. By "taking something out of one social frame and forcing it into a new one", by redefining meanings, enclosure involves something akin to translation.

When a concept is enclosed in the context of a radically alien language, something is inevitably "lost in translation". When what is lost is essential to the identity and livelihoods of a group, yet they are unable to use their native language to regain or defend it, their defences are weakened and they become victims. For women who have to use a language such as contemporary English with patriarchal elements and assumptions, there is often "nowhere to go in the language", no words or ways to express what is essential for them to express.[23]

Nor is it easy for people to develop and articulate resistance to enclosure unless they are able to maintain a cultural and linguistic space in which to do so — a fact of which West Indian and North American slave owners were well aware. As James C. Scott notes:

> "To minimize communication, plantation owners preferred to bring together a labour force of the greatest linguistic and ethnic diversity. When a dialect of pidgin developed that was unintelligible to the planters, the slaves were required to converse at work only in a form of English their overseers could understand."[24]

As slavery has declined, the slave owners' strategy has developed into something more subtle. Native tongues are deliberately infiltrated with Western concepts foreign both to the language and to the culture. For example, in the "villagization" campaign in Tanzania in the mid-1970s, in which people were encouraged to build Western style houses in new villages, the men were addressed as "you and your families". But, as P. Caplan observes:

> "In Swahili, the term 'family' in the sense of a bounded domestic group does not exist. Indeed it has been found necessary to take the English term and turn it into a Swahili form *'familia'*. Such a linguistic usage contains a number of premises — that the unit in

society is 'a man and his family', and that this unit requires a house and a unit of land. In other words, concepts foreign to this society . . . are being introduced."[25]

People who would oppose dams, logging, the redevelopment of their neighbourhoods or the pollution of their rivers are often left few means of expressing or arguing their case unless they are prepared to engage in a debate framed by the languages of cost-benefit analysis, reductionist science, utilitarianism, male domi-nation— and, increasingly, English. Not only are these languages in which many local objections — such as that which holds ancestral community rights to a particular place to have precedence over the imperatives of "national development" — appear dis-reputable. They are also languages whose use allows enclosers to eavesdrop on, "correct" and dominate the conversations of the enclosed.

This process of conceptual trapping has gathered pace through the eras of state-formation, colonialism, economic development and now environmental management. None of these dominant systems can afford a "live and let live" attitude towards the thousands of other, more or less independent languages which make up the social universe. They must expand to global scale; other systems with their messy multitude of goals and ways of settling conflicts just get in the way. When they do, they are enclosed — squeezed into the new, overarching system, trapping those within them in the process. All conflict is settled by criteria determined by the enclosers.

This conceptual trapping is justified morally only by persuading people that they have no right to refuse to abide by an alien translation of their words, practices and ways of life. Enclosure claims that its own social frame, its language, is a universal norm, an all-embracing matrix which can assimilate all others. Whatever may be "lost in translation" is supposedly insignificant, undeveloped or inferior to what is gained. As Stephen Marglin points out:

" What it cannot comprehend and appropriate, it not only cannot appreciate, it cannot tolerate . . . In the encounter of modern knowledge with [vernacular knowledge], the real danger is not that modern knowledge will appropriate [vernacular knowledge] but that it will do so only partially and will return this partial knowledge ... as the solid core of truth extracted from a web of superstition and false belief. What lies outside the intersection of modern knowledge and [vernacular knowledge] risks being lost altogether."[26]

Because they hold themselves to be speaking a universal language, the modern enclosers who work for development agencies and governments feel no qualms in presuming to speak for the enclosed. They assume reflexively that they understand their predicament as well as or better than the enclosed do themselves. It is this tacit assumption that legitimizes enclosure in the encloser's mind — and it is an assumption that cannot be countered simply by transferring the visible trappings of power from one group to another.

4 POWER

The Central Issue

Enclosure forces us to confront the issue of power, of who controls resources and decision-making, of how power is exercised, by whom and for whose benefit. If the beneficiaries of enclosure have been able to maintain their power, it is not because those who have been disadvantaged by the process are compliant — on the contrary, resistance to enclosure is a constant everyday phenomenon — but because enclosers have built up structures of social control that enable them to maintain their power and influence despite resistance from the commons. Understanding these structures — how they work and who the major players are — is vital to the struggle to reclaim the commons. For it is such structures, rather than "lack of political will" or "insufficient knowledge", which are the major barriers to reclaiming the commons.

Today, economic and political power is entrenched in a network of interest groups whose influence on policy lies in the scope and intricacy of the mutually-beneficial, though often uneasy, alliances that hold them together. Such alliances now bind industrialists to government officials, politicians to individual companies, companies to the military, the military to the state, the state to aid agencies, aid agencies to corporations, corporations to academia, academia to regulatory agencies, and regulatory agencies to industry. Although the alliances may be unequal, all the partners have something to gain from joining forces. The result is a web of interlocking interests that effectively ensures that what is deemed "good" for those interests is deemed "good" for society at large.

COMMUNITIES OF INTEREST: THE AGRO-INDUSTRY EXAMPLE

By way of example, consider the hold that agrochemical interests

have on farm policy, both in the North and in the South. That hold
stems not only from the control that the industry has developed
over inputs, but also from the networks it has formed with research
institutes, agricultural training colleges, regulatory agencies,
government ministries and aid agencies. Thus, there are few
agricultural research institutions in either Europe or the US which
do not now rely to some extent on agrochemical or farm machinery
companies for funding. With funding comes control over the
specific content of research projects and the power to suppress
research that might rock the agro-industry boat. As Henk Hobbelink
notes of funding in the field of biotechnology:

> "Monsanto has 'donated' $23.5 million to Washington University
> for biotech research; Bayer is contributing to the Max Planck
> Institute in Cologne for the same purpose; and Hoechst built an
> entire laboratory for the Massachusetts General Hospital where
> research on crop genetics is also carried out. Lubrizol has more than
> $20 million tied up in research contracts at 18 universities and other
> public institutions. These industry-university contracts have caused
> much controversy for obvious reasons. 'You don't need to know
> algebra to figure out how that committee works', says US [Senator]
> Albert Gore, talking about the committee that governs the Monsanto/
> Washington deal. 'No research can be done unless the company
> gives permission.' Of the Hoechst grant for a biotech laboratory,
> [one researcher has commented]: 'Essentially everyone in that lab
> is an indentured servant to Hoechst.' In most contracts, the trans-
> national company (TNC) has the right to the first look at the results
> and can delay publication of them until patent possibilities are
> investigated."[1]

Corporate grants give researchers leverage to gain additional
funds from government and even small amounts of corporate
funding can therefore have a disproportionate influence on public
research. Through the strategic placing of grants, industry can
direct public funds into research that best serves its own long-term
agenda. The process has gained its own momentum, and universities are embracing their own corporatist, profit-maximizing
vision. In the US, public universities allocate scarce resources to
research which it is hoped will yield patentable processes and
products to form part of the universities' future endowment.
Biotech research thus receives considerable funds, while research
on the environmental and social impact of industrial agriculture is

neglected or eliminated. As a result of what he terms "social sleepwalking", William Friedland of the University of California charges that US "land grant" universities, with their production-oriented approach, have in the past ignored a host of important issues:

"And the issues put aside have to do precisely with the more humanistic side of agricultural research. Thus while production scientists in agriculture argue that the humanistic elements are taken care of by the profusion of food production, its relative cheapness, its contribution to the US strength and political position in the world, other issues are not only set aside and ignored, but, indeed, actually suppressed."[2]

Inevitably, the pro-industry orientation of research within universities and other public institutions filters through into the curricula of training colleges and, thence, into the programmes promoted through agricultural extension services. In the US, for example, the Extension Service has pushed high-technology agriculture at the expense of less environmentally-destructive techniques and at great cost to smaller producers:

"Extension agents have acted as salesmen for the agricultural research generated by their colleagues in the land-grant college system . . . By persuading farmers to adopt expensive machinery developed by the agricultural research centres, the Extension Service has supported changes in the structure of agriculture that have driven millions of small farmers off the land and benefited only the largest and most prosperous survivors . . . [According to a report by the Agribusiness Accountability Project] 'The agents frequently are focused so intently on corporate needs that they literally have become tax-supported extensions of corporate agribusiness.'"[3]

At the international level, research and training is similarly dominated by industrial interests, working primarily through alliances with international development agencies. Thus, in its 46 years of existence, the UN Food and Agriculture Organization (FAO) has consistently derided traditional methods of agriculture and sought to modernize farming in the Third World (along with fishing, forestry and the other areas of food and agriculture that come under its remit).[4] In the 1960s, FAO agreed to set up a joint programme — the Industry Cooperative Programme (ICP) — with GIFAP, an agro-industry lobbying group, under which GIFAP representatives, drawn directly from agrochemical companies, would work hand-in-hand with technicians from FAO. The programme was housed in the FAO's Rome headquarters and joint FAO-ICP seminars were regularly organized in Third World countries to promote "new and better ways" of distributing pesticides.

In 1978, following growing criticism of the special relationship between FAO and the agrochemical industry, the ICP was closed down. Nonetheless, FAO has continued to "market" pesticides through its advisory programmes and, as Barbara Dinham of the Pesticides Trust reports, a cosy relationship still exists between GIFAP and FAO:

> "Involvement in FAO workshops . . . strengthens GIFAP's links with training structures in the Third World. For example, on a training course for plant protection and extension officers from the Ministry of Agriculture and local companies in Indonesia, the course programme used the GIFAP *Farmer Trainer Manual*. An FAO Workshop on pesticide management in West Africa in 1989 used a GIFAP resource person."[5]

With both research and training dominated by pro-industry networks, industry is able to operate in a climate that is broadly sympathetic to its aims and views. Those trained or employed in the mainstream can move freely between public and private sectors, universities and governments. The result is a "revolving door" relationship between industry and its supposed regulators.

In the agricultural sector, this cosy relationship is most conspicuous in the national committees which decide agricultural policy. In The Netherlands, over a third of the seats on the committee which decides on research funding for biotechnology are assigned to commercial companies.[6] At the international level, industry has a considerable influence on such bodies as the FAO/World Health Organization (WHO) Codex Alimentarius Commission, the organization which, if current proposals of the Uruguay Round of GATT go through, will be responsible for "harmonizing" pesticide standards worldwide. The pesticide committee of Codex has 197 participants: of those who attended a meeting in April 1991, 50 were from agrochemical companies, 14 from food companies, seven had no named or professional designation (which may or may not mean that they were consultants for industry) and just two were consumer representatives.[7] One study by Greenpeace USA found that Codex safety levels for at least eight widely-used pesticides were lower than current US standards, by as much as a factor of 25.[8]

The power of the agrochemical industry thus rests not exclusively in the economic clout of individual companies, but derives from the *network* of institutions, individuals and industries that have a stake in industrialized agriculture. A policy bias has been created that works not only to promote industrial agriculture but, just as importantly, to deliberately *undermine* other systems of production and distribution. The structure of subsidies to agriculture, for example, is invariably skewed to favour large-scale, intensive farmers who pick up the lion's share of support, thus disadvantaging smaller producers. Because many subsidies are tied to production or paid by head of livestock, the incentive to produce regardless of the cost to the environment is institutionalized — at the expense of farmers who would seek to minimize their use of agrochemicals or to farm without them. Similarly, throughout the Northern industrialized countries, governments have systematically underfunded research into organic and other environmentally-sensitive forms of farming, thus discouraging more widespread change to alternatives. As Joel Solkoff, a former assistant to the US Secretary of State for Labour, records, research aimed at "preserving the physical environment, encouraging rural community development and improving consumer nutrition" has been consistently discouraged by the US Department of Agriculture as being inimicable to business interests. Instead, research funding has been directed into such fields as "reducing human labour in agriculture, and, in general, increasing agricultural production per unit of output."[9]

ERODING THE COMMONS

The network of interests that now pushes agricultural policy in a direction favourable to agribusiness is not unique. Similar net-

The Power
of the Transnationals

- Seventy per cent of world trade is now controlled by just 500 corporations, which also control 80 per cent of foreign investment and 30
  per cent of world GDP.

- Shell Oil's 1990 gross income ($132 billion) was more than the total
  GNP of Tanzania, Ethiopia, Nepal, Bangladesh, Zaire, Uganda, Nigeria,
  Kenya and Pakistan combined. Five hundred million people inhabit
  these countries, nearly a tenth of the world's population.

- Cargill, the Canadian grain giant, alone controls 60 per cent of the world
  trade in cereals. Its turnover in 1990 was the same as Pakistan's Gross
  National Product.

- Just 13 corporations supply 80 per cent of all automobiles: five of them
  (General Motors, Ford, Toyota, Nissan and Peugeot) sell half of all the
  vehicles manufactured each year.

- US corporations spend more than one billion dollars yearly on
  advertising. The average US citizen views 21,000 television
  commercials every year.

Transnational Corporations (TNCs) epitomize the logic of enclosure.
Disembedded from any one culture and any one environment, they owe no
loyalty to any community, any government or any people anywhere in the world.
They are the most blatant example of what the anthropologist Roy Rappaport
has called the "special purpose institution". Such institutions — from the military
to government departments and international agencies — are driven by the
desire to promote their own interests, to perpetuate themselves and to increase
their power and influence. Decisions are not made because they are of benefit
to the community or on environmental grounds but because they serve the
institution's particular vested interest.

Employees are similarly disembedded from the real world. When acting for
the organization, company loyalty takes precedence over the moral and cultural
restraints that mediate the rest of their lives. Dennis Levine, a Wall Street high-
flyer who was imprisoned for insider trading, captures the detached world in
which much corporate decision-making takes place: "We had a phenomenal
enterprise going on Wall Street, and it was easy to forget that the billions of
dollars we threw around had any material impact upon the jobs and, thus, the
daily lives of millions of Americans. All too often the Street seemed to be a giant
Monopoly board, and this game-like attitude was clearly evident in our terminol-
ogy. When a company was identified as an acquisition target, we declared that
it was 'in play'. We designated the playing pieces and strategies in whimsical
terms: white knight, target, shark repellent, the Pac-Man defence, poison pill,
greenmail, the golden parachute. Keeping a scorecard was easy — the winner
was the one who finalized the most deals and took home the most money."

The power wielded by these organizations is greater than that of many, if not
all, governments and makes a mockery of certain countries' claims to democracy. With the world as their gaming-table, TNCs are beholden neither to local
communities nor to national electorates, but can dictate policy through their

control of markets and the economic havoc they can cause by withdrawing support from a government. As such, they are the chief obstacle to the resolution of our environmental and social problems. If incalculably more money has been spent in the last 40 years on nuclear power rather than solar energy, for example, this is not because communities or electorates have favoured nuclear over solar; it is because TNCs, acting in alliance with state corporations, stand to benefit more from nuclear energy, whereas solar power has a potential to put control of energy back into the hands of the community.

---

works dominate other sectors of the global economy, such as the military, the construction industry, the nuclear industry and the car industry. The important point is not merely that such networks exist but that they are *integral* to the process of enclosure; and, moreover, that their existence is incompatible with a healthy commons.

Firstly, it is only through creating such networks that interest groups have been able to override the cultural checks and balances that *limit* the power of any one group or individual within the commons. Once the authority of the commons has been superseded by the authority of outside interest groups, decisions are no longer grounded in the local needs of local communities, but in the cut and thrust of office politics, in geopolitics, corporate empire building and profit. The environment and local people become expendable because the new networks of power are neither based in any given locality, nor committed to any one community: once a forest has been logged, the logging company's concern is to find another forest to log; if wages can be undercut by moving a factory to another area, the factory is moved.

Thus, if the coastal commons of the Indian state of Kerala are now drastically overfished, it is not because of "overpopulation" or the "poverty" of local fisherfolk, but because an alliance of city-based entrepreneurs, aid agencies and the state government made it possible for commercial interests to cash in on the booming international market in prawns at the expense of the commons. Capitalizing on loans available from the aid agencies, the entrepreneurs built up trawler fleets whose operations were controlled not by the villagers whose livelihoods depended on fish remaining in the sea, but by state officials whose primary concern was to maximize state revenues from fishing. Whereas in the coastal commons, villagers had long protected their fishing grounds from overexploitation through elaborate rules on who could fish, when and where they could fish, and with what nets and tackle, the trawler operators were bound by no such constraints. Mechanized boats could be operated without any form of licence or registration; there were no restrictions on the nets used; and, initially, no limits to where the trawlers could fish. An activity which had been under the control of the commons was thus opened up to those who had no long-term stake in the health of the marine environment: as a result, the coastal waters of Kerala were exploited almost to the point of collapse, the landings of oil sardines and mackerel — once the mainstay of the fisheries — plummeting from 250,000 tonnes in 1968 to 87,000 tonnes in 1980.[10] Significantly, the state government only took action to restrict the trawlers after widespread protest from local fishing communities: equally significantly, such protest — together with declining profits — prompted many trawler owners to transfer their capital into other sectors.

GLOBAL REACH

Secondly, by removing decision-making from its local context, the networks that have emerged from enclosure have enabled vested interests to operate at a global level. TNCs have power not only because they have operations all over the world, but also because they have built up a web of political and personal contacts in the South and the North whose economic interests are grounded in those of the TNCs.

Creating such links has been key, not only to the strategy of the TNCs, but also to the post-colonial foreign policy of most Northern countries. As historian Gabriel Kolko has convincingly documented, "top US leadership spent the war years laying the groundwork for a postwar economic order firmly under its control. US needs were clear-cut: institutionalization of free trade and reconstruction of Europe and Asia, both to import US goods and capital and to export raw materials vital to the United States."[11] The World Bank and the other institutions set up at Bretton Woods were key to this strategy, and, from the outset, the Bank began to create "niches" within Third World countries through which it could cultivate factions and interests sympathetic to the North. By providing funds for "institution building", it fashioned autonomous agencies — national energy authorities, for example — "insulated from domestic political pressures (but responsive, of course to the nonpolitical pressures emanating from the Bank's own headquarters)."[12] The Bank also "quickly discovered its natural affinity with emerging transnationalist factions of Less Developed Country (LDC) states." It thus became established policy for the Bank to stipulate who would staff these autonomous agencies. "With the 1955 establishment of its own Institute (the Economic Development Institute), the Bank sought to assure a steady supply of technocratic counterparts."[13]

Where such "entryism" has failed to secure transnational regimes in the South, Northern interests have taken more direct action. In Brazil, for example, a transnationalist faction under General Castello Branco was propelled into power through a US-backed coup that toppled the nationalist government of João Goulart in 1964. Following the coup, the IMF quickly resumed loans under conditions that speeded the country's shift towards export-orientated industrialization.[14] Goulart's plans for land reform were abandoned, and the peasant groups which had campaigned for the reforms were suppressed. Meanwhile, the military regime opened the doors to foreign industry, initiating, among other projects, "Operation Amazonia", a vast plan to occupy and "develop" Brazil's forest interior. With the backing of the World Bank, subsidies, cheap land and new roads were used to encourage the landless into the forests and to set up ranches on forest lands. "Incentives were offered to the big companies to ensure that Amazonia was occupied in what the government saw as a modern and productive way. From 1973, car, steel and food-packaging magnates were encouraged, by means of credit and tax holidays, to diversify and invest, especially in cattle ranching. Companies were offered tax holidays for up to 17 years, grants totalling up to three-quarters of the value of their investment, and cheap credit (effectively, at negative rates of interest, given Brazil's high inflation levels)."[15]

As the transnationalist faction within countries such as Brazil has grown, coups and strong-arm tactics have become less necessary to ensure the dominance of the transnationalist agenda. Where Third World governments have agreed to the package of export-orientated policies and public expenditure cuts required under structural adjustment programmes, for example, it is not because they have been imposed by the IMF or the World Bank acting unilaterally, but because key ministries have come to be dominated by transnational factions whose interests are best served by structural adjustment — not least because it ensures a continued supply of credit. For the mass of the population, however, the consequences of lower wages, increased food prices, government health cuts and enforced cash-cropping are devastating.[16]

These transnational factions in the South have not achieved the position they have by accident. In the Philippines, when the IMF's efforts to persuade the government to adopt structural adjustment in the late 1970s were blocked by nationalist factions within the Philippines Central Bank, the baton was handed over to the World Bank. As Robin Broad records, by turning to allies in the Ministry of Industry and Finance, the World Bank was able to bypass nationalist factions within the Central Bank and put in place a $200 million structural adjustment loan package, "tied not to a specific project but to a set of policy stipulations consolidating an export-led course for the Philippine industrial sector":

> "By amassing a potent group of transnationalist allies elsewhere, it tilted the domestic power struggle in favour of transnationalist over nationalist factions . . . Within the state, nationalists lost every key foothold of influence on policy formulation, as transnationalists assumed hegemonic control of all major ministries. Within the private sector, economic nationalist factions whose enterprises depended on domestic markets were decimated as a class."[17]

In the wake of the agreement, free trade zones were established "with generous incentives to transnational corporations to exploit low-cost Filipino labour", tariffs on imports were slashed and domestic small-scale industries (textiles and the like) restructured to cater for the export market.

Similar programmes with equally severe consequences for the commons have been adopted elsewhere with the compliance of transnational factions in other countries. This is not to say that the principles behind structural adjustment did not originate in the World Bank and the IMF; nor that transnational factions would not have gained the hold that they have on policy-making without the patronage of the World Bank and other Northern institutions: nor that structural adjustment has gone unopposed from other factions within Third World governments: it is simply to point out that structural adjustment, like other development policies, is the result of specific interests from both North and South acting in *consort* and as *allies*. It is also to argue that without such alliances, and in the absence of direct rule, institutions like the World Bank would not enjoy the global reach that they do today.

Viewed from this perspective, the links *between* interest groups are more important than their differences. In that respect, the fundamental division within today's global economy is not between an ill-defined "North" and an equally ill-defined "South", but between those who benefit from being part of the new networks of power and those who do not. It makes little difference to a forest dweller from Guyana, for example, that the companies currently moving in to exploit the forests are, in many instances, from the South: what is of importance is that the forests are being taken over and destroyed. Conversely, it matters little to Palmaven, the Venezuelan company that has gained a concession to exploit 300,000 hectares on Guyana's Demerera River, that the Guyanese government has also opened the country's doors to companies from France, Canada and Australia.[18] What matters is that resistance to logging should be neutralized and that the flow of government subsidies and international aid for infrastructure should continue.

CONTAINING CHALLENGES

The conflict of interests is as old as enclosure itself. Throughout history, enclosures have been resisted: and throughout history, enclosers have sought to contain that resistance, where possible turning it to their advantage. Once again, alliances between different interest groups have played a key role in the enclosers' strategies. In the 1960s, Third World élites successfully blocked demands for radical land reform by entering into an alliance with agrochemical interests and Northern development agencies to promote "Green Revolution" technologies. By redefining the problem of rural poverty in terms of insufficient productivity (*solution*: high yielding varieties and agrochemicals) rather than lack of access to sufficient land (*solution*: land reform), land reform was thus given a new context: instead of being a means of freeing up land for peasant agriculture, it now became a means of freeing up land for the Green Revolution. As Roger Plant observes of the land reform programmes instituted in Latin America during the 1960s and 1970s:

> "Whatever the declared social objectives of the average land reforms, their real aim was rarely to provide land for the landless. Instead, their aim was to rationalize and modernize land use and production systems, and to replace semi-feudal and servile labour arrangements by wage labour systems. The land reform programmes tended to interpret the social function of property by the criteria of efficiency and productivity alone, declaring that all uncultivated land was liable to expropriation.

> " . . . They were premised not so much on the rights of the landless or near-landless, as on the obligations of the landed. Landowners who could turn into efficient commercial farmers were generally deemed to fulfil the social function of property."[19]

The demand to restore land to the commons — a demand voiced by numerous peasant movements — thus became used as a means of absorbing farming deeper into the market economy, as a means of further enclosure. Similarly, popular demands for local people to have a decisive say in the matters that affect their lives have been contained through the directed use of "participatory" processes.

Majid Rahnema, a former minister in the Iranian government in the late 1960s and an ex-officer of the UN Development Programme, summarizes how participation has been used to increase the control of enclosers over local people:

> " Grassroots organizations are becoming the infrastructure through which investment is made, or they help provide the human 'software' that makes other kinds of investment work ... [Participation] is now simply perceived as one of the many 'resources' needed to keep the *economy* alive. To participate is thus reduced to the act of partaking in the objectives of the economy, and the societal arrangements related to it."[20]

THE ENVIRONMENTAL CRISIS

Now comes the environmental crisis. The issues are not new: on the contrary, from the smokestacks of Victorian Britain to the logged-out moonscapes of modern-day British Columbia or Sarawak, environmental degradation has gone hand-in-hand with economic expansion, as commercial interests have sacrificed local livelihoods and environments in order to obtain raw materials, transform them into commodities, market them and dispose of the wastes. Nor has the destruction gone unchallenged. In the South, local cultures have fought attempts — first by colonial regimes and then by their "own" post-independence governments, acting in consort with commercial interests and international development agencies — to transform their homelands and themselves into "resources" for the global economy. Timber operations have been sabotaged, logging roads blockaded, dams delayed, commercial plantations uprooted, factory installations burned, mines closed down and rallies held in a constant effort to keep outside forces at bay.

Likewise in the North, the history of protest against the ravages of industrialization is a long one, coalescing initially around the machine-breaking and public health movements of the 19th century and emerging latterly in the many and diverse groupings now challenging environmental pollution, declining food quality, countryside destruction, health hazards in the home and workplace, and the erosion of community life. As in the South, such movements have expressed their concerns using whatever channels are available to them — from civil disobedience to legal challenges, boycotts and alliances of like-minded groups. Toxic waste dumps have been picketed, sites for nuclear power plants occupied, polluting pipelines capped, companies boycotted, whaling ships buzzed, and media campaigns mounted in an attempt both to combat environmental degradation and to put the environment on the political agenda.

THE THREAT OF ENVIRONMENTALISM

Where environmental destruction was limited to the local level — a clear-cut forest here, a leaking toxic waste dump there, a polluted river here, a salinized tract of land there — and where protest was restricted to isolated movements, the threat that such movements posed to established patterns of power could be contained with relative ease.

Commercial and industrial interests were able to follow a strategy of simply denying the problem or of justifying the destruction in the name of "the greater good" or the "national interest". Opposition could be met by force or played down as "uninformed", "reactionary", "Luddite" or "subversive". The reaction of the Velsicol Corporation to the publication of Rachel Carson's *Silent Spring*, the book which in many respects launched the "green" movement in the North, is illustrative. In a five-page letter to Carson's publishers, Velsicol accused her of being in league with "sinister influences, whose attacks on the chemical industry have a dual purpose: (1) to create the false impression that all business is grasping and immoral, and (2) to reduce the use of agricultural chemicals in this country and in the countries of western Europe so that our supply of food will be reduced to east-curtain parity."

Crude as such attacks are, they still persist. The vision may no longer be of a communist conspiracy but both corporations and governments are clearly worried by the way in which alliances are being formed between formerly isolated, local or national citizens' groups, in order to resist the powerful interests that are threatening their commons. Indeed, in a leaked memorandum, the US Environmental Protection Agency has described the "environmental justice movement" in the United States, best known for its work in opposing toxic waste dumps, as the greatest threat to political stability since the anti-war movement of the 1960s.

ACTIVISM WINS CHANGE

The threat is two-fold. On the one hand, environmental protest has forced the previously marginalized discourse of environmentalism into the political mainstream, transforming ecological destruction from a "side issue" that corporations and governments felt able to disregard into lost markets and lost votes. If the landfilling of toxic wastes in the US is now being phased out, for example, it is not because US companies themselves view landfill as an environmentally unacceptable means of waste disposal (US companies see no problems in landfilling wastes in Britain or the Third World, where standards are lower) but rather because the spread of popular protest in the US has made it clear that "Not In My Back-Yard" means "not in anybody's back-yard", leaving corporate executives with no option but to seek other waste disposal strategies. As Andrew Szasz notes, "popular pressure worked on two levels: in Washington, mainstream environmental groups and members of Congress facing constituency pressure recognized how salient and volatile the issue was and supported stronger regulations. At the same time, local opposition to new facilities interacted with these stronger regulations to drive up disposal costs, and thus to raise economic pressures for waste reduction."

But the threat of environmentalism goes deeper than simply upsetting individual corporate apple carts. Tighter environmental standards — not to speak of environmental degradation itself —

now threaten the throughput of resources in the global economy. But whereas economic contraction provides a space in which the commons can regain some of its authority, the prospect of such contraction becoming a permanent feature of the economy has caused alarm bells to ring in corporate headquarters and other centres of power. As the Brundtland Commission, whose report *Our Common Future* initiated the UNCED process, puts it: "We have in the past been concerned about the impacts of economic growth upon the environment. We are now forced to concern ourselves with the impacts of ecological stress . . . upon our economic prospects."

Environmental stress — and the pressure to ease it — is already denying resources to the global economy, whilst simultaneously depriving it of sinks into which the waste products of industrialization can readily (and cheaply) be disposed. As soils are eroded, so land is taken out of production; as the seas are overfished and rivers polluted, so fisheries crash; as forests are logged out or succumb to damage from air pollution, so timber supplies are threatened; and as the economic costs of mitigating damage rise, so capital is diverted away from "productive" growth. In the US alone, soil compaction — the direct result of modern mechanized agriculture — is estimated to have cost farmers some $3 billion in lost yields in 1980 alone. The damage already incurred through acid rain and pollution-related forest die-back in Europe and the US has been put at $30 billion, whilst the estimated cost of cleaning up the 2,000 worst polluting toxic waste dumps in the US has been put at $100 billion. No realistic figure can even be put on the social and economic disruption that will be incurred through global warming and ozone depletion. The likely loss of species alone makes the price tag incalculable. Both Northern and Southern governments — voicing the concerns of industrial interests — argue that such costs cannot be borne without sending the global economy into a tail-spin. Yet, for those who rely on the commons, such economic contraction is often to be welcomed since it can bring welcome relief from enclosure.

CONTAINING THE CHALLENGE

True to form, the networks of interest that have benefited from enclosure since World War II are now seeking to contain the threats posed to their interests by environmentalism, on the one hand, and environmental degradation, on the other. An element of restructuring is accepted as "unavoidable" if business is to retain public support, and outright resistance to change is giving way to the adoption of strategies for managing that change.

At one level, such strategies go no further than "damage control", with individual interests attempting to head off measures that would impose too heavy a cost on their individual industries, either by playing down their contribution to the problem or by playing up the action they have already taken to address environmental degradation. Within UNCED, for example, corporate interests effectively blocked discussion of the environmental impact of Transnational Corporations: recommendations drawn up by the UN's own Centre for Transnational Corporations (UNCTC), which would have imposed tough global environmental standards on TNC activities, were shelved and instead a voluntary code of conduct, drawn up by the Business Council on Sustainable Development, a corporate lobbying group, was adopted as the secretariat's input into UNCED's Agenda 21. The UNCTC's proposals were not even circulated to delegates.[21] Meanwhile, the UNCTC has been quietly closed down. Instead of being subject to a mandatory code of conduct, negotiated multilaterally, the TNCs have emerged from UNCED without their role in causing environmental destruction even having been scrutinized in the official process, let alone curtailed.

Indeed, governments of both North and South have done everything in their power to protect the interests of their industrial and commercial lobbies. The guidelines issued to US delegates negotiating the Climate Convention, for example, faithfully reflected the position of the oil industry. Delegates were advised that it was:

"not beneficial to discuss whether there is or is not warming, or how much or how little warming. In the eyes of the public, we will lose this debate. A better approach is to raise the many uncertainties that need to be understood on this issue."[22]

The negotiators were also told to stress that "the world community is making great strides towards understanding the science of global change, but many fundamental questions remain unanswered"; and that "more work is needed" on "the economic impacts of potential global changes and possible responses."

A similar approach was adopted in the negotiations on biodiversity, the main priority of US negotiators being to block any measures that might harm the interests of biotechnology companies or undermine the patenting of "intellectual property". During the fourth Preparatory Meeting for UNCED, for example, the US delegation insisted that references in Agenda 21 to the hazards of biotechnology should be deleted, arguing that the risks have been exaggerated. In this, the position taken by the US delegation was identical to that of the Heritage Foundation, an influential US think-tank with close links to the US administration. The US also deleted major sections of the Agenda 21 text which would have imposed safeguards against "the experimentation with unsafe fertility-regulating drugs on women in developing countries." A proposed ban on "medical technologies in developing countries for purposes of experimentation in reproductive processes" was also deleted at US insistence.[23]

Beyond such wrecking tactics, however, there is now a conscious attempt by corporate and other mainstream interests to "capture" the debate on environment and development and to frame it in terms that will minimize changes to the status quo. Thus, throughout the UNCED process, the great and the good have been making solemn noises about "the grave threat to our common future." The message is one that has rallied industrialist and environmentalist alike, many environmentalists seeing in it an opportunity for nudging business and government in a greener direction. But, now that the Rio conference has drawn to a close, it is clear that any hopes popular, movement-orientated groups may have entertained about working on an equal footing with the representatives of industrial interests have been delusions. Worse still, much of the rhetoric they have embraced is legitimizing an agenda that, if unchallenged, threatens a new round of enclosure as devastating to the commons as anything that has gone before.

5 *MAINSTREAM SOLUTIONS*

Further Enclosure

The degradation of earth, air, forests and water means different things to different people. For people who depend on the commons, such degradation means a loss of dignity and independence, security, livelihood and health. Defending the commons is thus often a matter of life and death.

In contrast, figures in government, business, and international organizations, whose livelihoods do not depend directly on what is around them, tend to view environmental degradation and the protests it provokes as threats to their political interests. For them, the environment is not what is around their homes but what is around their economies. Northern leaders, for example, are preoccupied with how to keep a growing South from tapping resources and filling up waste sinks which the North has grown accustomed to using, while simultaneously maintaining the global capital flows which help the world economy expand. Southern leaders, responding to prodding from Northern capital and hoping to benefit themselves as well, are equally preoccupied with extending the boundaries of their economies by bringing more land under the plough, logging more forests, diverting more water to industry, and so on.

Not surprisingly, the three groups approach environmental degradation differently. For people who rely on the commons, the only response that makes sense is to concentrate on what has proved to be effective in the past, a response that entails maintaining or creating a space in which local commons can root themselves. That involves pushing for an erosion of enclosers' power, so that capital flows around the globe can be reduced, local control increased, consumption cut and markets limited. While regaining the commons is undoubtedly a daunting undertaking, it at least has the advantage of building on the firm foundation of long-tested ways of life.

The preferred response of world leaders and mainstream environmentalists, however, is to seek further enclosure by the market, the state, the private and the public, in the hope that whatever troublesome environmental damage has been caused by previous enclosure can be remedied by more far-reaching enclosure in the future. This approach seeks to preserve economic expansion through a programme of global management of both the environment and people. It has never been attempted before on the scale proposed. Previous, less ambitious attempts, moreover, have not only failed to arrest environmental degradation, they have exacerbated it. Nonetheless, it is this path which has been chosen by the Secretariat and virtually all delegations at the United Nations Conference on Environment and Development, as well as by the World Bank, UNDP, FAO, and many scientific and conservation organizations. In that respect, the Earth Summit in Rio de Janeiro articulated the mainstream response to the "environmental crisis", which is now atttributed to six supposed "causes": poverty; overpopulation; continuing barriers to the operations of the free market; the failure to enclose the environmental debate within economic theory; and a lack of western technology, know-how and capital.

IS POVERTY THE PROBLEM?

Since the mid-1980s, dominant institutions have been redefining the concepts of poverty, the environment and development in order to make them fit with each other in a neat syllogism:

Poverty causes environmental degradation, while wealth cures it;

Development helps relieve poverty and create wealth;

Therefore,

Development helps cure environmental degradation.

This formula is typically accompanied by a skilfully selected array of images contrasting locust-like Third World peasants torching and chainsawing forests and Eastern Europeans burning high-sulphur coal in inefficient factories with the spotlessly white-shirted "ecological modernizers" of the West, showing off cities and rivers newly cleaned up with the latest green technology.

The problem with this syllogism is that both of its premises are false. There is no ground for saying that environmental degradation is caused by poverty which is not an even better ground for saying that it is caused by wealth. The only type of poverty which can be said to cause significant environmental degradation is that which is brought about by development itself. Other things which the North has learned to call "poverty" over the last half-century as a way of justifying development's assault on them — for example, the frugal, self-sufficient or risk-minimizing lifestyles associated with the commons — have had, by comparison, little impact. The notion that development is going to relieve environmental problems could therefore hardly be more wrong.

POVERTY: THE POLITICAL ECONOMY OF A WORD

In commons regimes, there can be many meanings of "poverty". Many of these survive in languages such as Persian, in which "there are more than 30 words for naming those who, for one reason or another, are perceived as poor"[1] — nuns who adopt voluntary asceticism, people who have been abandoned or excluded from their communities, the infirm, those who have lost status, and so on. The development industry, however, recognizes no such subtleties. By and large, people are defined as poor if their "standard of living" falls below that of "average" white, middle-class Americans. Peasants are deemed "poor" if they provide for themselves, rather than sell their crops and buy commercially-produced foods. They are poor if they wear handmade clothes rather than factory-made garments; if they build their own houses with the help of their neighbours rather than employing labourers; if their children are educated by family and friends rather than by paid teachers.

There are good reasons for this. Colonialists and developers have not always referred to such lifestyles as "poor". Before 1940, the preferred words were "undisciplined", "immature", "ignorant", "effeminate", and "unscientific", and the preferred approach, the "civilizing mission" which accompanied colonial plunder. Only after World War II, when former colonies demanded more respect and the "national security" requirements of the *pax Americana* necessitated a more far-reaching global economic mobilization, were the broad cultural standards which had been used to measure colonizers against colonized replaced with a specifically economic yardstick.

Placed against it, the majority of the world's peoples became economically backward rather than culturally inferior; thus today in the North a nominal "cultural tolerance" goes hand-in-hand with a sense of economic superiority. The battle against "poverty" rather than the "improvement" of customs and religions became the North's excuse for intervention, expropriation and incorporation, a way of establishing a relationship with the South, based on imputed Southern "needs", which Northern publics could grasp. The same societies which viewed Christian proselytizers or colonial armies in Asia and Africa as a relic of a racist past, and which now pronounced themselves appreciative of variegated cultural traditions, thus began dispatching a new sort of "mission": hundreds of economic advisers charged with the task of retooling and "correcting" the "backward" economies of the Third World to ensure "prosperity for all". Former colonial possessions were "freed" only to take their assigned places in a single world economic race led by the United States.

It was to underscore the importance of entering this race that Northern agencies tried to subsume as many important characteristics of Southern societies as possible into the single omnibus category of "poverty". As Colombian sociologist Arturo Escobar puts it, life in the South was reduced "simply to conditions of 'misery', overlooking its rich traditions, different values and life styles, and long historical achievements."[2] Its people were "seen as no more than crude matter, in urgent need of being transformed by planning." Ways of life revolving around the commons were run together with the destitution caused by colonialism, the modern market, military incursion or natural disasters. Traditionally-protected forest commons were confused with "open access" areas which, following enclosure attempts on the part of state or business, had evolved into free-for-all zones looted by both marginalized peasants and business. What for the commons were "integral components of viable social and cultural systems, rooted in different, non-modern social relations and systems of knowledge" were translated by the economist into "indubitable signs of poverty and backwardness."[3]

Simultaneously, efforts were made to reduce this omnibus category of "poverty" (as well as the lifestyles it concealed) to one or another quantifiable "indicator". In the 1940s and 1950s, the World Bank pioneered the comparison of per capita cash incomes of different countries. Many other indicators have since appeared: gross national product, distribution, "literacy", "availability of public health institutions", "degree of satisfaction of basic needs", degree of adoption of settled as opposed to "slash and burn" agriculture, "empowerment", "improvement of social choices", "sustainability" and "well-being".

The type of indicator has never been particularly important, however. What matters is that there is one. If a society can be made to measure itself against other societies along a common yardstick, it will soon have to admit that many of its "differences" with them are actually "deficiencies" requiring "aid" and susceptible to technical attack. It will have to acquiesce in its definition as a "winner" or "loser" according to its position along some single (generally numerical) scale.

The commensuration of countries and peoples through a criterion of economic achievement was a brilliant solution to the problem of how to justify the enclosure of alien societies within the framework of the world market and the nation-state. By promoting the view that different societies share a single principle for resolving conflicts ("Does this improve the national social and economic development indicators?") rather than many ("What effect will this have on our community?" "Will this offend the spirits?"

"What do our friends say about this?" "Does this accord with the *akhazang*?"), the architects of development suggested that decision-making could be placed in the hands of experts without losing its "democratic" and "uncoerced" quality. "We are not telling you what to do," aid officials and technicians could say, displaying sheaves of calculations and graphs, "but don't you see that according to the standards which you yourself have endorsed, electrification of your country will remain inadequate unless you do what we suggest?" Measurement thus replaced discussion. No group could legitimately protest against being reorganized to become a part of the money economy, since such "growth" was, by definition, what enabled people to "reach their potential" as exemplified by those with higher "indicators". Exploitation and liberation had been defined out of this language, resistance could be treated as the frustration of the have-nots aspiring to the condition of the haves, and social interaction became merely a means of carrying out predetermined objectives. (A section on the "limitations and costs of participation" in the World Bank's current *World Development Report* notes with unconcealed dismay that "extensive participation . . . can delay decision making" since "communities with political influence sometimes reject proposals to construct facilities such as waste disposal centers.")[4] Instead of having to be vulnerable to the surprise and change involved in encountering alien cultures, leaders bent on enclosure grew more assured that they would not be challenged by alternative values, accused of dictatorship, or compelled to revise their plans. "Development indicators" furnished them with that power which is, in the words of Karl Deutsch, "the capacity not to have to learn".[5]

Comparing societies by means of a common "wealth–poverty" yardstick carried another comforting implication for enclosers: provided that the source of value lay in whatever the yardstick measured, what was measured became replaceable. To choose one possible society over another was not to neglect the separate and unique value of the rejected option, but merely to prefer a larger amount of the same value. "Everything has a cost and everybody has a price", World Bank representatives often reassured their

Southern interlocutors; "you have to make trade-offs". Risk mini-
mization, aspirations for political liberation and other aspects of
lifestyles with "low income" were rendered invisible or dispensa-
ble. Local knowledge, too, was acknowledged only insofar as it
could be commensurated with that of the West: a Cambodian
buffalo cart became merely a "primitive" form of pick-up truck
and the Nepali brush dam a defective version of a concrete slab.

"POVERTY" AND CONSERVATION

The political agenda behind blaming environmental destruction on
poverty is thus clear. But if frugal, self-reliant ways of life are what
is meant by "poor", then it is false to maintain that poverty causes
environmental degradation. It is not peasant farmers, for example,
who have eroded biodiversity in agriculture, but modern
agribusinesses which aim to maximize output of a single crop
through monoculture. Peasants deliberately plant a wide range of
crops to suit different needs and in a conscious attempt to spread
risks by minimizing the possibility of crop failure. In India, prior
to the Green Revolution, some 50,000 varieties of rice were
cultivated. Each had its special use: some were rich in minerals and
thus well suited to nursing mothers, others more suitable for the
elderly, others specially adapted to deeply-flooded fields, others
helpful in stopping encroachment by wild rice and so on.[6] Similarly, it is not the "poor" peasants and "poor" forest dwellers of the
commons who have been responsible for degrading forests: on the
contrary, over centuries, they have not only evolved ways of life
that conserve the forests but have been at the forefront of resistance
to their destruction by outside interests. "Poor" farmers in *Baan*
Toong Yao in Thailand's Lamphun Province, for example, have
responded to forest destruction by strengthening the communally-
sanctioned rules and social arrangements that have served to
protect their community forests in the past:

> "Trees can only be cut down for genuine necessities, such as to build
> houses for newlyweds. Those who chop down trees for sale on the
> market or for other purposes face penalties handed down by the

village government. These penalties cannot be treated as mere 'costs' by budding timber entrepreneurs, moreover, as they might be within the modern market economy, since they also involve a considerable social stigma. The group of villagers who govern the local traditional irrigation system also inspect the forest, keeping tabs on who is using it, for what, and when, and preventing outsiders from exploiting it. But all villagers are responsible for doing whatever is necessary to ensure that the forest is protected as a source of water, food, medicine, and wood. In carrying out this task, *Baan* Toong Yao villagers do not desire the assistance of the government. 'All the government has to do is recognize our rights to it', says one leader. 'We want to take care of it ourselves, and we can do that better than anyone else.'"[7]

WEALTH AND DESTRUCTION

"Poverty" in the sense of frugality obviously has little to do with the large-scale degradation which has fired environmental activism across the globe and forced world leaders to assemble at the Earth Summit in Brazil. Nevertheless, there is admittedly a type of poverty — destitution and uprootedness — which has contributed in some degree to forest clearance, ill-adapted forms of agriculture, and so on.

It does not follow, however, that wealth and development are the cure. One reason is that even this sort of poverty, when viewed in perspective, is far less environmentally damaging than the direct effects of wealth. The rich industrial countries, with a small fraction of the world's people, are responsible for 83 per cent of accumulated carbon dioxide emissions since 1860 and even more of its toxic waste production, while multinational corporations are reckoned to be responsible for half of global warming.[8] The average American meanwhile consumes 137 times more paper — with all the tree-cutting and chemical applications that this implies — than the average Indian. The World Bank's own figures show that both municipal waste and carbon dioxide emissions increase in direct proportion to per capita income and that "environmentally benign activities usually contribute a much smaller part to national income than do environmentally malign ones."[9] Per

Does Wealth Cure Environmental Degradation?

Wealth is always able to buy itself some "environmental quality." The élites of Mexico City or Manila can shut themselves inside air-conditioned Mercedes-Benzes or high-rise apartments while fumes choke their less-fortunate compatriots. The Netherlands or the United States can afford to demand that domestic industries install the latest in pollution-control equipment while their subsidiaries elsewhere continue business as usual. But in an expanding global market economy, where even air is an "economically scarce good" and atmospheric and terrestrial sinks are filling up with industrial waste, a better quality of life for one person is generally only purchased at the expense of someone else's. The Mercedes, even if equipped with a catalytic converter, is hardly an environmental boon to those walking behind its exhaust pipe or living where the oil it needs is drilled or refined. Northern schemes to spirit some of their own cities' emissions away — to say nothing of plans to profit from exporting "green" technology Southwards — might well be begrudged by those in the South whose own surroundings have been plundered to pay for or construct the equipment.

Buying Back Nature

While money can buy remedies for local pollution here and there, no amount of up-to-date technology is going to bring back the things which have been annihilated permanently by the North's much-vaunted "wealth-creation machines." It will take more than money to restore the fertility of the 17 per cent of European soils seriously damaged by mechanized farming, acid rain, and the like or the other soils permanently eroded away in the Americas, Asia and Africa. No infusion of cash will speed up the centuries-long process of natural replenishment of the aquifers now being drained in the American West. And no wizardry of biotechnology can restore the varieties and species of plants which are being lost from agriculture, gardens, steppes and forests in what specialists Cary Fowler and Pat Mooney call the "biggest single environmental catastrophe in human history." Trying to reconstruct nature with building-blocks made of capital is a Sisyphean task.

Obvious as this fact is, it is often denied in UN agreements and publications. A good example is the World Bank's latest *World Development Report* released in May 1992 for UNCED. The report acknowledges that the "earth's sources are limited and so is the absorptive capacity of its sinks", but argues that the compensatory ability of "substitution, technical progress and structural change" allow us to assume that no "bounds" need be placed on the "growth of human activity." The only reasoning offered in support of this claim is that, due in part to substitution, the prices of minerals have declined over the past 100 years, from which it is concluded that their supply is effectively infinite. If the scarcity of water, forests and clean air were reflected in market prices with similar accuracy, says the Bank, they too would cease to be "under siege." The document inspires little confidence, however, that technical substitutes for water, air, genes and soil will be found quickly enough to prevent the "irreversible damage to the biosphere" which the World Wide Fund for Nature (WWF) predicts will result from the tripling of global productive output that the Bank projects for 2030.

Growth for Environmental Protection?

The report also claims that the rising income brought about by development "will make environmental protection affordable." There are five good reasons why this is not so.

- First, the rising income in one country often causes environmental damage to other countries. Increases in dividends for shareholders of Rio Tinto Zinc may well enable them to set aside extra acres of woodlands near their homes, but this is hardly a gain if it entails contaminating the people, soil, air and water of Oceania and Africa with radioactivity from mining operations.

- Second, rising average income, particularly in the South, is typically accompanied by growth in the numbers of marginalized people, who, as the WWF points out, are then encouraged by élites to clear forests and migrate to infertile frontier land "as a means of defusing . . . social discontent" among the "most vulnerable sectors of society."

- Third, to generate the money to "clean up" the environmental mess generated by past "wealth creation" in turn creates additional environmental damage. Moreover, it cannot be assumed that mitigating the effects of, say, one tonne of carbon dioxide emitted today will cost the same as mitigating the effects of an additional tonne emitted tomorrow. If global warming begins to feed back on itself, it will become an accelerating process, the impact of each additional molecule of carbon dioxide becoming greater and greater — and the damage done more and more difficult to contain.

- Fourth, continued growth makes even the most impressive gains in efficiency and "clean production" meaningless in the end. Although energy intensity — the amount of energy consumed per unit of GDP — improved by 23 per cent in OECD countries between 1973 and 1987, the total amount of energy consumed by these countries increased by 15 per cent between 1975 and 1989.

- Fifth, the claim that wealth will cure environmental degradation is often based on figures showing, for example, that the number of people without safe water or adequate sanitation declines as per capita income rises. Wealth cannot, however, bring back lost species, an altered atmosphere, or ruined soil — and these are what are at issue.

---

capita share of "dirty production" in rich and supposedly "clean" Western Europe is meanwhile over three times that of the poorer East. The claim that environmental degradation can be cured by creating more and more wealth thus has little factual foundation, even if one accepts the assumption that wealth cures destitution and uprootedness.

But this assumption also is ungrounded. Destitution and

uprootedness, on the scale on which they exist today, are in fact the *result* of the operations of wealth and development. It is modern wealth moving across frontiers (and not traditional self-reliance), which backs the wholesale enclosure and destruction of forests, land and water by corporations and development agencies for the sake of distant markets, depriving many ordinary people of livelihood and independence and pushing them to clear forests, migrate to mountains, deserts and slums, and hitch their fortunes to an exploitative labour market. It is merchants, profiteers and land speculators who generally entice or push villagers into opening up export crops or logging operations. And as Norman Myers notes, that well-known villain of Northern environmentalist demonology, the "shifting cultivator", is often in fact a "shifted cultivator" — shifted by force, economic differentiation or development projects.[10]

Environmental degradation, in fact, rather than being the result of destitution, is often the means through which modern wealth creates poverty. Thus six million people who have been uprooted from their lands to make way for dams in India now live in slums,[11] while local people are destitute in Bougainville in Papua New Guinea where Rio Tinto Zinc's copper mining operations have devastated the environment. As one landowner affected by the mining observes, "We don't grow healthy crops any more, our traditional customs and values have been disrupted and we have become mere spectators as our earth is being dug up, taken away and sold for millions."

Since the early 1970s, even top development officials such as Robert McNamara have been forced to confess that urban-rural gaps and numbers of marginalized increase in the shadow of development. Succeeding efforts to redefine "growth with redistribution", "fulfilment of basic needs", "rural development", "improving the well-being of people", "human resources development", and now "sustainable development" have not changed the basic picture. In country after country, gaps between the enclosing rich and the enclosed poor continue to grow, with devastating social and environmental consequences. In Brazil, scene of an early development "miracle", nine million households are landless while 82 million acres of farmland lie idle. In Thailand, one of the shining success stories of development in the 1970s and 1980s, the share of national income of the top fifth of the population increased from 49 per cent in 1975 to almost 55 per cent in 1986, while the share of the poorest 20 per cent (which includes thousands of forest colonizers) dropped from 6.1 per cent to 4.6 per cent.[12]

Gaps are growing on the international level as well. Two centuries ago, incomes in Europe were perhaps twice those of India.[13] Yet in 1965 nations classified by the World Bank as "high income" were on average 15 times richer than their "low-income" counterparts and, in 1990, 33 times richer.[14] Even in the unlikely event that the global economy achieved the five- to ten-fold increase in industrial growth called for in the Brundtland report, it would take several hundred years for per capita income in current "low-income" countries to equal that of "high-income" countries. In the process dozens of spare planets would have to be found to provide the necessary resources and waste sinks.

The only plausible interpretation of the claim that "poverty causes environmental destruction" is therefore one that indicts an entire economic system. For in getting rid of the types of "poverty" which preserve local commons (self-sufficiency, frugality, common property regimes, and so on) development can only *create* more of the sort of "poverty" that destroys them. Insofar as there are any significant connections between poverty and environmental degradation, it is poverty-as-development, not poverty-as-underdevelopment, that is the problem.

OVERPOPULATION OR OVERCONSUMPTION?

"Overpopulation" is frequently cited as a cause of poverty. But as with environmental destruction, there are few grounds for blaming increasing human numbers on poverty which are not even better grounds for blaming it on the operations of wealth. To single out

"population" as "the greatest threat to the environment" — a view
that dominated many commentaries on the Earth Summit — is to
downplay the destruction caused by consumerist lifestyles, the
workings of the market and the activities of commerce. Although
the bulk of the increase in human numbers in the last fifty years has
been in the countries of the South, these countries are not the major
emitters of greenhouse gases, either today or historically. Indian or
Chinese peasants cannot be blamed for the ozone hole when they
have never seen a refrigerator or an air-conditioned car. The US,
however, with just four per cent of the world's human numbers, is
responsible for some 24 per cent of global carbon dioxide emissions, while India is responsible for just 2.2 per cent of emissions
and is home to one sixth of humanity.

PEOPLE AND THE COMMONS

To single out "population" is also to ignore the critical role that
economic growth and development, by enclosing the commons,
have played in *causing* the increase in numbers. Contrary to what
Malthus suggested, population growth is not an inevitable phenomenon that is only checked by famine, pestilence and plague.
Where people themselves managed and were intricately connected
with their surroundings, they were conscious of the limits of their
environment; decisions as to how many children they raised were
taken in the light of this. In the Himalayan region of Ladakh, for
example, which was relatively isolated until recently:

> "People were consciously aware of the fact that *this* piece of land
> is where our food comes from, *these* pasture lands are where our
> animals graze. They could clearly see the limits of that land, and
> they were conscious of the fact that they needed to adapt their
> numbers and practices to that limited resource base . . . In Ladakh,
> as was the case in early Europe and in many agrarian societies, the
> land was passed on intact, in one piece, from generation to genera-
> tion. The human populations had to adapt themselves to that land.
> One's whole sense of self was connected to it — even your name
> might be the name of the house and land-holding."[15]

While disease and warfare played their part in many societies in regulating numbers (as accidents and pollution-related deaths do in the West today), cultural factors were also decisive. Again, Ladakh provides an example:

". . . adaptation to very scarce resources sometimes involved polyandry, which means several husbands to one wife. A number of Ladakhi brothers would marry the same woman — and that, of course, helped to keep population down, because although the gender ratio was roughly 50/50, many women didn't marry and bear children . . . This practice was supported by the status given to the Buddhist religion and members of the religious community. An unmarried woman had a very comfortable position as a nun, and both the nuns and the celibate monks further helped support the relatively stable population growth rate . . . There was enormous social flexibility . . . one actually had the possibility of polyandry, or polygamy, or in some cases, monogamy. Keeping these social relations so flexible made it possible to optimize the relationship to *resources*, because from generation to generation, you couldn't be sure just how many sons and daughters you would have, what demographic situation you might be in, and hence what arrangements would work for the best."

Although much traditional knowledge of contraceptives and abortifacients was lost in Europe several hundreds years ago and in colonized countries more recently, non-invasive ways to limit the number of births were and still are used in some cultures. A prolonged period of breast-feeding can prevent conception because ovulation is reduced during lactation, leading to longer intervals between births. In addition, in polygynous marriages in Africa, for example, coitus is taboo while a woman is breast feeding, often for up to two years. Other cultural patterns also influenced the stability of the numbers of people, including sexual abstinence, the segregation of the sexes, a later age for marriage and restrictions on widows remarrying.[16]

DISLOCATION CAUSES MORE BIRTHS

As soon as many traditional societies are forced on the path of economic development, however, the number of people begins to climb dramatically. In Britain, for example, the birthplace of industrialization, the number of people was around 6 million in 1700, rising to 6.5 million by 1750. By 1800, however, it had jumped to 9 million and by 1850 it had reached 17 million.[17] The beginning of the "population explosion" in India dovetailed neatly with the expansion of British rule in India when resources, rights and livelihoods were taken away from people. In 1600, the number of Indians is estimated at between 100 million and 125 million, a level which hardly altered until 1800. Then the rise began: 130 million in 1845, 175 million ten years later in 1855, 194 million in 1867 and 255 million in 1871.[18]

There are many interacting economic, social, cultural and personal reasons behind such increases in human numbers. One aspect, however, is clear: high birth rates are often a distress signal that people's survival is endangered.[19] Enclosure accentuates distress because people's connections with their surroundings and with each other are lost. It is no coincidence that during the periods of rapid increase in the number of people, both in India and elsewhere, land became concentrated in the hands of a more powerful minority. In agrarian societies, access to land determines a family's survival and sense of security. As one Indian peasant has put it, "Without land to feed my family, I go hungry, no matter how much food the country produces."[20] In Ireland during the 18th and early 19th centuries when numbers quadrupled, much of the arable land was enclosed by big estates to grow crops for export. The peasants had to resort to potatoes as the only food which could grow on the small plots of degraded land left.

The dislocation caused by enclosure deprives people of a sense of security gained from belonging to various social groups and from having access not only to land but also to agricultural methods which provide a guaranteed, if limited, yield. Children can make up for this lost sense of security in many ways. "Having a larger family is an eminently rational strategy of survival. Children's labour is a vital part of the family economy in many peasant communities of Asia, Africa, and Latin America. Children help in the fields, tend animals, fetch water and wood, and care for younger brothers and sisters, freeing their parents for other tasks.

Quite early in life, children's labour makes them an asset rather than a drain on family income."[21] The security derived from children can also be critical in times of crises due to illness, drought, floods, food shortages, land disputes and political upheavals, and when the parents are older.

As the viability of agricultural and rural life declines, networks of support *outside* the village grow more important. Parents hope that at least one child will get a well-paid job in the city, bringing not only the protection of an income to support the rest of the family back home, but also connections with urban-based patrons. A recent study in Pakistan, for example, found that rural villagers, although aware of the local impact of an increase in the number of people, wanted to have more children as a conscious strategy of establishing a variety of urban contacts.[22] Within cities, too, children can be an asset. Poor urban dwellers can rely on their children to earn money in various ways including begging, garbage collecting, petty trading, working as servants or messenger boys, or else to stay at home to care for younger children. Even in the cities, therefore, children provide security. One study showed that unionized workers had fewer children than those workers who were equally-paid but not unionized for whom children were the only insurance of a roof over their heads in their old age.[23]

FROM WITCHES TO HOUSEWIVES

Considerations of power, security and survival aside, many women have more children than they would wish for. One reason for this is that women's power has been undermined by enclosure. The dismantling of the commons has invariably exacerbated or created patriarchal structures, depriving women of their self-determination and control in every sphere, but particularly over their bodies. Control has shifted towards men who have determined in many instances that women should be confined to child-bearing.

As a consequence of the witch-hunts which raged throughout Europe and North America for at least four hundred years until the 18th century, a new image of women was created:

"that of the child-bearer excluded from the public economy. The productivity of women, which had been high in many fields in the Middle Ages, was reduced to their wombs. This reduction means a biologization of the woman: she appears primarily as a child-bearing instrument."

This reduction was reinforced under industrialization as women became "housewives", economically dependent on a male breadwinner, a model which was then exported under colonization:

"Just as (women's) knowledge was systematically annihilated in Europe by the persecution of witches and the patriarchal alliance of Church and State, so too in countries of the South women have been dispossessed of their traditional means of birth control."

In many colonies, "missionaries declared birth control and unrestricted sexuality to be sinful . . . (they) did their best to drive out polygyny and spread the model of monogamous Christian marriage."[24] Women in the South were dispossessed of their economic independence as well.

This particular colonial legacy, reinforced by other patriarchal forces, is a key factor behind the growth in the numbers of people. Women's subordination to men means reduced power to avoid sexual intercourse or delay pregnancy. A wife's tentative decision to limit the number of mouths to feed is often interpreted as a challenge to her husband's power over her — and thus to the very crux of his virility.[25] But women themselves can be trapped because having children is often the only source of prestige and respect society accords them and which, in many instances, they therefore accord themselves:

"For women . . . their capacity for childbirth is frequently the only capacity left to them. In many societies women played a key role in the subsistence economy and drew social recognition from this. With the marginalizing of subsistence production came a devaluation of women's work and a loss of prestige for women in their social context. Women have practically no access, however, to the new sources of social power: money, education, technology. Therefore for them, the significance of motherhood has relatively increased. Children are their only capital."[26]

Clearly, in such circumstances, "the desired number of children is bound up with the status of women and women's image in a society." Yet, within the population control industry, the deeper structural changes required to reclaim women's power within society are being glossed over in favour of technologies that can only enclose them further.

THE MYTH OF DEMOGRAPHIC TRANSITION

Also glossing over the issue of women's power and the links between development and increasing human numbers is the theory of demographic transition. It is assumed that a shift from a rural economy to an urban, industrial one will bring higher incomes and greater financial security, leading to a decline in birth rates. Population experts point to the countries of Europe where industrialization in the 18th and 19th centuries caused a massive surge in the numbers of people, but now after decades of increase, the growth rates are levelling off. The low-income countries, which have experienced the highest rates of increase in human numbers in the last 50 years, are expected to follow the same pattern; economic growth is therefore promoted as a linch pin of any strategy to slow this increase.

Numerous statistical examples run counter to the theory. The link between a drop in the rates of increase in human numbers (a combination of lower death and lower birth rates), and higher incomes and economic security in Third World countries is tenuous. In Mexico, for example, a 37 per cent decline in the average number of children women produced started in 1960, *before* the country's 1970s' economic boom, a decline which continues despite the current economic downturn. Recent studies in Brazil and Colombia indicate that declines in the average number of children women gave birth to not only occurred during an economic depression, but were most pronounced in poorer, rather than richer, communities. A decline not only in the rate of increase of human numbers but in the total number as well has taken place in Hungary and Bulgaria, which are middle-income economies, while the US has not yet achieved "demographic transition", despite having one of the largest per capita GNPs in the world. It is expected to gain another 50 million people, equivalent in consumption terms to two billion Indians, before there is not growth rates.[27]

Statistics aside, the theory of demographic transition is flawed on other grounds. The levels of affluence supposedly responsible for stabilization in the growth rate in Northern countries have been achieved only at tremendous cost to the environment — not only in those countries but also in the South. If every citizen in the world were to require the same standard of living before "fertility" rates declined, the resulting ecological stress would be intolerable. Attempting to reduce the rate of growth in the numbers of people through increased economic growth is thus self-defeating. Indeed, by degrading the environment, it can only undermine livelihoods and cause further dislocation.

ECONOMY AND ECONOMICS

"Establishing economic value requires the disvaluing of all other forms of social existence . . . The time has come to confine the economy to its proper place: a marginal one."

Gustavo Esteva

If the wealthy tend to blame environmental degradation on the poor, market enthusiasts like to blame it on not enough markets and market thinking. The best hope for preserving air, earth or water, they insist, is further enclosure by the industrial economy, and the best hope for society, more and better economics.

"Improved environmental management" is to be achieved through greater "integration with the global economy", trumpets the World Bank's 1992 *World Development Report*. "Liberalized trade fosters greater efficiency and higher productivity, and may actually reduce pollution by encouraging the growth of less-polluting industries and the adoption and diffusion of cleaner technologies."[28] Only by selling goods in the growing markets of the North, adds a recent document from the General Agreement on Trade and Tariffs (GATT), will the South be able to pay for environmental protection and poverty alleviation. UNCED, too, has enthusiastically joined in the chorus assuring us that an "open trading system" will be "of benefit to all trading partners".[29]

COMPARATIVE ADVANTAGE?

A central defence of economic integration at UNCED and elsewhere has been that such a system leads to an equitable and mutually beneficial distribution of global production in accordance with the doctrine of comparative advantage. This doctrine, developed in the 18th century by David Ricardo, holds that no matter how broad the resource endowment of a country, it will benefit from specializing in only a few of its industries and using the earnings gained from the export of these goods to import other products. To use Ricardo's example, even if Portugal happens to be better than Britain at making both wine and cloth, it will be of benefit to both countries for Portugal to channel its capital only to the production of wine, which it can then export to Britain in exchange for cloth.

One problem with this theory is that it takes for granted a bygone world in which investment is national, not international. Faced with Ricardo's example, today's British investors would be likely, instead of investing in domestic cloth manufacture, to transfer their capital electronically to Portuguese cloth concerns, leaving Britain in the lurch. For this reason alone, as World Bank Senior Economist Herman E. Daly points out, the "confident assertion that an open trading system will benefit all trading partners is utterly unfounded."[30]

The invasion of international capital also often undermines precisely those "advantages" which are supposed to secure benefits for a country. A nation's "advantage" in minerals may well lead to their swift exhaustion when transnational corporations arrive and foreign exchange has to be found to pay for imports. Investment in renewable commodities such as coffee and cocoa, meanwhile, tends to glut markets, lowering prices. Due in part to

United Nations enthusiasm for the doctrine of comparative advantage, traditional commodity prices in 1987 were only 62 per cent of their 1960 figures in real terms.[31]

Technocrats in capital-poor countries are often pressured by the decline in commodity prices into increasing the rate of plunder or ransacking their countries for other possible "comparative advantages". Forests may be cleared to plant non-traditional upland crops which are enjoying temporarily high prices; demand for international sex-tourism may be built up to cash in on young girls' feelings of financial responsibility toward their impoverished rural families; and traditional patron-clientage may be exploited to help provide cheap labour for international investors.

EXCHANGE AND EXTINCTION

The environmental effects can be devastating. Resource economist Richard Norgaard has written persuasively, for example, of how pursuit of "comparative advantage" leads to extinction of species and varieties. As the "global exchange economy" extends its network of roads, ports, airports and processing depots, more and more traditional farmers take up specialized export-orientated agriculture.

> "The reduction in the number of crop species grown results in an even larger reduction in the number of supporting species. The locally specific nitrogen-fixing bacteria, fungi that facilitate nutrient intake through mycorhizzal association, predators of pests, pollinators and seed dispersers, and other species that coevolved over centuries to provide environmental services to traditional agroecosystems have become extinct or their genetic base has been dramatically narrowed. Deprived of the flora with which they coevolved, soil microbes disappear . . . Participation in the global exchange economy also . . . forces farmers to stay competitive with other farmers who have been put in the same bind. This encourages use of inputs common to modern agriculture worldwide—fertilizers, pesticides, and high-yielding seed varieties — thereby eliminating many of the remaining regional differences in selective pressure. The global exchange economy also induces temporal variation for which species have not evolved the strategies needed to cope. Crop

failures, new technologies, changing tastes, variations in interest rates, changes in the strength of cartels, and variations in trade barriers — all these redefine comparative advantage."[32]

This redefinition, Norgaard continues, is accommodated, at least in theory, by a shift in the specialization of people, tools and land to different lines of production and by a new pattern of exchange. But biological species are generally less able than people to shift between lines of activity: they cannot coevolve to fill their supporting niches as fast as the global exchange economy leads farmers to shift crops. Land cannot move between uses like people and tools — "environmental services cannot freely shift from the support of rice to the support of cotton, to suburban lawns, to concrete, to alfalfa, to marsh habitat for waterfowl, and back to rice much the same as a reasonably adaptive person might shift from being a farmer to an urban gardener, to a game warden, and back to being a farmer."[33]

Nor is it easy for local commons regimes to safeguard their environments in the face of the changing demands of the global economy. As subsistence goods are made available for trade and as pressures to consume increase, rural villagers' market dependency and indebtedness grow. Encouraged to clear land and to treat their homes as potential items for exchange, villagers learn to disregard local conservation practices geared to long-term local subsistence rather than profit. The environmental consequences of "free trade" are again precisely the opposite of those suggested by UNCED and the World Bank.

GREEN ECONOMICS — A WHITE KNIGHT?

Replying to criticisms of the market economy, environmental economists argue that environmental problems are due not to economic integration itself, but to a defective type of market economy. They hold that integrating more forests, fields and societies into the economy need not result in their destruction as long as environmental concerns are simultaneously enclosed within economics. The "primary cause of environmental problems", they

How Free is "Free Trade"?

Market solutions to environmental problems are often understood to enhance independence and oppose tariffs, subsidies, inefficiency, regulation, protection, compulsion or monopoly. They do not. In fact they merely favour some types of centralization, compulsion and subsidies over others. Like other approaches which stress heavy intervention by states, "market solutions" typically require communities to sacrifice many of their goals and ways of life to the requirements of small élites.

Open investment policies, for example, merely replace tariffs or subsidies protecting local or state production with negative tariffs or subsidies for international capital. In order to open up a country economically, ports, roads, pipelines, canals, and airports have to be built in order to tempt prospective investors and traders with cheap transport, electricity and water. Local people invariably have to pick up the tab through taxes and environmental damage.

While often ostensibly devoted to an ideal of fairness, free traders are very careful about what sort of level playing field they advocate. Tariffs are supposed to be made uniform internationally, but Northern countries are allowed to start the trading contest with the advantage of the immense subsidies provided by colonial and post-colonial plunder.

Nor is there at present a level playing field with respect to environmental regulations. As attorney Stephen Shrybman points out, the absence of environmental regulation

> "is itself a form of subsidy, even though the various trade regimes do not recognize it as such, since it permits industry to freely externalize the environmental costs of production. And it is a subsidy that developing countries hard-pressed to attract foreign investment have often been willing to offer, even at the cost of serious damage to the environment and public health. The Brundtland Commission estimated that in 1980 developing nations would have had to expend over $14 billion in pollution-control costs to establish the same standards that are in place in the United States. For many an industry, this subsidy provides a very strong incentive to relocate".

The World Bank's Vice President and Chief Economist, Lawrence Summers, has recently confirmed his institution's commitment to maintaining such subsidies and its opposition to the idea of a level playing field in which human beings in the South are regarded as the equals of human beings in the North. "Just between you and me," Summers writes in a now-notorious memorandum of 11 December 1991, "shouldn't the World Bank be encouraging more migration of the dirty industries to the less-developed countries?" Southern workers who sicken and die from pollution forego few earnings since their wages are low, anyway; hence "the economic logic of dumping a load of toxic waste in the lowest wage country is impeccable and we should face up to that." "Underpopulated countries in Africa are vastly underpolluted," Summers adds, and "their air quality is probably vastly inefficiently low [in pollutants] compared to Los Angeles or Mexico City". Arguing against such claims on moral grounds, Summers notes correctly, would entail having to argue against "every Bank proposal for [economic] liberalization", since they all have similar practical implications.

While attempts by a country to relax its environmental standards or worker protection to levels lower than those of its neighbours is encouraged under the doctrine of free trade, attempts to impose stricter standards are labelled with the emotionally-loaded terms distortion or inefficiency. Free trade thus tends to lead to a worldwide lowering of standards and progressive global environmental degradation. The North American Free Trade Agreement, for example, has compelled Canada to relax its regulations on pesticides to bring them into line with those of the US. As Herman Daly observes, such moves may buy some time for polluters whose domestic waste sinks are filling up, "but at the cost of eventually having to face the problem simultaneously and globally rather than sequentially and nationally". Free trade as usually defined is incompatible with a policy of internalizing environmental costs within nations — although both, ironically, are often advocated by proponents of market solutions to environmental problems.

Free traders are also selective about the sort of protection they oppose and the type of competition they promote. In Southern countries, tariff protection for domestic producers is often reduced only to be replaced by state protection of Northern companies selling proprietary goods. While free trade laws encourage the sort of competition which forces people with low incomes to fight in the market-place with the rich for food and consumer goods, the concept of intellectual property is used to stifle competition in areas in which Southern countries might have an advantage, for example industries which rely on availability of a wide variety of genetic materials. Nor, contrary to cliché, are free traders hostile to regulation or bureaucracies. On the contrary, since the days of gunboat diplomacy they have been solidly in favour of big government, global enforcement and big bureaucracies such as international trade organizations. All of these are indispensable in helping the market system make headway in hostile or difficult environments and in helping it moderate its own self-destructive effects. Like the market itself, economic integration is, in the words of Gustavo Esteva, a "result of a conscious and often violent intervention by the government". It requires only that large bureaucracies restrict themselves mainly to assisting the market to enclose other societies rather than enclosing too much for themselves.

---

insist, is not the price-making market, but rather "the failure of markets and governments to price the environment *appropriately*", taking into account the "costs of environmental damage to society".[34] On this view, assigning proper prices to currently unpriced or underpriced aspects of the environment and social life will effectively curb the market's destructiveness. Conservation, once it becomes profitable, will finally fall into place as one part of economic development. As increased economic integration blurs national and local boundaries by enclosing the world within a single framework of exchange, so environmental economics will erase borders between economic and non-economic ways of thinking by enclosing decision-making within the framework of cost-benefit analysis.

The central question of environmental economics concerns "externalities". These arise when economic actors shift "uncertain social costs . . . to other social groups or to future generations."[35] A factory creates an externality when it uses the air as a free waste dump, a logging operation when it silts up streams used to feed farmers' fields.

In a sense, the temptation to create externalities is universal. Other things being equal, people usually find it agreeable to push the bad effects of an action off on somebody else. What makes commons regimes work is their check on this impulse. Only when commons regimes have been broken down into private property and "open access" areas is it possible for people to get away with externalizing. Only where one party has acquired sufficient power and overcome moral restraint and other users are not organized or powerful enough to intervene can land, water and air be turned into enclosed "resources" and "waste sinks" for infinitely-expanding production.

This is precisely the state of affairs the modern economy encourages. As powerful producers seek to immerse themselves "in large spaces which can absorb their wastes without visible costs",[36] individual ownership multiplies the number of boundaries across which such "costs" can travel. Lands which are not privately owned become free-for-all zones open to plunder. It is partly because of such tendencies, indeed, that the state is forced to create an expanded notion of the "public" to protect the system from its own rush to create externalities.

MORE AND MORE ECONOMICS

Instead of addressing the economic organization of modern society at the root, however, environmental economics seeks to address externalities by the application of more and yet more economics. In the words of Dieter Helm and David Pearce, the "free-market approach identifies the problem of externalities as the *absence* of markets and the associated property rights."[37] It seeks to make environmental protection "visible" to economics and economic actors. That means setting in motion a centralized mechanism to "internalize externalities" — to reclassify them as "costs" so that they can be set against "benefits". As much as possible, environmental protection is to become synonymous with efficiency in the allocation of resources and waste sinks.

Here as elsewhere, enclosure means exclusion and the erasing of traditional boundaries. The whole river valley in which a polluting factory is situated must be placed under unified management, either by granting the factory property rights to it, thus giving it an incentive to protect it, or by creating an administration capable of forcing it to pay for the damage it causes outside its property. The former means monopoly ownership. The latter means state controls in the form of pollution standards, enforcement of tax regulations, or creation of property rights in waste sinks through pollution permits. Thus the economic system, while it creates an "abundance of opportunities" for the "rise of externalities", also gives rise to "the need to address these externalities with collective action (the state) or with anti-competitive firm consolidation."[38]

The environmental crisis thus brings out the tensions of modern economies in a particularly stark form. More than ever before, its atomizing, competitive ideals collide with its need to enclose, centralize, colonize, dominate, monopolize and to create an investing and regulating state to look after its interests. Its imperative of unbounded accumulation is countered by the need to set limits to production or throughput; its need to internalize costs in one area creates pressure to externalize them elsewhere. Broader and broader areas of social life are forced into dependence on more and more precarious science and ambitious techniques of centralized control. Trying to establish markets for the thousands of polluting substances released into air and water daily by industry would call for bureaucracies whose size would mock the market's pretensions to efficiency; trying to "cost" the effects of global warming would entail an army of expert economists in constant disagreement with one another.

THE PRICE IS RIGHT: ACCORDING TO WHOM?

Many of these tensions are visible in recent efforts to internalize externalities by finding the "right prices" of environmental goods or the "full costs" of environmental damage. What are these "right prices" and "full costs"? Some years ago Herman Daly observed acerbically that conventional market prices for natural resources *in situ* were "largely arbitrary". "All that economic theory can tell us about the price of resources in the ground is that they must fall between historical cost of production and present cost of replacement — ie. approximately between zero and infinity for non-renewables."[39]

The pricing mechanisms advocated by environmental economists would result in resource prices higher than conventional ones, but would these prices be any less arbitrary? Or, to put the question more precisely: under what circumstances is the hope these prices offer for a liveable community sufficient to suggest that activists should concentrate their efforts on enclosing the environmental debate within economics instead of working to roll back the dominance of the market economy?

To advocate the former unconditionally on the ground that prices can be made "ecologically correct" is to beg the question. "Ecology" cannot determine prices; only human beings can. No hedgehog, mangrove swamp or virus is capable of telling people what its price should be to ensure its survival within the market economy. To reply that some of the human beings who will set the new prices are "scientists" hardly removes the problem. Spending years becoming intimately acquainted with a lemur species' interactions or a river valley's cycles cannot equip one to determine whether it is "equivalent" in value to a steel mill, a stealth bomber, or the maize crop of Belize. Practically speaking, the sense of the phrase "ecologically correct prices" cannot come to anything more than "prices which enable the market economy to keep ticking over while taking a bit more account than hitherto of the concerns of environmentalists, ecologists, business people with long views, and others with interests in 'natural resources'."

Consider the grab-bag of attempts by environmental economists "to construct hypothetical or simulated markets for ecological services, or to derive demand for those services from the observed demand for marketed goods and services."[40] One method is to calculate the net economic effects of deforestation, high-tech agriculture or pollution by looking at what they do to water supply, soil structure, long-term farm output, or income forgone due to illness. Prices for minerals or soil fertility can be concocted by estimating how much it would cost to develop substitutes or buy fertilizer to replace depleted nutrients. The value of clean air can be estimated by finding out how much extra home-buyers would pay for property in unpolluted areas. Prices for game eaten without being marketed can be set partly by looking at the cost of marketed animals; for wildlife by asking ecotourists how much they would be willing to pay to see elephants or tigers; for a water supply by asking rural villagers how much they would be willing to accept for having it ruined by a dam.[41] Once prices are determined, they can be moulded into the economy through taxes, subsidies or regulation.

Alternatively, governments can indirectly determine prices by fixing maximum emissions levels for a region and issuing "permits to pollute" which award corporations property rights in atmospheric waste sinks. Companies who find it hard to reduce pollution will then buy up these permits at a high price from companies who find it easy. The price of the permits, in theory, will approximate the "optimal pollution tax" which would otherwise have to be imposed by the government. Giving property rights in the atmosphere to governments so that they can trade them has also been proposed during international negotiations on the environment. Applying a similar idea on an even grander scale, Herman Daly and John Cobb suggest setting in advance the "resource flows that are within the renewable biospheric capacities of regeneration and waste absorption . . . Imposing sustainable biophysical limits as a boundary on the market economy will lead to changes in market prices that reflect these newly imposed limits . . . These new prices would have 'internalized' the value of sustainability."[42]

OBSCURING THE CONFLICTS

In addition to their many technical problems, both these sets of methods obscure underlying and radical conflicts over rights, interests, beliefs, goals and demands. Different valuation methods aggregate different groups' preferences and take different attitudes toward existing income distribution. Different pricing mechanisms and scientific conclusions yield conflicting "right" prices, "right" emissions levels, "right" amounts of throughput in a particular industrial economy, "right" taxes and subsidies, "right" ways of specifying which people are to pay them, "right" areas over which to limit emissions, "right" numbers of pollution permits to give, and ways of determining the "right" polluters to give them to.

Who is to decide which of these conflicting pricing techniques is right? This question cannot be settled by technical economic means, but only by free-wheeling discussion or political decision. Small wonder that cost-benefit analysis, far from being an "aid to decision-making", generally merely touches off new rounds of debate. By its very nature, it is a tool for special interests.[43]

To compound the problems, both the pollution taxes and pollution permits approaches, as well as cost-benefit analysis, are susceptible to abuses resulting from their heavy reliance on central authority. Regulators and cost-benefit analysts are chronically susceptible to the influence of the most powerful groups in society, particularly transnational corporations, with their arsenal of lobbyists, persuasive friends, political action committees and economic threats. Permissible standards or tax levels may be set very loosely in order not to cripple industry or (even more blatantly) in response to bribes or political contributions. Companies who have polluted most in the past may be disproportionately favoured by pollution permits, elevating a history of depredation into a right. And pollution trading may lead to pollution rights being sold to "dirty" utilities in the poorest and least politically empowered areas of a region or country.[44]

THE PROBLEM WITH PRICING

If the idea of "right" prices raises the question of who determines "rightness", the idea of pricing itself raises an even more fundamental question: Who determines whether things should be costed at all? Environmental cost-benefit analysis, no matter how high a value it assigns to "the environment", is often in itself a threat both to democracy and to the commons.

One reason for this is that weighing the costs of an action against its benefits requires commensurating all the values which are assigned to its effects. But it is part of the structure of many values that they *cannot* be commensurated with others without being lost entirely. To apply cost-benefit analysis is simply to bulldoze these values.

This point is obvious to anyone who feels the repugnance of reducing the value of a person to a price, or who understands that many actions — from raising children to playing basketball — are worth doing for their own sake, not for the contribution they make to some external or abstract end. But in many places in the world, such attitudes extend to nature and conservation as well. Andean peasants, for example, tend to look at their land and crops in personal terms and to farm through a dialogue with them rather than by manipulating them instrumentally, as machines for maximum production. A mountain may be viewed as a grandfather; rock outcrops may suggest how a terrace should be built; and different varieties of potatoes will reveal to the peasant over time which type of beans and maize they are best cultivated with. In South-East Asia, activities connected with agriculture and forest conservation are generally valued not only because they provide food, but also for their own sake. Labour-sharing is an occasion for talk and jokes; breaks for prayer are part of the leisurely rhythm of work in the fields; a sense of self-worth is developed from the fine performance of particular chores; protecting an upland forest is a way of respecting spirits of place as well as ensuring a water supply. Not incidentally, this intricate interlacing of concrete social ends supports local autonomy, and vice versa. In the preindustrial Malaysian *kampong*, for example, "personal promptings and the task-orientation of rural work, rather than external impositions," are what guide passage through the day, and people who devote large amounts of time to unfulfilling tasks for the sake of money-making face the sanction of mockery for having broken "implicit time codes".[45] To commensurate the values of everyday actions in such a context is both to alter them and to lay the basis for an undermining of local independence.

FROM CONVERSATION TO MEASUREMENT

Cost-benefit analysis also threatens democracy and the commons by attempting to replace craft and conversation with measurement. Just as the goals of an essay change in the course of its composition, depending on what one finds one can express and what one discovers in the course of writing, so, in commons regimes, the goal of (for example) providing "enough" for each community member is open to constant reinterpretation in the light of what means are available and what other ends the community shares at the moment. If one of these ends is the survival of each member of the community, then in a bad crop year, "enough" for even the richest person may amount to starvation rations. Similarly, if a leader's idea of "enough" entails sacrificing the freedom, independence or pace of life of other members of the community, then their resistance is likely to whittle it down. Reliance on cost-benefit analysis precludes any such way of harmonizing ends or of reaching any such sense of "enoughness". As Wolfgang Sachs says, "economists will never tell you what ends you will finally achieve 'managing wisely' your means; for them ends are faceless, they have only one, just formal character: they are infinite."[46]

A third threat to democracy and the commons arises from the fact that the only way that cost-benefit analysis can take account of a community's values is to aggregate individual preferences. Many communities will regard this so-called "neutral" methodology as itself in conflict with their values. "Don't you dare aggregate our values about our land with those of people elsewhere," community leaders may say. "Our views must have special weight, since this is where we live." Other communities may even view with abhorrence the aggregation of individual preferences *within* their community, insisting that consensus can only be reached through a process of mutual persuasion and learning in which these preferences themselves are constantly open to question.

ECONOMICS AND RIGHTS

Viewed from another angle, environmental pricing and cost-benefit analysis are often incompatible with notions of rights which have evolved out of defence of the commons: rights to place, to subsistence, to free discussion and to use of local nature. In commons regimes with a "safety-first" orientation, degradation that would threaten the ability of water and soil to support every member of the community is not accepted at any price. Neither insiders nor outsiders are held to have the right to degrade local water and soil for certain reasons or beyond certain points — which are determined by the community and not by a clique of experts. Thai *muang faai* communities, for example, do not allow sanctions forbidding felling of trees in community forests feeding rice fields to be interpreted as prices on the trees, even hypothetically. And in many places in the world, people do not allow their homes to be assigned even the highest monetary value, since they feel they have a right to occupy the familiar landscape of their ancestors and kin. Such people would dismiss David Pearce's postulate that "every decision implies a monetary valuation",[47] as a threat to their subsistence and ways of life. For them, the notion that cost-benefit analysis might be an "aid to decision-making" could only be a joke.

Even in industrialized societies, the notion that an industry can buy the right to pollute is bitterly disputed. Community activists across the US are incensed by the assumption implicit in pollution permits that industry has a "preordained right to pollute their neighbourhoods".[48] "Clean air should be protected, not traded and sold like a used car," says a representative of one citizens' group.

"What's next — the Los Angeles Police Department trying to buy civil rights credits from Wisconsin?"[49] Even where no concrete community exists and the issues are far from being life-and-death, there is a strong sense that such rights are to be granted or denied only through free discussion and not merely assumed as a basis for market bargaining. In the late 1970s, University of Wyoming economists attempted to show how "aesthetic" values could be translated into economic "existence" values by asking people how much they would accept in compensation for loss of visibility caused by power-plant emissions in desert regions of the American South West.[50] Over half of the sample rejected the premise of the question outright by refusing to cooperate or by demanding "infinite" compensation.

Unwilling to believe that the premise of their discipline has been challenged, environmental economists often take such demands for "infinite" compensation at face value. Such demands are absurd, they go on, since they trump all others automatically, leaving no room for the weighing of alternatives against each other. To regard environmental assets "as priceless . . . is devoid of policy implications unless it is to preserve the existing structure of environments untouched", complain Dieter Helm and David Pearce.[51] "Due allowance" for "noninstrumental values . . . produces stultifying rules of behaviour", adds R. Kerry Turner, since if one does not regard nature as an instrument one will not be able to modify it to provide any "function or service to humans".[52]

The confusions here are worth exposing, since they are common among not only economists but also some "deep ecologists" and many other members of modern industrial societies. A refusal to discuss prices, while it may be a "stultifying constraint" on *economic* reasoning about, and *economic* exploitation of, a forest, does not prevent people from reasoning about — or using — that forest in other ways. Forest commons which no local person will allow to be priced or treated as commodity, capital or instrument often provide game, fodder, building wood, water, shelter, beauty, mystery and a variety of other things of benefit to human beings, without any financial assessment being involved. It may even be decided — without the use of any form of cost-benefit reasoning whatever — to convert the whole forest to some other use. The type of reasoning used to reach this decision will be one in which many different ends and norms of conflict-resolution are accepted to be relevant simultaneously, some relating to social life, others to food needs, religion, property and personal rights, aesthetics, and so forth. The conversation which embodies this reasoning will be one in which no single yardstick is allowed to dominate and in which ends as well as means are up for continual re-evaluation, discovery and rediscovery.[53] Finally, refusing to discuss prices is, *pace* Helm and Pearce, far from "devoid of policy implications". One implication is that policymakers must be prepared, when this is requested by local people, to set cost-benefit analysis to one side, speak the local language and let their power erode.

THE ENCLOSURE OF PRACTICAL REASONING

Environmental economics, in sum, follows a familiar pattern of conceptual enclosure in its offensive against other forms of practical reasoning. To begin with, it announces that all practical reasoning of whatever social context revolves roughly around the problem of economics defined by the early 20th century British economist, Lord Robbins: the allocation of scarce means among given ends. Two claims are involved. The first is that, because scarcity is inevitable, so are difficult sacrifices. The second is that the choice of sacrifice can only be made by commensurating the alternatives and then choosing the one with the highest value. That is, all choice involves implicit or explicit cost-benefit analysis. These two claims are neatly encapsulated in a slogan from the World Bank's latest *World Development Report*: "Measurement is essential, since trade-offs are inescapable."[54]

Both clauses of this slogan are false. First, the notion that "trade-offs are inevitable" — that any given forest or homesite must eventually be threatened with conversion into an economic resource — is true only within an economic system expanding under the rule of scarcity. Only in such systems are choices inevitable between, say, economic growth and sacrificing children's lives. Most societies in history, by contrast, have been organized around avoiding such choices — including the new commons regimes now emerging on the margins of the market economy. As Gustavo Esteva notes:

> "The basic logic of human interactions inside the new commons prevents scarcity from appearing in them. People do not assume unlimited ends, since their ends are no more than the other side of their means, their direct expression. If their means are limited, as they are, their ends cannot be unlimited. Within the new commons, needs are defined with verbs that describe activities embodying wants, skills and interactions with others and with the environment. Needs are not separated into different 'spheres' of reality: lacks or expectations on one side, and satisfiers on the other, reunited through the market or the plan."[55]

Second, it is seldom that rational choices are made about complex matters by comparing the alternatives using a measuring-stick of value. They are more likely to be made, for example, by deciding, like a court, if and how a rule applies; or by acquiring, like an artist, critic, student, or revolutionary scientist, a new language, taste, perception or goal which shares no criterion of value with the old but, rather, recontextualizes or comments on it.[56]

MARKETS, ECONOMICS AND TACTICS

Both the market economy and environmental economics set their face firmly against the commons. But commons-oriented movements can make tactical use of both. Few such movements, for example, would want to argue against removing the massive and disproportionate state subsidies which shield the nuclear industry from market competition.[57] Many, too, would presumably welcome the persuasive evidence which physicist Amory Lovins has accumulated over 15 years to show that energy efficiency is a more profitable investment for utilities, communities and nations than new power stations; that abating global warming and air pollution, instead of costing money, as is automatically assumed by UNCED, the US government, and others, would actually save industry and governments hundreds of billions of dollars a year; and that saving electricity is usually cheaper than constructing a new hydroelectric dam, and often even cheaper than operating an existing dam.[58]

Similarly, when economists talk about modern agriculture's "efficiency", commons movements often find it tactically useful to reply "Efficiency over what period? Taking into account what costs?" as one step in their efforts to discredit the dominance of the notion of efficiency altogether. Taxes on energy, emissions or agrochemicals could also relieve some pressure on the commons. Environmental economics, finally, has sometimes come in handy as a face-saving device by which governments and corporations can explain their cancellation of projects resisted by local communities.

Movements to defend and regain the commons, however, are under no illusions about what happens to their ideas when they are transformed into a "green economic" version for "policymakers" to chew over. It is only by protesting against such translations that people can begin to make their real views known.[59] Politicians who have been taught by economists to respond only to cost-benefit arguments will never be able to represent movements for the commons. In the future as in the past, these movements will rely on their own forms of words and action — meetings, demonstrations, refusals, uprisings, silence, petitions, sabotage, foot-dragging and hundreds of other types of resistance — to defend what they find of value.

GLOBAL MANAGEMENT

"Properly speaking, global thinking is not possible."
Wendell Berry

Managers, like economists, are in the business of splitting the world up into fixed ends and available means. Then, in a process they take to be synonymous with rationality, they match the one to the other. In doing so, they transform nearly everyone and everything into tools whose effectiveness in "helping us get from A to B" it is the prerogative of the managers themselves to measure. Acting on "objective data", managers plan, mobilize and "clear space for action". Others, whose lack of skills and autonomous ends are either assumed or enforced, are "tapped", "mobilized", "brought out of traditional isolation" and "empowered" so that they can carry out the managers' designs.

From the rise of the market economy and the state to that of colonialism and industrialism, the scope for management has steadily increased in both "public" and "private" spheres. Since World War II the expansion of transnational corporations, medical therapies, high-tech weaponry, war machines, and "big technology" have been accompanied by ever newer kinds of management. Development has brought one of the most extensive deployments of all, from the onset of national planning in the 1950s to that of sectoral and regional planning in the 1960s, local-level planning in the 1970s, and planning to incorporate women and "the grassroots" in the 1980s.[60]

MANAGING PLANET EARTH

Management today has a new object, its biggest yet: Planet Earth. Everything in the world is now viewed as a potential instrument, ostensibly for achieving the overriding goal of "human survival" or the "balancing of the global economic system with ecological limits".

The projected dislocations are unprecedented, the schemes dreamed up by the new global managers ever more remote from the reality of the lives of those who are to be managed. Today, grown men and women convene in air-conditioned rooms in Washington and Geneva to discuss such topics as whether the global warming caused mainly by industrial emissions in the North should be "managed" by "rejigging" the world's irrigation and hydropower systems or by establishing carbon dioxide-absorbing tree plantations covering a dozen times the area of Great Britain in the tropical zone.[61] Northern donors and experts supporting the Tropical Forestry Action Plan, which has been described as a "Marshall Plan for the forests" of over 80 countries, routinely divide their meetings into two parts: one on "objectives", in which experts decide, on the basis of "scientific data" and "industrial and conservation requirements", what forest zones which are home to hundreds of millions of people should look like; and another on "implementation", in which they decide how to get everyone else to carry out their vision. Given the scale of such schemes, it is not surprising that more of the world's people than ever before are now viewed by managers as "obstacles" to be removed or "social factors" to be cajoled into "collaboration".

It is easy to snigger at such solemn megalomania. But if one accepts economic development and the institutions and premises on which it relies, the logic of "global environmental management" is impeccable. Development, after all, entails an uncompromising drive toward a single global social structure fitted out with mechanisms for global surveillance and global resource conversion to feed unlimited material advance. "Sustaining" this process through damage control requires an equivalent level of surveillance and intervention. The flip side of global prospecting for resources and waste sinks is global environmental monitoring, accounting and enforcement.

Whose Common Future? questions the entire project of development and thus, implicitly, the whole justification for global environmental management. But it is worth asking an additional question: could management on the scale envisioned succeed even on its own terms? A glance at its structure suggests that, of three conditions necessary for its fulfilment — universally-applicable knowledge, workable global enforcement, and a worldwide culture of "global concern" — none can be satisfied.

GLOBAL MANAGEMENT NEEDS GLOBAL KNOWLEDGE

Global management, like other forms of bureaucratic administration, is the "exercise of control on the basis of knowledge".[62] In the words of one of its champions, William D. Ruckelshaus, it involves "converting scientific findings into political action . . . trying to get a substantial portion of the world's people to change their behaviour".[63]

Ruckelshaus's last phrase is perhaps too crude even to describe as "paternalistic". Few parents would go so far as to regard their children as objects to be manipulated until they conformed to some external standard. Issues of democracy aside, however, can the project of rescuing the environment by making humans act in accordance with "scientific findings" be made intelligible even on its own terms? If the findings in question describe worldwide phenomena such as global warming, they are likely to be both uncertain and extremely controversial in their implications for *local* political change, as climate negotiators know only too well. If, on the other hand, such findings relate to, say, agricultural practice, their applicability in any given local situation is likely to be inversely proportional to their universality — or the degree to which they are interesting to global managers.

It is not simply that the science Ruckelshaus refers to is ragged and inadequate even in its own terms, although this is certainly true of many disciplines ranging from tropical forestry to atmospheric science. Nor is it just that this science overlooks much of the wisdom accumulated by people who have been living in dependence on particular landscapes for thousands of years, although this is also true. Nor is it even merely that, as David W. Orr points out, "grand scale requires islands of ignorance, small things that go unnoticed, and costs that go unpaid".[64] More important, manager-friendly knowledge is in *principle* not local-friendly knowledge. Kentucky farmer and writer Wendell Berry explains that good farmers can make use of expert advice only by translating it themselves from the abstract to the particular:

> "This translation cannot be made by the expert without a condescension and oversimplification that demean and finally destroy both the two minds and the two kinds of work that are involved. To the textbook writer or researcher, the farm — the place where knowledge is applied — is necessarily provisional or theoretical; what he proposes must be *generally* true. For the good farmer, on

the other hand, the place where knowledge is applied is minutely particular, not *a* farm but *this* farm, *my* farm, the only place exactly like itself in the whole world. To use it without intimate, minutely particular knowledge of it, as if it were *a* farm or *any* farm, is, as good farmers tend to know instinctively, to violate it, to do it damage, finally to destroy it."[65]

The sort of abstract knowledge in which global managers put their faith, in other words, is useful to individual farmers only in the *absence* of management. The broader the managerial project of "getting from A to B" becomes — and there is no broader "B" than "global sustainability" — the more ignorant managers become of the locally-embedded knowledge they would need to check environmental destruction. Richard Norgaard concludes that "it is unreasonable to expect to find universal principles for renewable resource systems even apart from people, let alone with people involved."[66]

GLOBAL MANAGEMENT MEANS GLOBAL POLICING

A second problem for global managers revolves around the fact that, as Ivan Illich points out, "commons can exist without police but resources cannot".[67] Once commons are transformed into resources through enclosure, control over them must be exercised from outside. At that point, conserving them may require even more brute force than plundering them, since the process of enclosure will have made those who benefit and those who lose from their preservation strangers to each other, reducing incentives for local stewardship.

Yet if conserving distant sources of raw materials requires police, so would any move to limit the consumption of manufactured goods in the North. As Hans Magnus Enzensberger saw two decades ago, keeping the limitless hunger for commodities which industrial economies require for their functioning in line with ecological imperatives could "only be done by force".[68]

It is hardly surprising, then, that what might be called "war-room environmentalism" is on the rise among would-be global managers. In a recent booklet on *The Crisis of Global Environment: Demands for Global Politics*, Germany's Foundation Development and Peace proposes with a seriousness which is deadly in more ways than one that:

> "Global environmental policy . . . calls for fast-acting intervention instruments, such as an international environmental police force, which should intervene whenever and wherever ecological threats are posed in or by a given country for the international community of nations."[69]

On the other side of the Atlantic, Senator Al Gore of the US says that treating environmental crises as if they were "military threats to our national security . . . is precisely the kind of political, personal and emotional response that . . . is required."[70]

The concentrations of power such militaristic sentiments imply can only be justified by global managers' presenting themselves as "executives of the inevitable"[71], guideposts to impersonal "limits" given by "nature" or "science" rather than defenders of a particular economic system or culture. The notion of "carrying capacity" is invoked, for example, to justify managerial interventions to "control population", and that of "safe minimum standards" to sanction industrial pollution.[72] Western worries are presented as "global concerns", while those of the majority of the world's people become "merely local". All pronouns except the all-encompassing "we" disappear from managerial pronouncements. "Sustainable development" becomes the subject of history, and statements begin "The task is . . .", "The challenge is . . .", as if these abstractions no longer need to be tied to human actors at all.

Those who have been on the receiving end of large-scale management in the past have good reason to doubt whether the actors masked by such abstractions are capable of looking after a system of any size, much less a global one. Having witnessed previous "international police actions" such as those undertaken during the Gulf War, they know in whose interests such actions would be taken and what the social and environmental consequences would likely be.[73] They understand that the managerial preoccupation with "getting from A to B" — or even "B" itself — cannot be meaningfully discussed without talking about the institutions involved, their interests, their commercial links, their background and their abilities. They know too that no amount of brute force — no matter how much abstract science it is combined with — can replace local traditions of care and stewardship.

Witnesses to previous managerial policing operations can testify, in addition, to how such notions as those of "carrying capacity" (*see* Box: "Carrying Capacity", "Overpopulation" and Environmental Degradation) and "overpopulation" are used by institutions such as the World Bank to license programmes of staggering human and environmental impact. Indonesia's Transmigration Programme, for example, ostensibly undertaken to relieve "population pressure" on Java, has marginalized hundreds of thousands of people, heightened social conflict, and ruined vast expanses of forests and land.[74]

Finally, as scholars of conservation movements such as Tariq Banuri and Frederique Apffel-Marglin observe, whenever managerial initiatives to conserve the environment have been taken, they "have always *followed* rather than led popular expressions of concern over environmental degradation".[75] The globalization of management and the accompanying policing operations, because they lessen the chances of those concerns being heard, thus actively undermine hopes for genuine conservation.

GLOBAL MANAGEMENT NEEDS A UNIVERSAL CULTURE

A third prerequisite for successful planetary management is the ability, in the words of Lester R. Brown, to "mobilize the world" around concern for such abstract entities as climate, "population" and tropical forests.[76] To do this requires not only police but popular enthusiasm. In the eyes of managers, this is lacking worldwide. In addition, in societies where a sense of "the public" is weak, environmental laws are often ineffective, and the economic and political costs of using police to enforce them prohibitive. Hence the constant laments from Northern would-be global managers about the "policy failures", "irrationality", "lapses in

"Carrying Capacity", "Over-population" and Environmental Degradation

The term "carrying capacity" originally derived from the biological sciences, where it was used to denote the optimum number of a given species that a specific ecosystem is able to sustain without interfering with its basic structure and stability. For global managers, it is a concept that has a particular appeal since it provides a seemingly "objective" measure of how many people can survive or flourish on a particular area of land at particular levels of consumption and technology. If "carrying capacity" is exceeded, the reasoning goes, then population can be said to be "objectively" excessive relative to land, consumption and technology.

It is not as easy as all that, however, to remove the concept of "overpopulation" from the realm of moral criticism and debate. Outsiders' claims that a given area of land has a certain "carrying capacity" are open to criticism in three different ways. First, the number of people who can live on a piece of land depends largely on their culture, which determines both their needs and their ways of life. The nature and success of their farming systems, for example, cannot easily be predicted in advance on the model of outsiders' cultures. Second, the fact that the question of consumption and technology levels must be raised in any discussion of "carrying capacity" means that the normative issues of what sort of society or economy people desire cannot be evaded when talking of "overpopulation". Third, a given land area's "carrying capacity" will depend largely on what happens outside its borders: upstream deforestation, global commodity price fluctuations, greenhouse gas emissions, acid rain and so forth. Local inhabitants will always be justified in pointing out that their land could support a great many more people if damaging external influences were curbed, and, on this ground, in calling into question the presumption of those partly responsible for such influences in suggesting "proper" local population levels.

This latter problem might be evaded, of course, by an attempt to determine global carrying capacity. However, this is usually acknowledged to be technically far-fetched even if the world's peoples could be induced to accept uniform global consumption levels and technology. And it would of course leave wide open the question of which local "populations" would have to be "adjusted" to meet the purported "global" requirements.

Lack of Explanatory Power

One response to such arguments is that, while "overpopulation" cannot be precisely or "objectively" defined, there are at least unambiguous statistical correlations between "population" and environmental degradation on a national scale. On close examination, however, even this assertion turns out to be problematic. Malaysia, for example, although it has only a tenth as many people as neighbouring Indonesia, has cleared fully 40 per cent as much forest as Indonesia has done. Central America, with a "population" density of only 57 persons per square kilometre, has cleared 410,000 square kilometres of forests, or 82 per cent of its original forest cover, while France, covering the same land area with double the number of people, has cleared less. And those who would explain the destruction of half a million square kilometres of Brazilian Amazonian forests between 1975 and 1988 in Malthusian terms "overlook the inconvenient fact that although the Amazon forms over 60 per cent of Brazilian national territory, less than 10 per cent of Brazil's population lives there".

If "population" and "population" density are poorly correlated with specific examples of environmental degradation, "population" increase is equally poorly correlated with rates of environmental degradation. Costa Rica and Cameroon, for example, are clearing their forests faster than Guatemala and Zaire, respectively, in spite of having lower "population" growth rates. Thailand's rate of forest encroachment, similarly, has varied less closely with the rate of population increase than with changes in political climate, villagers' security, road and dam-building, and logging concessions.

To confuse the issue still further, there are many instances of environmental degradation resulting from the outflow of people from a given area of land. In Africa, for example, there are many areas where fallow periods have been reduced, not because there is a shortage of land, due to "population pressure", but because there is a shortage of farm labour due to urban migration. The longer a plot of cleared bush is left fallow, the more labour is required to clear it again for agriculture: hence, it makes economic (if not ecological) sense to reduce the fallow period. In such cases, the problems associated with reduced fallow periods result not from overpopulation but from local depopulation.

Exploitative Relations

Indeed, the closer one looks at the relationship between human numbers and environmental degradation, the clearer it becomes that, at root, the key issue is not simply how many? but *how is society organized*? In the case of deforestation, for example, the periods of most rapid destruction "have not necessarily been at the times when population was most rapidly expanding. They have occurred when the exploitation of subordinate groups (as well as of resources) has intensified." The halving of Central America's forest area between 1950 and 1990, for example, is due not to a "population explosion" but to the concentration of land in the hands of a limited number of rich ranchers and landowners raising bananas, cotton, coffee and cattle. Peasants have been used as land-clearers only to be pushed into the hills, where they displace others and are forced to cut yet more forest. Elsewhere, transnational corporations such as Finland's Jaakko Pöyry Oy, the US's Scott Paper, and Japan's Marubeni often supervise forest plunder, with additional destruction resulting from expropriative cattle-raising, road, hydro-electric and industrial projects.

In the Amazon, most land cleared of forest produces little in the way of food and often was not cleared for that purpose. Migration into the forests has much more to do with structural changes in the regions of emigration than with "population" growth. Thus, decline in access to land, as it occurred in North-Eastern Brazil, stimulated emigration. In the case of migrants from the South of Brazil, the expansion of mechanized agriculture and the flooding of enormous areas of agricultural land forced small farmers out of their holdings. Finally, the threat of violence and lack of employment have also expelled farmers from their holdings. Since more than half of all agriculturalists in Brazil rely on wage labour as well as cropping for their income, activities like mechanization which reduce rural employment are often as disastrous to peasants as brute expulsion from their lands.

For those who would avoid such issues, the concept of "carrying capacity" offers a welcome life-belt. Seemingly objective, it depoliticises what is a highly political issue by reducing the debate to one of mathematics. In its recommendations to UNCED on sustainable agriculture, for example, the UN Food and Agriculture Organization (FAO) argues that governments should "evaluate the carrying and population supporting capacity of major agricultural areas", and, where such areas are to deemed to be "overpopulated", take steps to change "the man/land ratio" (sic) by "facilitating the accommodation of migrating populations into better-endowed areas". Elsewhere, FAO is more candid, specifically recommending "transmigration" programmes. Peasants who have been forced onto marginal lands as a result of the best quality land being taken over for intensive export-oriented agriculture may thus be liable to resettlement because officials calculate that they are a threat to local "carrying capacity": yet nowhere in its Sustainable Agriculture and Rural Development policy paper does FAO consider the alternative option that ecological stress in marginal areas might be better relieved by reclaiming the best farm land for peasant agriculture. In effect, far from being a neutral and objective measure of ecological stress, carrying capacity is already being used as a means of preventing radical social change.

---

governance", "personal fiefdoms" and "corruption" of the Southern officials who are supposed to carry out their instructions.

In order to tackle such difficulties, champions of global management such as Brown and Maurice Strong are calling for "new attitudes", "new political will" and a "revolution in individual values". In their more visionary versions, such calls amount to a proposal for the adoption of a new "global consciousness". Among other things, such a consciousness could play the role of a sort of internalized environmental police force which would lighten and smooth the task of the real police. Active within each world citizen, it would compensate for the loss of the multitude of moral sanctions which ensure the preservation of land, water and living things in traditional commons regimes. It would complement the exercise of global environmental management in much the same way that the development of the culture of the factory worker, with its sensitivity to clock-time and other forms of modern discipline, complemented the efforts of the first industrial managers.

To be effective in this way, what would such a "global environmentalist culture" have to look like? First, it would have to be a culture in which an expanded notion of "the public" was universally recognized and respected, while the idiosyncratic moral feelings connected with the commons — which often stand in the way of the smooth operation of that "public" — were encouraged to fade away.

Second, in order to safeguard the position of managers against "irrational protests", this culture would have to view them as mere agents of a unified world economic-ecological system, not in themselves morally responsible for any past or future environmental disasters it might unavoidably bring about but simply facilitating the system's optimal operation. The general public, meanwhile, would be trained to an extremely high level of moral responsiveness to the global system itself. Individuals would willingly consent to the managerial application of conclusions concerning "climate", "population" or other abstractions to their consumer habits, cultivation methods, sex lives, and so on. As a recent popular book on environmental management says, "every action of 'normal daily life'" would be put "in question".[77] Local, personalized traditions of mutual scrutiny which apply in the commons would need to be replaced by an utterly general, impersonal surveillance.

Last, the new culture would inculcate new attitudes toward nature. Ordinary people would have to stop loving and protecting the land, streams and woods they know — as people do who rely on the commons — and instead learn to love and protect nature only in the abstract. Only then would they become willing to trade a local forest or stream for something else if required to do so by "systemic needs", yet at the same time cherish enough of an abstract "love for nature" to be interested in managed environmental protection efforts.

The required attitude toward nature is epitomized in a photograph in a new periodical called *Tomorrow*, which bills itself as "The Global Environmental Magazine" and is funded by Asea Brown Boveri, an engineering company involved in the construction of the bitterly-disputed Tehri project in India and other large dams. The photograph depicts a young, blond Western model in a bathing suit standing waist-deep in a sunlit sea. Like the women of the Chipko movement in India, she is hugging something — only in her case it is not a tree threatened by state forestry managers but a colourful giant inflatable plastic globe. Rather than expressing reverence, defiance or humour, her face, with its closed eyes and soft smile, communicates passivity and bliss. She is pictured, as her cheek rests on the North Pole and her arm embraces Africa, trying to show love for an abstract "world" which is in fact connected with her life only through impersonal mechanisms and expert explanations. By calling to mind the Chipko movement, the picture implicitly equates this non-rooted, impersonal affection, which according to the managerial mentality is required to save the world, with the highly particular, personal moral feelings which derive from relationships which govern the commons. It crystallizes in visual form the sense of the oxymoron "global commons", now so widely used by managers to describe their new area of expertise.

GLOBAL CULTURE FAILS GLOBAL MANAGERS

The photograph suggests not only why the managerial appeal for a new culture of abstract "global concern" is sentimental and wrong, but also why it is impracticable. In reality, cultures capable of stirring dedication and "political will" of the order which global managers are hoping to enlist are most likely to be ones in which people and things are viewed not as means to "survival", "economic-ecological balance", or "the good life" as defined by international bureaucrats and scientists, but ones in which people and things, rooted in particular pasts and landscapes, are loved for themselves. Reliance on a disembodied "culture of global concern" is no less problematic for environmental managers than dependence on a disembodied, abstract science.

While it may be part of the moral self-understanding of World Bank executives that they are not responsible for the development projects they plan and execute, similarly, this understanding is not likely to catch on widely among those affected. Managerial hopes that a Northern-directed "revolution in values" will "reduce corruption" and toughen up so-called "soft states" in the South are refuted by the lack of a Western concept of the public through most of the world as well as by the hard logic justifying Southern élites' incorporation of Western capital flows into their own personal networks. "You have taught us about meritocracy and accountability," such élites can reasonably say. "Are we less qualified than those of you who earn ten million dollars a year? Are Northern advisers who come to our country 100 times more qualified than the local counterparts who earn 100 times less? Are the World Bank, FAO and GATT you founded accountable to the people whose lives they affect? Are Wall Street bankers or Secretaries of Defence?" One of the drawbacks of attempting to impose a universal culture on others is that they tend to take it seriously.

Ivan Illich foresaw a decade ago that "the coming steady state society [without the commons] will be an oligarchic, undemocratic and authoritarian expertocracy governed by ecologists".[78] He could well have added that such an expertocracy cannot work even on its own terms. This failure is hardly a matter for regret. It is merely the other side of the coin of the success of the commons. Arturo Escobar concludes a recent essay by expressing the hope that in the future, the "plurality of meanings and practices that make up human history will again be made apparent, while planning itself will fade away from concern."[79]

"POPULATION CONTROL"

One area where the managerial approach now reigns supreme concerns "population". Instead of addressing the social, economic and political roots of increasing human numbers, population controllers focus primarily on preventing births through technical means that are often coercive, and which injure women's health and undermine their self-determination. The "population issue" is being used politically to control groups of people who are considered a threat by those who have benefited from enclosure. Moreover, "population control" is being used to enclose women still further: it takes away their power to determine how many children they have and to choose a method of regulating births which they control and which does not threaten their health. It also erodes their power to decide when and how they have sexual intercourse.

"Earlier our bodies were controlled by our men," comments one woman in Bangladesh. "Now they are controlled by our men and our government."[80]

Even those who acknowledge the devastating impact of the development process on the environment often take the "pragmatic" view that reducing human numbers must take priority over addressing the structural roots of the environmental crisis because it is more urgent and easier than curbing consumption or adopting environmentally-sound technologies. As Paul Harrison puts it:

". . . the poorest one billion must increase their consumption. The middle three billion will not rest with the odd radio, bicycle or fridge they now have. They will go on aiming for the Western dream — including cars. The richest billion will not readily renounce even part of their affluence . . . Technology must be softened. But don't let's expect miracles . . . Technology changes must be backed by slower population growth. Population is actually the easiest of the three knots to cut."[81]

Easiest if one forgets that the knot is real live people, ignores what "population control" really means and assumes bullying the powerless is preferable to redressing the balance of power. But the word "population" no longer means people.[82] It typically has connotations of a *bomb* which has released an *explosion* of mainly poor, brown- or yellow-skinned people, who are creating *pressure*, so must be *controlled* — regardless of the methods used. As the Bombay director of family planning during the 1970s, Dr. D.N. Pai, said, "If some excesses appear, don't blame me. . . You must consider it something like a war. There could be a certain amount of misfiring out of enthusiasm. There has been pressure to show results. Whether you like it or not, there will be a few dead people."[83]

COERCED TO CHOOSE

India's population control programme, one of the first and largest in the world, dramatically illustrates the use of coercion. In 1976, under a state of emergency, a variety of laws and regulations on sterilization were enacted. Fines and imprisonment threatened couples who were not sterilized after three children. Men were rounded up with brute force for sterilization in mass vasectomy camps. These abuses helped to bring down the government in 1977 and contributed to a predictable backlash against family planning. The number of sterilizations dropped to 900,000 in 1977 compared to 6.5 million in just the last six months of 1976.

Today, the sterilization programme continues, but with a shrewd change in strategy: women, who have less political power than men, are the main targets. Since 1977–1978, women have accounted for 80 per cent of sterilizations, even though tubal ligation is riskier than vasectomy. Brute force may be rare, but other forms of coercion and pressure are used. As during the state of emergency, the salaries of various public employees or civil servants are withheld unless they bring in a target number of "acceptors" each month; each "acceptor" earns them a bonus as well.[84] A woman herself is paid 200 rupees to be sterilized, a man 180 rupees. Over-zealous recruiters are known to compel or trick women into unwanted contraception and sterilization, including post-menopausal women and widows.

Women in India, as elsewhere, have always sought ways to limit births, but the existence of these various incentives would indicate that the methods on offer are not their method of choice. Christa Wichterich points out that "under conditions of poverty where the premium (for sterilization) is greater than the monthly wage of an agricultural worker, it is pointless to describe the women's decisions as voluntary."[85]

WHO CONTROLS?

Even the World Health Organization (WHO) has acknowledged that sterilization and contraception have been forced upon vulnerable groups who for various reasons (ethnic, cultural, political, economic) threaten the interests of powerful decision-makers, whether national or local.[86] Consistently justifying such actions has been the concept of "overpopulation". The concept sounds scientific and can be applied in a flexible range of circumstances according to the convenience and interests of those who use it. For the foreign and domestic companies who have usurped 40 per cent of Kenya's arable land to grow coffee, tea and sisal for export, for example, "overpopulation" occurs when peasants outside the plantations begin to covert land for their own subsistence. Prior to mechanization, when states found that labour, not land, was in short supply, the complaint across Africa and South-East Asia was of "*under*population".

"Population control" policies aim not to control people as such but to limit human production — of future people. They involve a dominant group deciding *who* will be born, *how* many will be born, and of *what* race, class, sex and "quality". Farida Ahkter, an activist from Bangladesh, recalls a story narrated by a family planning officer to a group of poor and illiterate women in a remote village in Bangladesh:

> "You see, there are only nine cabins in the steamer launch which comes from Dhaka to Patuakhali. In the nine cabins only 18 people can travel. The ticket is expensive, so only the rich people travel in the cabins. The rest of the common passengers travel in the deck. The latrine facility is provided only for the cabin passengers. But sometimes the passengers from the deck want to use the latrines. The cabin passengers allow them to use the latrine because they are afraid that if the poor deck passengers get angry then they might go down and make a hole in the launch. Then the launch will sink; they will die no doubt but the rich cabin passengers will not survive either. So, my dear sisters, do not give birth to more children as they cause a problem for the cabin passengers."[87]

CONTROLLING WOMEN'S FERTILITY

"Population control", "family planning", "family welfare" and "birth control" are euphemisms for what is really happening: control of women's fertility.[88] Although methods of contraception could be assumed by either men or women, or both together, the emphasis in population control is on reducing *women*'s reproductive capacities. In 1978, 78 per cent of public sector expenditures for the development of new contraceptives was for female methods, as opposed to only seven per cent for males.[89] This is slowly changing after pressure from women's groups, but the deep-rooted bias persists. While women alone bear the risks of childbirth, and thus have an obvious incentive to be concerned about contraception, the disproportionate focus on controlling their procreative abilities cannot be attributed solely to this concern. The underlying assumption behind the focus on female contraception is revealed in the justification given for it by Dr. Hugh Gorwill, a researcher in human reproduction, that "females create population problems," a statement he backs up by saying the "common pathway to turn off having people is females."[90]

Women do not produce children on their own. The involvement of men in the human reproductive process, however, is virtually unacknowledged and unchallenged in the contraceptive field; it is an "illegitimate speciality within reproductive biology"[91]

Contraceptive research has therefore been directed into technical, systemic and surgical ways of preventing women conceiving. These often interfere not only with women's health but also with their libido, sexual enjoyment and ability to say "no". In contrast, men's libido and pleasure in pursuing unrestricted "normal" heterosexual intercourse is not to be disrupted. One woman has remarked of the hormonal pill that it seemed to have been developed "to enable women to be sexual at *any* time, but to me it was like a statement that I had to be sexual at *all* times. The pill seemed less to do with not getting pregnant than with being sexually available."[92] Some health workers defend the use of the injectable contraceptive, Depo-Provera or NET-EN, on the basis of women's powerlessness and male opposition to contraception, claiming that it is the only way for some women to have any control over any aspect of their lives. This approach, however, can undermine efforts to change the fundamental social and economic conditions that are responsible for women's powerlessness in the first place. Much as the injectable and other contraceptives may free women from pregnancy, they do not free them from unwanted sexual intercourse. Ironically, Depo-Provera has proved an effective male contraceptive, but has not been promoted as such because of complaints of loss of libido — although women complain of the same thing.[93]

EFFICACY AND EFFECTS

This patriarchal bias of modern contraceptive technologies — the "tools" of population control which "embody the values of their creators" — is apparent both in their design and in the ways in which they are administered in population control programmes.[94]

The single overriding goal in contraceptive research is to develop a fail-safe product that prevents pregnancy: the health effects on women using the contraceptive are of minor importance to researchers. Studies assessing safety have often proved less than rigorous, if undertaken at all; when adverse effects and long-term risks finally come to light, often after a long struggle by the women affected by them, they tend to be trivialized by population control agencies; women are generally not fully informed of all these health risks when they "choose" a method; and, in population control programmes, women are not given adequate medical screening or follow-up care.[95] The Office of Population of the US Agency for International Development has argued against standard medical screening and follow-up procedures for the pill: "With respect to contra-indications, we prefer not to even use the term" as it may have "very negative connotations."[96]

Indeed, many population controllers seem to consider that concern about the debilitating effects of modern contraceptives on women, although regrettable, should not be allowed to interfere with preventing women getting pregnant in an "overcrowded" world. As Dr. J. Robert Weston remarked upon the revival of intrauterine devices (IUDs):

> "[IUDs] are horrible things, they produce infection, they are outmoded and not worth using . . . [but] suppose one does develop an intrauterine infection and suppose she does end up with a hysterectomy? How serious is that for the particular patient and for the population of the world in general? Not very. Perhaps the individual patient is expendable in the general scheme of things, particularly if the infection she acquires is sterilizing but not lethal."[97]

Not *lethal* perhaps, but for women who use an IUD or any other method as a *reversible* form of contraception, such enforced sterilization can not only be a deep personal tragedy but, in many societies where women's only status and capital comes from having children, it may be a cause of social ostracism, abandonment and ultimately destitution.[98]

Depression, menstrual irregularities, headaches and other adverse effects of hormonal contraceptive technologies (pill, injectable, implant) are dismissed as "minor" or "personal side effects" or due to "psychological factors", even though "depression is a minor side effect which merely destroys the entire quality of a woman's life."[99] Not menstruating, far from being a blessing, may be a cause for anxiety because it is a natural indication of pregnancy, not of its opposite. Unusually heavy or intermittent bleeding is often an indication of a problem, not of health. Heavy bleeding can also be particularly serious for anaemic and undernourished women, while intermittent bleeding can not only be physically inconvenient but socially restrictive as well. In cultures where menstrual blood is considered "unclean", menstruating women are restricted from social and household activities, such as going to the temple or cooking. For prostitutes, it can mean not being able to work.

A QUESTION OF CONTROL

The latest generation of fertility regulation methods undermine women's control of their reproductive capacities still further. The trend in contraception is away from short-acting (24 hours for the pill) towards long-acting methods: three to six months for the injectable and five years for the implant, Norplant®. Some women may feel this is a relief; they know they are protected. But if a woman experiences adverse effects, or decides she would like to have a baby, she can only wait for the effect to wear off or, in the case of Norplant®, get it taken out — if she can.

This long-acting trend coincides with another which dominates population control programmes: provider dependency. One reason why safer barrier methods, such as the condom and diaphragm, and natural family planning, have been neglected in terms of research, promotion and distribution — even though they have no adverse impact on breast feeding, are suitable for birth spacing and, in the case of the condom, help to prevent the spread of sexually transmitted diseases — is that they are under the *user's*, not the *provider's*, control. Not so the new technologies. Whereas a woman can decide each day whether to take the pill, or to put in a diaphragm, and a man to use a condom, a woman has to go to trained medical personnel for a Depo-Provera or NET-EN injection or for insertion and removal of an IUD or Norplant®.

The president of the US Population Council, the developer of Norplant®, advocated in 1969 the establishment of involuntary fertility control which would include, "Temporary sterilization of all girls by means of time-capsule contraceptives, and of girls and women after each delivery, with reversibility allowed only upon governmental approval."[100] His proposal has come close to being realized. In January 1986, the Brazilian Ministry of Health prohibited further trials of the implant in the country because they did not follow basic international norms of ethics and safety required for human clinical trials of new products. One woman's experience is illustrative:

> "I didn't go to (the clinic) for Norplant®. I went for a preventive. But I was sent to a girl who said she was a nurse. Then she started talking about Norplant®. Nowadays I know what 'inducing' means. They induce people. That day I met various girls, young girls who had never had children and were using Norplant®."[101]

The lack of removal on demand of Norplant® is where the main potential for abuse lies. Women in countries such as Brazil, Thailand and Indonesia are among those who have wanted to have the implant removed but have been unable to find a doctor trained or willing to do so. One woman in Ecuador cut it out herself in a procedure that in some cases in Finland has needed general anaesthesia because the implant is so deeply embedded in fibrous tissues.

Women in the US, particularly poor women and "women of color", are now particularly concerned about the punitive or coercive use of the implant in the country. "Two days after the FDA (Food and Drug Administration) approved Norplant® for public use (in December 1990), a *Philadelphia Inquirer* editorial suggested the implant should be used as 'a tool in the fight against black poverty.' The fact that some policy makers and opinion makers . . . see this drug as a potential tool to be 'used' against the poor, and those victimized historically by racism, sexism, unequal pay, discrimination, and other injustices is not only inhumane — it is unconscionable."[102]

The potential for abuse is considerably greater with the anti-pregnancy "vaccines" now being researched. The "vaccines" are designed to work by inducing in the body an immune response towards natural body constituents which are essential to reproduction, such as hormones, human eggs, sperm or the early embryo. For example, the immune response generated by a "vaccine" developed in India targets the human pregnancy hormone and thus interferes with the implantation of the fertilized egg. These immunological contraceptive methods may have a lifelong effect — auto-immune reactions are difficult, if not impossible, to stop — but this seems not to concern the researchers, some of whom consider the "vaccines" an "attractive alternative to surgical sterilization."[103]

Even WHO, a sponsor of some of the "vaccine" research, warns that:

> "the fact that [the anti-pregnancy vaccine] is administered by injection makes it easy to confuse, intentionally or unintentionally, with other preventive or curative injections . . . The advantage of being long-lasting will be a problem instead of an advantage if the vaccine is given without the woman's informed consent."[104]

The potential for misleading women about injections they receive is often enhanced by the mystique of injections in many societies. Despite these warnings, however, the developers insist that the "vaccine" should be a high priority in contraceptive research because of the "urgency of the demographic crisis".[105]

CHOICE? WHAT CHOICE?

For women who are informed in an unbiased way about the pros and cons of each method, who have the back-up of an available, effective, safe and hygienic health service and who have the option of changing to another method if one is unsuitable, the range of contraceptive technologies may offer a choice. In many countries with population control programmes, however, such choice is an illusion. Farida Akhter has little confidence in this so-called "cafeteria" approach of the population controllers:

> "We are inundated with devices (high dose pill, IUD, injectables, implants or sterilization) to render our reproductive organs dysfunctional. I see dumping and inundation before I see the point many Western women are trying to raise through the demand of reproductive rights. I have no illusion that there is any right involved in the population control programme of Bangladesh . . . even those who distribute the contraceptives . . . do not have adequate information to share with the users. They do not have the necessary skills or equipment to check and inform women what they should be careful about . . . The concept of a cafeteria approach . . . is meaningless in Bangladesh. How are women going to choose if they do not have the information to judge and compare methods?"[106]

Not surprisingly, the feeling of many women in the Third World regarding contraception runs counter to their perceptions of Western women's liberation. "Under conditions of insecurity and a patriarchal culture . . . (contraception) is not a means to liberation or self-determination but determination by others: an instrument of control from outside."[107] With the present "choice" in India between sterilization or "the mess of IUDs", some groups feel trapped in a punishing dilemma concerning the proposed introduction of Norplant® in the country, despite knowing the adverse effects, long-term risks and ways in which the implant is administered in other population control programmes. Which mess is less bad? What choice do women have? If the contraceptive users had been consulted about the methods to be developed, would they have chosen those with the characteristics of the present technologies?

FAILURE

The irony is that population control policies rarely work. "In spite of immense efforts and financial expenditure, population controllers in many countries have only been marginally successful.

Many women resist the measures or only take preventive steps after they have had five or six children."[108] Suffering from unexplained and untreated adverse side effects, and disillusioned with contraception and the lack and quality of service, a high percentage of women stop using the contraceptives and avoid health and family planning centres altogether. The approach of focusing solely on targets — the number of "acceptors" or sterilizations — backfires. Even in countries where the birth rate has gone down, no direct link can be established between the programmes and the decline.[109]

Many women are "interested in the abolition of the social reduction of their personality to child-bearers", and contraception may have enabled some of them to gain more control over their lives. But the majority, particularly poorer, Third World and black women, are well aware that their emancipation:

> "will be not be produced by an intrauterine pessary, or by tubal ligation, if there are no changes in the state of poverty of their life and work, if they do not overcome the sexist exclusion from all resources — land ownership, money, education and political power — and the patriarchal dictate of bearing sons, not daughters."[110]

Unwanted pregnancies and unwanted abortions can indicate not just a lack of contraceptive techniques but the powerlessness and missing self-determination of women in all spheres — social, economic, political and personal. As Christa Wichterich says:

> "I should like to emphasize yet again: of course I am in favour of women in the Third World determining for themselves their reproduction and having control over their lives and bodies. But what is happening at present in most population control arenas is in my opinion a deprivation of self-determination and power from women and at the same time a comprehensive intervention in human reproduction. With the standardization of fertility and the family, whether reproduction is restricted, selectively guided or artificially achieved, the path towards the industrial production of humanity in this one world has been entered upon."[111]

Yet the response of population controllers to the failure of their programmes is not to reform the programmes to meet women's needs, but to intensify further population control efforts. "The policy of the multinational organizations is characterized by an unshakeable belief in the political feasibility of fertility control with the aid of methods developed in the West."[112] It is a path that leads only to further attempted enclosure of the majority of the world's people — women.

TECHNOLOGY TRANSFER

The technocratic approach to contraception is only one example of the more general view that more Western science and technology is indispensable for curing the world's environmental ills. This view is often expressed in the form of a beguiling syllogism:

> Only Western science and technology can solve the world's environmental problems.
>
> The developing countries, by definition, are lacking in scientific and technological resources.
>
> *Therefore*,
>
> a massive transfer of science and technology is required from North to South, involving in turn a massive transfer of funds.

This argument has been almost universally accepted in the UNCED discourse. Any disagreements — and there have been many — have centered around secondary concerns, such as how much money should be transferred and what particular technologies should be employed.

SCIENCE VERSUS IGNORANCE

Central to the logic of technology transfer is the presupposition of the recipient's ignorance. "Ignorance" according to the World Bank, "is an important cause of environmental damage and a serious impediment to finding solutions . . . Frequently, especially in developing countries, decisions are made in the absence of environmental information. Collecting basic data can be expensive, but the rewards are usually high."[113] And again: "Poverty, uncertainty and ignorance are the allies of environmental degradation . . . Better-educated people can more readily adopt environmentally sound but complicated techniques such as integrated pest management."[114]

It is predictable that the World Bank should have chosen an agricultural example — pest management — to illustrate their point. The peasant farmer, "especially in developing countries" has always been represented by experts as an archetype of ignorance, "backward" and bound by tradition. In the words of E. Alvord, an agricultural missionary to Rhodesia in the 1920s and 1930s, "we have in my opinion little or nothing to learn from native agriculture" which he characterized as "wasteful, slovenly, ineffective and ruinous to the future interests of Rhodesia," while the natives themselves were "heathens who were grossly immoral and incredibly steeped in superstition."[115]

The language used today by World Bank policy-writers is every bit as racist, if not as crude, as that used by Alvord, and it reinforces similar attitudes further down the hierarchy: for example, Zambian extension agents, working on a World Bank project in the 1980s, described local farmers as "ignorant peasants, too lazy to farm."[116] The word "ignorant" is pregnant with contempt. It epitomizes an attitude that is consciously or sub-consciously held by all those who consider that Western technology is a *sine qua non* of environmental stability and human comfort; those who assume, without question, that a small, noisy, polluting refrigerator must inevitably be better than a large, cool larder, that a two-litre motor car must inevitably be more efficient than a two-pedal bicycle, or that an expensive tractor-drawn plough must inevitably be superior to the nimble mattock.

THE SCIENCE OF THE COMMONS

The assumption, implicit in the World Bank's allegations of "ignorance", that scientific research and technological advance cannot exist outside the research laboratories and computer networks of the developed world is inherent to the logic of technology transfer. Yet until quite recently, even in Europe, almost all scientific research and technological advance took place in the field or on the shop floor. Waterproof suits made from fish-gut and watertight bowls made from grass were not developed in research laboratories; nor were the junks of China, or the kayaks of the Aleut: nor even the traditional "wootz" steel of India, which in the 1840s was judged to be better than anything produced in Britain.[117] The technological advances of the English "agricultural revolution" were originally developed, not by theorists such as Arthur Young who propagated them in the 18th century, but some two or three hundred years earlier by a succession of nameless farmers.[118] This tradition of vernacular science is still very much alive, though its disdain for publicity and the written word have led many academic scientists to doubt its value and even its existence.

Human beings are for the most part curious, experimental and concerned for their own well-being. It should therefore come as no surprise to us that groups of people who have lived in an area for generations should evolve systems of agriculture and ways of living that are congenial, effective and sustainable — unless they are prevented by someone else from doing so. This process of native scientific selection and discovery is not always as slow as we have been led to believe. Winin Pereira has described how when the *dandavan* tree, from Australia, was introduced to an area north of Bombay, in the first year that it came into flower the local Warli tribals discovered that its seeds could be used to stupefy and catch fish; and subsequently started using it as a medicine as well. The following year a paper describing experiments by two scientists on the effects of the seed on two species of fish confined to a laboratory aquarium was published in *Environment and Ecology*. Not only did the tribals beat the scientists — their research needed no expensive equipment, no submission of reports and budgets, no academic accolade and was tested on the fish that needed to be caught, in their natural environment.[119] This was research carried out by and for the commons — rather than in the enclosed and jealous world of the academic institution.

The intimate knowledge of the properties of plants is reflected elsewhere in the widespread practice of intercropping. Whereas Northern agriculture finds it easier to cope with one crop at a time — and frequently with one crop all the time — in many parts of the tropics farmers have found it advantageous to grow two or more crops together in one field. In West Africa, 80 per cent of all farmland is intercropped, with up to 60 crop species being grown on any one farm.[120] N.S. Jodha notes a tradition in India "that every farmer should plant nine crops in at least one of his plots. This ritual practice known as *nava dhanyam* (nine grains) is guided by a belief that it is the duty of every farmer to preserve the germplasm which nature has provided."[121]

There are many advantages associated with intercropping. Often there is simply a net gain in yield over growing a single crop on the same area of land. Certain combinations of plants complement each other, by providing shade or windbreaks, and by exploiting nutrients at different levels of the soil. They can also protect each other from pest attacks. Intercropping also minimizes the risks of farming. The more crops and cropping schedules used, the less the likelihood of total crop failure; and staggering different crops means that there will be something to eat in the uncertain period before the main harvest. Also, the work load is spread evenly throughout the year rather than concentrated in a few critical periods. This can be the crucial limiting factor to the amount of food that a farm produces. Paul Richards argues that West Africans are turning increasingly to intercropping techniques, as a response both to land shortages and to labour shortages caused by out-migration. In this respect, "it might be better to view intercropping . . . not as a set of 'traditional' techniques, but as evidence of progress towards an agricultural revolution."[122] Certainly the fact that one observer counted no less than 147 distinct intercrop combinations in three villages in northern Nigeria suggests that much experimentation is taking place.[123]

The sophistication of vernacular science may also be observed in the numerous indigenous irrigation systems that are still operating throughout the world. For example, the *qanats* of the Middle East constitute a vast network of underground conduits stretching over 170,000 miles in Iran alone. In contrast to modern pumped irrigation technologies, they only tap spring water from mountain areas conveying it by the force of gravity. As a result, the aquifer cannot be depleted and the quality of the water is maintained. Though some of the channels were built thousands of years ago, many are still functioning: until recently they supplied 75 per cent of the water used in Iran both for irrigation and for household purposes.[124] Many other smaller-scale systems, such as that of the Chagga people on the slopes of Mount Kilimanjaro, have impressed Western engineers with their technical sophistication.

The most intractable problem faced by many irrigating societies is salinization of the land caused by the evaporation in the soil of unnatural amounts of water. Farmers know that overwatering and poor drainage threatens the whole community: there are thus a raft of sanctions and social arrangements that work to safeguard against salinization by giving the whole community a stake in preventing abuses. Different cultures have also developed rotations to control salinization. The farmers of the Euphrates, for example, do so by fallowing their lands with two wild legumes, *shok* (*Proserpina stephanis*) and *agul* (*Alhagi maurorum*), which, besides supplying nitrogen to the soil, draw moisture from the water table and dry out the subsoil, thus preventing water from rising and bringing salt to the surface. J.C. Russell has described this system as "a beautiful procedure for living with salinity", adding that the "villagers understand it, in that they know it works, and they know how to do it and they insist upon it."[125]

Of course, not all indigenous technologies have been sustainable. Some of the ancient irrigating civilizations became over-ambitious and sacrificed ecological stability for the increased short-term output they could gain by abandoning fallows and adopting perennial irrigation.[126] But those that were not sustainable have perforce died out; while those that have survived represent a vast repository of human knowledge, too large to be documented by any academic system.

A LITANY OF DISASTERS

For those who rely on the commons, defending this body of vernacular knowledge is fundamental to defending the commons.

For them, the experience of technology transfer is not that it solves problems so much as that it creates them.

Technology transfer has led to an influx of experts and other outsiders determined to impose their "solutions" on the commons. Since the 19th century, when the scientific academies blossomed and universities acquired departments of agriculture, physics and chemistry, the credit for innovation and the licence to innovate have been progressively lifted out of the public domain and placed in the hands of the professional scientist. New breeds of expert have appeared — the architect, the soil engineer, the planning officer, the conservationist, the health and safety officer, the agricultural extension officer — educated in the classroom and the laboratory, entitled with paper qualifications, and entrusted with the enforcement of a growing body of legislation that has been formulated in those same institutions.

No one has suffered more from this invasion of experts than those who have been most consistently stigmatized as ignorant, the poor of the Third World. In the words of Bill Rau, "The widespread failure of agricultural and rural development projects in Africa is largely due to the failure of planners to work with and reflect the complexity and diversity of rural and urban realities." Or indeed to understand them. "The dreams and myths of development 'experts' have been repeatedly altered or rejected by peasants, artisans and the urban poor because the projects were irrelevant, impractical or directly threatening to their well-being."[127]

The schemes devised by these experts have so far led to a litany of ecological and cultural disasters — and there is no reason to suppose that they will not continue to do so. Most frequently the problems are caused not by one or two basic miscalculations, but by a fundamental failure to comprehend the complexities of the local ecology and culture.

The Kano River Irrigation Project, for example, is an attempt to modernize a local farming community in northern Nigeria. In 1911, E. M. Morel wrote, "There is little that we can teach the Kano farmer . . . they have acquired the necessary precise knowledge as to the time to prepare the land for sowing; when and how to sow;

how long to let the land be fallow; what soils suit certain crops; what varieties of the same crop will succeed in some localities and what varieties in others ... how to ensure rotation; when to arrange with Fulani herdsmen to pasture their cattle upon the land."[128] Sixty years later the Nigerian government and agencies such as USAID and FAO thought differently. A project was initiated to replace the local *shadoof* bucket-irrigation system with water supplied by the new Tiga dam, which was completed in 1975. The main object was to supply wheat to make western-style bread for sale in the cities.

Although the area had been identified as being suitable for wheat, after the first five years of the project yields were only about 15 per cent of the amount predicted.[129] Farmers were pressurized to give up intercropping guinea corn with millet, because the harvest date interfered with the wheat crop, and were encouraged instead to grow maize, which is more demanding on the soil and more dependent on fertilizer. Soil fertility dropped as intercropping declined, and erosion increased because of the work involved levelling the land.

The project drastically altered the people's way of life. The co-operative arrangement between the farmers and the nomadic Fulani herders, mentioned approvingly by Morel, was stopped by project organizers who considered the cattle disruptive, and consequently *fura*, a vital food for both groups made out of milk and millet, could no longer be made. Poultry was banned from domestic households and there was a decline in foodstuffs such as sorghum, dates, locust beans (a weaning food), vegetables and other crops dependent upon the defunct *shadoof* irrigation.[130] The increase in men's income and the growing integration into the market economy resulted in a power imbalance between men and women, which led women to remove themselves "as much as possible from the household economy, creating a separate women's world into which to place their energies and generate independent resources, however meagre, with which to endow their daughters."[131]

Despite these problems and repercussions, the Kano River Project is regarded as more successful than others. A similar project in neighbouring Bakolori encountered determined resistance from peasants, culminating in 1980 in the massacre of at least 23 and probably over 100 farmers by the Nigerian police.[132]

The Kano story is just one of a now familiar stream of disappointments and failures that does not seem to be drying up. A report published in May 1992 by the UK National Audit Office found that of 17 recent aid projects funded by the Overseas Development Administration, (some in conjunction with the World Bank), the ability of more than half to survive after the project teams left was in doubt, and two were already written off as complete failures. In one drainage scheme in Pakistan, designed to alleviate the salinization of cotton fields in the Sind caused by the British-built irrigation systems, only three out of the projected 79 drainage sumps were working properly, and in these three cases "the water table had fallen below the optimum level and crop yields had reduced."[133]

TECHNOLOGY AS TROJAN HORSE

In the wake of such disasters, advocates of technology transfer have adopted two lines of defence. The first of these insists that it is not the technologies themselves that have caused the problems but the manner in which they have been applied. The UN Food and Agriculture Organization, for example, argues that "since farm chemicals are essentially tools in farm management, environmental problems stem from their misuse rather than being inherent characteristics."[134]

Even on its own terms, this statement is false: numerous pesticides are carcinogenic to consumers and dangerous to wildlife, regardless of how they are used in the field: that is why many of them have been banned. But the suggestion that pesticides are "environmentally neutral" — that is to say that they are not inherently dangerous, there is simply a right way and a wrong way to use them — is at the same time an admission that they are *not* socially neutral. To use pesticides safely, it is not enough for farmers simply to mix them up and spray them: they must adopt a "pesticide culture", with *its* prescriptions for "safe practice", "agricultural management", "wildlife protection", "food quality" and so on. In effect, pesticides, like other Western technologies, act as a Trojan horse for Western assumptions, practices, beliefs and social relations.

The networks of interest that promote technology transfer are well aware of this, and use it to their advantage. The use of technology-transfer to change cultural attitudes is made explicit in a text prepared for a pre-UNCED seminar organized by the Norwegian government and attended principally by representatives of the large dam-building industry. This states that hydropower projects — euphemistically renamed "waterfall technologies" — "are often very appropriate vehicles for introducing an appropriate mechanical culture into a developing country."[135] Significantly, the seminar had been called primarily to discuss how dam builders could best exploit any funds generated by UNCED for technology transfer.

ENVIRONMENTALLY-FRIENDLY ENCLOSURE

The second line of defence adopted by the agents of development is more complex and involves a grudging acknowledgement of past failures and of the value of vernacular knowledge and technologies. The World Bank, alongside its denunciation of "ignorance", now concedes that "the belief that traditional knowledge of the environment is simple and static is changing rapidly. More and more development projects are taking advantage of local knowledge about how to manage the environment . . . Development projects that do not take existing practices into account often fail."[136]

These admissions, however, are coupled with a generalized assumption that vernacular systems are inadequate to the task of "saving the planet". In its recent policy document on Sustainable Agriculture and Rural Development (SARD), for example, the UN Food and Agriculture Organization states that "low-input production is probably the most environmentally-friendly system and has

Wood Stoves and the World Bank

The reluctance of modern science to acknowledge the expertise of the commons is illustrated by a curious sub-plot that runs through the World Bank's 1992 report *Development and the Environment*. In at least seven separate places the report refers to what it calls "indoor air pollution".

> "For hundreds of millions of the world's poorer citizens, smoke and fumes from indoor use of biomass fuel (such as wood, straw and dung) pose much greater health risks than any outdoor pollution, and its effects on health are often equivalent to those of smoking several packs of cigarettes a day."

Put in scientific terms, this means that "studies that have measured biomass smoke in household kitchens in poor rural areas have found suspended particularate matter (SPM) levels that routinely exceeded by several orders of magnitude the safe levels of World Health Organization guidelines". The World Bank therefore sanctions programmes to introduce "smokeless" wood or charcoal stoves into rural homes: "Recent research has found that the eco-nomic value of the environmental and health benefits of improved stoves amount to $25–$100 a year per stove". However the Bank also acknowledges that "progress in dealing with indoor air pollution has been disappointing" though it does not suggest why.

Domestic Science

Anyone used to cooking on wood stoves and open fires will know that both systems have their advantages and disadvantages. Stoves are less smoky, and can be more fuel-efficient, though this is by no means always the case. They are particularly useful in cold climates where they can also serve to heat the room and keep a constant supply of hot water. On the other hand open fires are more versatile than stoves: they can be easily moved, they can be used for smoking food, they can accommodate a wider range of cooking implements, and the heat can be directed and adjusted more easily. In this sense they can be more fuel-efficient than stoves. A skilled cook can keep a pan of soup simmering evenly with three smouldering sticks. Open fires also give off light and can provide a focus for the household.

The importance of such factors as the cook's skill and the fire's function as a hearth means that, in the words of one chemical engineer, "the problem of evaluating the performance of wood-burning stoves is very complex indeed. This is because it is difficult to stipulate any test that adequately and precisely simulates the processes used in actual cooking." Nonetheless he goes on to stipulate several tests and arrives at some impressive formulae, for example:

> "The view-factor depends on the distance between the fuel bed and pan (Hp), the radius of the fire bed (Rf) and the radius of pan bottom (Rp) according to the formula:

160

$$F= \frac{[Hp2+Rf2+Rp2—(Hp2+(Rf+Rp2))0.5.(Hp2+(Rf—Rp)2)0.5]}{2Rf2}$$

From these formulae it is clear that radiative heat transfer will decrease with increasing distance between the fuel bed and the pan".

In other words, the nearer the pan is to the fire, the hotter it will get.

The supreme intellectual effort invested in assessing what any normal person learns through experience, is judged necessary because the stoves are required to conform to scientifically determined standards. Indeed any deviation from these centralized standards is frowned upon. When the Deccan Development Society was promoting stoves funded by the Indian Institute of Technology, it found that "the funding agency would not permit any alterations to suit local requirements and good habits. The same model is for application all over the country. We were told that these changes would reduce the fuel-efficiency and it was suggested that we embark on changing the food habits and cooking practices of the people".

In fact, it is questionable whether many of these stoves achieve an increase of efficiency at all. Ian Smillie recounts:

> "At Sylveria House, a Jesuit Training Centre on the outskirts of Harare, there is a small appropriate technology workshop and a house where several experimental stoves have been installed. There is a *Lorena* stove, developed in 1976 by an appropriate technology organization in Guatemala, a *Tso Tso* and other locally designed mud and ceramic varieties. At lunchtime, three or four women cook their lunch at the house, but they do not use any of the 'model' stoves. They sit on the floor around a traditional grate fire. Sylveria House discovered that by lowering the grate from fifteen to eight inches and by protecting the fire from the wind, it was as efficient as any of the exotic designs attempted by donor agencies and the Ministry of Energy."

The women, presumably, were gathered around the fire, not for reasons of efficiency, but because they preferred it. Patricia Stamp has collected some of the complaints voiced by African women about their new stoves: "they have lost smoke for chasing insects or waterproofing roofs . . . a centre for conversation and a symbolic focus for the household." The three stones of the original open fire "offer the flexibility of being moved due to the weather etc., and of cooking with pots of different sizes."

> "Stove projects also fail because they do not take account of polygynous households. Replacing the traditional three-stone fireplace in each hut with a single stove for the 'family' raises the question of where to locate the stove and how to allocate cooking time. Given that separate hearths structure polygynous marriages, the promotion of technology that undermines this practice is bound to fail or, worse, seriously disrupt the marriage institution."

Stamp also quotes the Kenyan poet Okot p'Bitek:

> "I really hate the charcoal stove!
> Your hand is always dirty
> And anything you touch is blackened . . .
> I am terribly afraid of the white man's stove
> And I do not like using it

Because you stand up
When you cook
Whoever cooked standing up?
You use the saucepan and the frying pan
And other flat-bottomed things
Because the stoves are flat
Like the face of a drum
The earthen vegetable pot
Cannot sit on it
There are no stones
On which to place
The pot for making millet bread."

Risk Assessment

In short, the advantages of wood-stoves are relative, and are specific to site, culture, family and individual; this probably accounts for the fact that attempts to impose them have been "disappointing".

The World Bank's ideological onslaught against traditional cooking practices takes no account of such complexities. It is based on the assumption that ordinary people are incapable of taking responsibility for their own lives: in other words, that cultures which have achieved a considerable degree of sophistication in the fabrication of fireproof earthenware or copper pots are incapable of designing a stove that suits their diet and their way of life; that local people cannot, given access to land, organize their own wood supply; that poor people are too ignorant to assess the relative dangers and benefits of indoor smoke for themselves; and that they are too ignorant (as opposed to too impoverished) to be able to devise smoke-alleviating measures such as ventilation or chimneys, should they so desire. The World Bank makes this revealing statement:

"When the public has a well-informed grasp of environmental issues, there is a better prospect of developing positive rather than defensive policies. Without such knowledge, people tend to focus on causes of death (for example, technological hazards and nuclear accidents) that are sensational and are caused by somebody else and to worry less about the probability of death from causes that are less dramatic and often under an individual's own control, such as cigarette smoking and wood fires."

This passage reveals the Bank's bewilderment and irritation with the self-evident fact that people do not mind taking risks themselves, but object to having risks imposed upon them. It also betrays the logic behind the Bank's sudden surge of propaganda against traditional cooking methods: when people are "uneducated", they accept a greater degree of environmental risk if they feel that risk is under their control; "education" leads them to the view that there is, in scientific terms, no difference between risks that are chosen and risks that are imposed; they are therefore more easily encouraged to sacrifice control over their lives.

The improved stove movement is an "intermediate" technology in the fullest sense of the term. It is, in the World Bank's words, a "stepping stone between traditional stoves and modern fuels". "Higher incomes and improved distribution systems for commercial fuels and electricity will bring about a switch away from biomass . . . In the meantime, improved biomass stoves, which increase efficiency and reduce emissions, can make an important contribution." The "white man's stove" obliges the users to buy the white man's aluminium cooking ware, adopt the white man's stance and eat the white man's food, in preparation for the day when they will graduate to genuine "white goods", the modern electric cooker, the fridge and the dish-washer.

The power for these machines arrives:

> "via a network of cables and overhead utility lines, which are fed by power stations that depend on water pressures, pipelines or tanker consignments, which in turn require dams, off-shore platforms or derricks in distant deserts. The whole chain only guarantees an adequate and prompt delivery if everyone of its parts is staffed by armies of engineers, planners and financial experts, who themselves can fall back on administrations, universities, indeed entire industries (and sometimes even the military)."

This electricity network is, by its nature, an enclosing technology whose nerves are reaching to the heart of every household. It saps people of their self-reliance, forcing them to cede control of the risks that affect them and sign that control over to a priesthood of professional risk-takers, the same people, incidentally, who brought us global warming, the ozone hole and Chernobyl. The desire to enclose every last outpost of local culture within this unifying grid is what lies behind the World Bank's sudden enthusiasm for wood stoves.

---

been practised since time immemorial, but every country has abandoned this practice during the process of development due to its low productivity and inability to meet the food requirements of an ever-increasing population."[137]

Rather than considering the possibility of reclaiming for peasant agriculture land currently used for export crops, FAO uses the population argument to justify the further intensification of agriculture. The technologies that it recommends for transfer are those of the Green Revolution, which has caused such damage to the environment and to society. Nonetheless, alongside the call for a 50–60 per cent increase in the use of pesticides, SARD also calls for greater use of biological husbandry. In the same vein, the Agenda 21 text on technology transfer repeatedly stresses the need for "environmentally [safe and] sound" technologies.[138]

But what is environmentally-friendly to the development industry is not necessarily environmentally-friendly or culturally acceptable to those who rely on the commons. The belief that intensive development can be rendered "safe and sound" by the infusion of a little vernacular technology — by "taking advantage of local knowledge" as the World Bank puts it — poses a new, more insidious threat. Far from being rescued, the technology of the commons is likely to be "chewed up and spat out by the big development agencies, its original aims masticated out of all recognition."[139] In that respect, the "appropriate technologies" now being promoted for transfer can be just as powerful tools for enclosure as the inappropriate technologies that are to be cleaned up with post-UNCED funding.

For example, the National Research Council (NRC) of the US National Academy of Sciences has issued a report entitled *Alternative Agriculture*, half of which is given over to eleven farm case-studies.[140] As Jack Kloppenburg reports, "the conclusions reached in the report relate almost entirely to the need for the application of more *scientific* effort to the development of alternative agriculture, and the report's recommendations focus on how this strategy might best be accomplished. Farmers are regarded as the recipients of technology, advice and information. The authors of the NRC report simply do not conceive of any potential for farmer-generated knowledge except in connection with or translation through 'science'."[141]

Similarly, "integrated pest management" is now being promoted by the World Bank and other agencies as a means of reducing the damage done by pesticide use. "Integrated pest management" has, of course, been practised for centuries by farmers whose inventories include techniques such as mixed cropping, fallowing, selection of resistant varieties, decoy crops, pest-deterrent plants, predator-attracting plants, natural pesticides, burning, flooding and manual labour. The integrated pest management proposed by the World Bank, however, differs in three respects.[142] Firstly, it uses toxic chemicals in "small, carefully timed applications". Secondly, it keeps the farmer dependent upon chemical companies, for whom he or she must earn or borrow money to pay for the input. And thirdly, the farmer is no longer in control, but must bow to the opinion of "experts", who will be hovering round the farm, checking that the applications are small and carefully timed. The farmer is integrated into the scheme — but only as one of a number of factors in a pest-management process determined largely by outside experts.

Forced in this manner into a marriage of convenience with development, "alternative agriculture", "integrated pest management" and similar "appropriate" techniques become complicit in the further enclosure of vernacular science. Indeed, as the conventional technological solutions, such as large dams, become discredited, other more acceptable technologies must be found to take on the role of a Trojan horse. One agronomist, David Norman, explains frankly how mixed cropping improvements are used by extension agents to get a foot in the door and gain the confidence of farmers:

> "... once the farmer has adopted an innovation that does not conflict too much with his present traditional outlook, e.g. improvement of his returns from mixed cropping, it will then be easier for the extension worker to suggest more radical changes, e.g. sole cropping, if evidence obtained under improved technological conditions indicates that this is desirable as far as farmers are concerned."[143]

This is not to imply that appropriate technologies can never be successfully exchanged, but rather that, as David Burch has pointed out, there is no permanent place for appropriate technology in a society that is committed to the standard models of technological growth. The pressures of a market fuelled by the consumption patterns of a wealthy minority are too great. "What is produced within a country is not determined by some objective assessment of needs . . . Patterns of income distribution biased towards the middle- and upper-classes produce a structure of effective demand for products that can only be produced by capital-intensive technologies."[144]

The current nod in the direction of vernacular science should be regarded in this light. As long as a wealthy minority of people concentrated in the North and within Southern élites continue to exert an effective demand throughout the world for exotic foodstuffs, Western-style clothing and other luxuries, and as long as they rely upon an ever-expanding market for produce such as fertilizers, pesticides, machinery and wheat, we can expect a further enclosure of vernacular science, a continuing succession of hare-brained schemes to drag the "ignorant peasant" into the 21st century, and the relentless growth of an environmentally unsound industrial economy. When cultures develop alongside each other on an even footing, they can and do benefit by borrowing ideas from each other. But this process is in no way linked to the systematic colonization of knowledge that is taking place under cover of the term "transference of technology." As SONED, an umbrella organization for Southern NGOs, has stated:

> "From the Southern point of view, technology is a product of diverse cultures and environment and therefore should not be transferred . . . Technology must reflect people's culture, environment and science. Northern technology, which is the root cause of the environment and development crisis, is rejected. What is sought is an alternative science and technology reflecting the traditions, cultures and achievements of Southern peoples."[145]

CAPITAL FLOWS: INVESTING IN ENCLOSURE

Just as enclosing as the technologies that UNCED seeks to transfer to the South is the capital that will be loaned to pay for those technologies. In the same way that technology transfer has been used as a Trojan horse through which industrial values and relations of production are foisted upon the commons, so capital transfers have been used to enclose the commons within the global economy.

TIED AID

Firstly, as Cheryl Payer notes in her remarkable book, *Lent and Lost: Foreign Credit and Third World Development*, aid and credit have been used as "a cleverly designed tool to bribe nations with money to give the creditors or aid donors access to the home markets of the recipient."[146] One means by which this has been achieved is through tying aid to the purchase of goods from the donor countries. Eighty per cent of Canadian aid, for example, is "tied" aid, whilst two-thirds of British aid is said never to leave Britain (some put the figure as high as 98 per cent). Of Japanese government aid, Richard Forrest notes:

> "To promote Japanese goods in the 1960s, aid was tied to purchases of Japanese goods and services, creating markets for Japanese goods and introducing Japanese banks and trading companies into developing countries. Starting in the 1970s, Japanese funds have been used to build large-scale facilities for exploiting and processing raw materials in resource-rich countries, such as Indonesia and Brazil, and to relocate hazardous and energy-intensive processing facilities to offshore sites, usually in South-East Asia. Reports by Japan's overseas development agencies highlight how projects provide supplies of crucial materials for Japanese industry, such as oil, aluminium and pulp. Aid to Pacific island nations has been used as a tool to secure access to fishing grounds for Japanese fleets. Aid has also been used to help 'phase out' particular industrial sectors that are no longer economic in Japan."[147]

Even the officially "untied" loans of the 1970s were frequently made *de facto* conditional on the recipient country's or corporation's awarding business to a corporation from the country lending the money. As Payer remarks, "The use of credit to pry markets open is also obvious in the 'conditionality' of the IMF and the World Bank. The *sine qua non* of conditions required by these organizations is import liberalization . . . Import liberalization represents the surrender of all or part of the domestic market to foreign sellers and is, incidentally, about the worst possible policy that can be imagined for any country short of capital. But to the sellers, credit is considered a cheap way to buy markets."[148]

CREDIT AND THE ENCLAVE ECONOMY

Secondly, the supposed need for capital has provided transnational élites with a rationale for imposing forms of enclosure that go beyond simply tying the South to the use of Northern equipment. In order to attract capital, for example, Southern governments have been willing to offer companies tax breaks, the freedom to repatriate profits, cheap labour, bans on trade union activity, the right to import duty-free, raw materials and components from abroad, low-cost access to land, and (where hydroelectric schemes have been involved) below-cost electricity. To that list has increasingly been added the "freedom to pollute", an incentive that has proved of particular appeal to those industries which are under pressure to clean up their activities within the North. Such concessions reach their apotheosis in the numerous Free Trade Zones (FTZs) that have been set up throughout the Third World since the mid-1960s. Exempted from virtually all legislation that might impinge on their profitability, companies operating within FTZs not only enjoy minimal pollution standards but are guaranteed cheap, largely female, labour and the right to enforce the most draconian working conditions. Human rights abuses are common, as is widespread pollution. In effect, through the lure of capital investment, transnational interests have been able to create enclaves within the South where enclosure is complete.

CREDIT EQUALS DEBT

Thirdly, as Payer points out, debt and capital flows are inextricably linked: they are the reverse sides of the same coin. The loans that transnational élites in the Third World take out on behalf of "their peoples" are not free gifts: they have to be repaid. There is nothing remarkable about this: on the contrary, it is intrinsic to the nature of loans. If as a result of having to repay those loans, the Third World is now a net exporter of hard currency to the North, "it is not *in spite of* but *because of* the unquestioned faith that foreign capital is essential to development." In effect, the current flow of capital from South to North — now put at some $51 billion — "is the natural, logical and above all legal consequence of the very belief that foreign capital is essential to Third World development."[149]

With debt comes political bondage as "the real sovereignty of the nation [is] handed over to foreign creditors and their governments."[150] For the South's transnational élites, this causes few problems, their interests coinciding with those of their foreign creditors. For them, the only problem lies in the possibility that their credit might run dry, bringing a backlash from the urban middle-class for whom foreign credit means the availability of Western goods. Hence, the resistance of such élites to repudiating debts and the willingness instead to accept IMF structural-adjustment programmes. As Payer puts it:

> "While it is overwhelmingly to the benefit of the country as a whole to repudiate, the individuals and classes which are in control of the governments of most debtor countries still see their own interests as lying in obedience to the interests of creditor countries. The minister of finance who crosses the will of creditors, for example, cannot expect a cushy job at the IMF or World Bank when he or she leaves office, as more obedient colleagues can. Similarly, these narrowly based groups stand to benefit more from the small trickles of aid and forced lending that pass through their fingers as they come in than they pay as their share of the larger sums that go out."[151]

For the rest of the population, however, debt translates into further enclosure. To service the loans that have been taken out in their name, they must suffer the despoliation of their environment and the indignities and injustice of structural adjustment. The policies of the Free Trade Zone are extended to cover the entire country: new loans become conditional on expanding export-crop production, removing import controls and cutting public expenditure on health and other services.

MORE OF THE SAME

Taking out the new loans on offer after UNCED may temporarily stem the South's current credit crisis, enabling debts to be serviced in the short term, but it will not resolve it. For, sooner or later, these new loans will also have to be repaid. In that respect, the new capital flows to the South are likely to exacerbate environmental destruction rather than reduce it. For if the new loans are to be repaid, the capital loaned must ultimately be used to yield hard cash. As Payer points out in a passage that destroys the whole logic of "greening the earth" through increased capital flows:

> "Capital is a term for assets, whether in the form of money or otherwise, which are used for the purpose of making more money. Land may be capital if it is exploited for the purpose of making money. Factory machinery is capital. So are inventories of raw materials and the products of the factories. Capital may be embodied in many forms, but it is capital *only* if it is employed in the quest for more money."[152]

A loan to "restore" a deforested watershed *requires* that a restoration strategy be adopted that generates sufficient money to service the loan: not surprisingly, most watershed restoration programmes involve commercial reforestation. Alternatively, the money is generated by increased productivity in some other sector of the economy. Either way, the loan necessitates further enclosure: instead of the watershed being restored to meet the needs of the commons, it is "restored" to meet the demands of the creditors. This is inescapable.

Moreover, the North's new concern to secure pollution sinks, on the one hand, and the resources it requires to keep its industries going, on the other, threatens to take past enclosure a step further. Thus, by designating the atmosphere and biodiversity as "global commons" (sic), the World Bank and other agencies have overridden the local claims of those who rely on the real commons, and effectively asserted that local people have no more right to the air around them or the biodiversity of their forests, streams, and hills than a corporation based on the other side of the globe. It is surely no coincidence that 59 per cent of the projects selected for financing under the Global Environmental Facility (GEF) should involve "biodiversity protection" or that the chair of the GEF, Mohamed El-Ashry (previously of the World Resources Institute), has singled out areas which "include important gene pools or encompass economically significant species" as the priority for funding. Protecting biodiversity thus means protecting biodiversity for the global economy. The conditionalities attached to new capital loans will undoubtedly be the means through which that agenda is imposed.

For the poor, the landless, those who have been marginalized by the development process and those whose livelihoods are under threat, however, "new and additional funds" hold no attractions. The solutions they seek are not financial, but political. It does not cost money to reclaim large plantations for peasant agriculture or to plant the trees that will restore their ravaged homelands. But it does require political change.

6 RECLAIMING THE COMMONS

It is midday and in the village of Nagami, in the foothills of the Himalayas, a group of villagers sit cross-legged in the heat of the sun listening as Sudesha, a woman in her late thirties, sings to them. Her song tells how she was jailed for attempting to stop timber merchants from felling the trees near her village and of her willingness to go to jail again if it furthers her protest against enclosure of the forest commons. Sudesha is prominent in Chipko, a village-based movement that takes its name from the Hindi word for "to hug", villagers literally hugging trees to prevent them from being felled. She is speaking at the end of a two-day meeting, organized by local villagers to discuss how best to prevent the destruction of their forests and to encourage the regeneration of those areas which have already been logged. Already many villages have set up tree nurseries, growing fruit and other trees of the villagers' own choice, and hundreds of hectares of denuded hillside have been replanted. In one village, a single villager, Vishweshwar Dutt Saklani, has planted more than 20,000 trees, all native species, creating a little oasis of forest in an area which has been devastated by the timber industry. Streams have begun to flow again, birds and other animals have returned in large numbers and the hillside is no longer eroding.

On the southern edge of Brazilian Amazonia, where the savannah of Mato Grosso meets the rainforest, the Xavante Indians are slowly restoring their ancestral commons, devastated by years of illegal logging and ranching. In 1982, after the authorities refused to expel the timber merchants and ranchers from Xavante land, the Xavante took matters into their own hands, burning down the local sawmill and giving the loggers and ranchers their marching orders. Since then, the Indians have worked to restore their degraded commons. The savannah is naturally rich in a wide variety of nutritious plants and fruits, which the Xavante have begun to grow and market. They have also begun to experiment with new techniques for encouraging forest regeneration. Efforts are being made to restore the local wildlife, which has been seriously depleted through illegal hunting by colonists. Once the numbers of wild animals have been restored, the Xavante hope they will be able to give up keeping cattle and obtain their protein through hunting, as they did in the past.

In the US, numerous communities, having fought successfully to protect their commons from being used as a dumping ground for toxic waste, have joined together to lend their support to others facing the same threat. Their fight is not simply to protect their own backyards, but to reduce the production of waste so that no one's backyard is used for dumping. In 1980, there were just a few hundred such anti-toxics groups: today there are over 5,000, a network that stretches from coast to coast and covers every state in the Union. The movement grew out of the Love Canal disaster in 1977 when hundreds of families demanded that they be evacuated from a housing estate built over a leaking toxic waste site near Niagara Falls in upstate New York. The evacuation came about only after a prolonged campaign by local residents, mainly women; few of them had been involved in politics and many had family members working for the companies which had dumped the polluting waste. Stonewalled by officialdom, the local residents took up civil disobedience to apply pressure on their elected representatives to take action. Only then were they evacuated.

THE COMMONS RESURGENT

In seeking to defend their local environment, to restore the damage done to it and to thwart the strategies of would-be enclosers, community groups opposed to toxic dumping or movements such as Chipko are part of a long tradition. Throughout history, commons regimes have resisted the enclosure of the forests, rangelands, fields, fishing grounds, lakes, streams, plants and animals that they rely upon to maintain their ways of life and ensure their well-being.

Such resistance has taken many forms, and its focus has been as various as the commons being defended. Machinery has been sabotaged, hay ricks burned, landlords and officials satirized and threatened, experts lampooned, loyalties shifted and bureaucratic defences tested in an endless flow of effort to stall enclosure. Whether overt or subterranean, thwarted or beaten down, channelled into ideology or action, this resistance has been opportunistic, pragmatic and resourceful. Frequently using local traditions as an arsenal, constantly faced with reversals, it always finds fresh ground to fight from, some of it created by the very systems in opposition to which it must constantly transform and renew itself. Willing to adapt new developments to its own purposes, it is nonetheless uncompromising when the bounds it has set are overstepped.

It is through such resistance that the ideology of economic growth as the only concrete solution to poverty, inequality and hardship is slowly being dismantled. Millions of people in both the South and the North who know first-hand of its false promise need no convincing. Whilst most participants in UNCED and similar forums are interested only in "solutions" that will permit industrial growth to continue, the movements that have been spawned through resistance to enclosure are carving out a very different path. Their demands centre not on refining market mechanisms, nor incorporating text-book ecology into economics, nor on formulating non-legally binding treaties, but on reclaiming the commons; on reappropriating the land, forests, streams and fishing grounds that have been taken from them; on reestablishing control over decision-making; and on limiting the scope of the market. In saying "no" to a waste dump, a dam, a logging scheme or a new road, they are saying "yes" to a different way of life: "yes" to the community's being able to decide its own fate; "yes" to the community's being able to define itself.

What begins as a fight against one form of enclosure — a proposed incinerator, perhaps, or a plantation scheme — often becomes part of a wide struggle to allow the community to define its own values and priorities. As Triana Silton notes of the movement to oppose toxic wastes in the United States,

> "Many community groups have moved from simply fighting off an incinerator to looking around at themselves, at the community they are part of, identifying what they don't like and attempting to solve those problems. The empowerment that accompanies a success, whether that success is having your voice heard or actually stopping the facility, allows people to have some control over the things that happen to them."[1]

In California, for example, "Concerned Citizens of South Central Los Angeles is looking for ways to reinvigorate their community economically, to create after-school activities for the kids, to clean up the neighbourhood, to prevent certain factories from entering their community. This is a case where the community was able to come together around one issue, become empowered, and then continue as a community to address other issues."

DEFENDING THE COMMONS

Often making use of what James Scott calls the "weapons of the weak",[2] groups, communities and individuals the world over are successfully resisting the web of enclosure and reclaiming a political and cultural space for the commons. The search is generally not for "alternatives" in the sense that Western environmentalists might use the term: rather it is to rejuvenate what works, to combine traditional and new approaches and to develop strategies that meet local needs. In that respect, the debate is not over such technocratic issues as *how* to conserve soil or *what* species of tree to plant — for those who rely on the commons, the starting point for addressing such questions is invariably, "Let's see what has worked in the past and build on that" — but rather over how to create or defend open, democratic community institutions that ensure people's control over their own lives.

For some communities, the immediate issue is *defending* existing commons against enclosure. In Sarawak, for example, Dayak peoples, denied legal or political means of defending their lands, have set up barricades across the logging roads to defend the forests around their longhouses. The government has responded with mass arrests and by passing a new law making all interference with logging roads a criminal offence. Yet despite the intimidation and threats, the blockades have been persistently re-erected, halting timber extraction on the concessions of prominent politicians such as the Minister for the Environment and Tourism.

Another celebrated example of resistance to forest destruction concerns an International Tropical Timber Organization project for "sustainable logging" in the Chimanes forest of Bolivia, which was promoted on Indian lands under a debt-for-nature swap without steps being taken to secure the Indians' involvement or their land rights. When it became clear that the international funds were merely accelerating the logging and invasion of Indian lands, the Indians embarked on a 750-kilometre march from their forests to the Bolivian capital, La Paz, to demand a halt to the project and the recognition of their territorial rights. As a consequence, the government took steps to recognize on paper the Indians' rights to land, although the legal status of the "indigenous territories" that were created by the Presidential Decree remains ambiguous. Funds for the project have now been frozen while new management plans are evolved that give the Indians some control over the development process.[3]

In India, Chipko is only one of thousands of popular movements that have challenged enclosure. Widespread mobilizations against hydropower programmes that are displacing thousands of communities and flooding their farmlands and forests have sprung up all over the country. In September 1989, a rally of some 60,000 people against "destructive development" was held at Harsud in the Narmada Valley, the site of one of India's largest hydropower projects. The slogan of the march was "Our Villages, Our Rule". Mass marches of protesters have led, in some places, to the cancellation of proposed dams and, in others, have resulted in police firings and deaths.

Popular mobilization against forestry plantations has also developed in Karnataka State in South India. Here, attempts to take over common lands for commercial plantations of fast-growing eucalyptus for paper pulp and rayon led to a "pluck and plant" movement, in which the eucalyptus seedlings were uprooted and replaced by indigenous species that provide products useful to the local peasants.

In Thailand, where as many as ten million people live in forest reserves, the government has a long history of policy shifts to accommodate various vested interests. Popular pressure helped lead it to declare all timber extraction illegal in 1989, after floods and landslides attributed to logging led to a number of deaths and wiped out villages. Since then, the government has been promoting commercial tree plantations on "degraded" forest lands, which threaten to displace hundreds of thousands of people. Concerted action by peasants has brought a number of such plantation schemes to a standstill.

Resistance to imposed development has been very widespread in the Philippines as well, the most topical example being the Bagobo peoples' resistance to government plans to build geothermal power plants on the forested slopes of Mount Apo, held sacred by the Bagobo as the domain of the "god" Sandawa. Mobilization against the project has linked the indigenous people with local environmental organizations. The protests have been met with intimidation by the Philippine army.

In some areas, relations between the national government and local peoples have become so bad that the affected populations, denied other means of protest, have expressed their opposition through organized armed resistance. A tragic example involved the World Bank-supported Chico dams project in the Philippines which threatened to displace some 80,000 Kalinga and Bontoc people from their ancestral lands. When the locals protested against the project, the Marcos regime responded with brutal violence, leading to an escalating conflict. Many tribals took to the hills and joined the New Peoples' Army in defiance of the imposed development programme. The conflict endured long after the World Bank pulled out of the project. Villages were repeatedly bombed and subjected to counter-insurgency programmes as a result.

North of the Chico, the resistance of the Tinggian people of

Abra to the Cellophil Corporation logging of the pine forests on their watersheds, escalated into similar armed confrontation. In Mindanao, Higaonon resistance to the logging operations of the Nasipit Lumber Co., led to indiscriminate aerial bombardments of their communities and the displacement of hundreds of tribal refugees into the lowlands.

RECLAIMING THE COMMONS

For other groups and communities, the focus of their struggle is not the defence of an existing commons but the reclaiming of those commons that have been enclosed or, in other cases, the taking over of territory on which to build a new commons.

In Brazil, disillusionment with the government's abject failure to implement its promised programme of land reform has led to land "take-overs" by peasants. At Espigao d'Oeste, near Rolim de Moura, for example, over 300 families (some 1,400 people in all) have occupied 10,000 hectares of land previously held by an absentee landlord. The occupation was organized by peasants belonging to the Movimento dos Trabalhadores Rurais sem Terra (MST, or Landless Peoples' Movement). As Carlos Reyes reports:

"In June 1989, 125 families began to move into the area. Within two weeks, they were driven off by the police. Instead of dispersing, as the police had expected, they camped in a group at the headquarters of INCRA, the Institute for Colonization and Land Reform, in Pimenta Bueno. INCRA expected the movement to fizzle out, but it grew to 250 families.

"The pressure succeeded. INCRA decided to buy the land and divide it into 318 plots of 30 hectares each. On 25 July, the people moved in. They had hardly any belongings and nothing to eat, and survived in those early days only thanks to the solidarity of neighbouring towns."[4]

The MST (whose slogan is "Occupy, Resist, Produce") is one of three major peasant movements — the others are the United Workers Union and the Comissao Pastoral da Terra — which together have organized the reoccupation of some 4.5 million hectares, benefiting over 100,000 families.[5] In 1991 alone, occupations secured land for 13,844 families, many of whom had come from urban slums, prompting the unions to ask, "Are we witnessing the opposite of the rural exodus of the past?" In addition to land take-overs, the unions' cause has been promoted through the occupation of government offices, demonstrations, encampments outside the offices of provincial governors and pilgrimages (in Mato Grosso, 530 people marched 230 kilometres after being forcibly expelled from an occupation; in Rio Grande do Sul, 250 people marched 500 kilometres to Porto Alegre, culminating in a rally of 3,000 people).[6] "The courage and stubbornness of these people in their desperation is hard to imagine," says Paul Ekins, director of the Right Livelihood Foundation, whose Alternative Nobel Prize was awarded to the MST in 1991. They are regularly attacked by the military police. One occupation (Fazenda Santa Almira, March 1979) was sprayed by aircraft with a potent pesticide and four children subsequently died. The 500 families were attacked by 1,200 soldiers who fired 2,500 rounds of ammunition, wounding 19 peasants.

At the Fazenda Hollandese in Rio Grande do Sul, occupied in 1985, 23 of the farmers work the land collectively, sharing everything. Two other groups, of five and four farmers, do the same. Three farmers farm individually. The 23 farmers have further set up a co-operative open to other farmers in the area, which now has 176 members. Between them, they farm 700 hectares, of which 25 per cent is original forest, which, through their deeds of association, they have committed themselves to protect.[7]

That commitment to keeping a sizeable part of any land taken over as forest or wilderness is general to all 600 settlements set up by the MST, a ground rule being that 20 per cent of the land occupied should be "ecological reserve". Aware of the ecological damage done by industrialized farming, the MST and its partners also encourage farmers to reduce the use of pesticides and fertilizers and to move towards more sustainable forms of agriculture, although there is a recognition that many farmers are not currently in a position to move off the treadmill. In that respect, the struggle to establish land rights is seen as part of a larger struggle to achieve a more ecologically-sound society. As a joint statement by the three groups at the forefront of the land take-over movement put it:

"The modernization of Brazilian agriculture has occurred from one perspective only: to increase productivity without considering social and environmental questions . . . The system of large farms has been the main cause of rural violence and human and environmental degradation. Faced with this reality, we again propose land reform . . . A successful land reform programme is a necessity in order to allow millions of politically excluded people to exercise their citizenship. To think about democracy also means to think about the redistribution of power, which today is concentrated in the hands of a few. Therefore, land reform is a *sine qua non* condition for the achievement of democracy."[8]

The demand for land reform is by no means restricted to Southern countries like Brazil. In the North, too, land speculation, the loss of land to urban development and the trend towards increasing concentration of landholdings, has led to some groups and communities evolving new patterns of land ownership. The US, for example, has a growing movement in which farmers or other land owners sell or place their land in "land trusts". Whoever farms the land is granted the long-term right to use it under whatever conditions are agreed by the trustees: the sale of the land, however, is forbidden. In effect, as Marty Strange of the Centre for Rural Affairs notes, "the fundamental character of family farm agriculture — owner-operatorship — is preserved, but what the farmer owns is not the land but the long-term right to use it."[9]

Once considered outrageously radical, land trusts and similar forms of land ownership are now gaining support within conventional quarters. "In some urban states within the US," reports Strange, "legislatures have authorized the state to take what amounts to an ownership interest by purchasing the right to develop the land from the owner. The owner gets the cash, pays lower taxes because he or she no longer owns all the rights to the land, and keeps the land as a farm base. The purpose is to preserve farmland by preventing non-farmers from buying it for condominiums, parking lots and hotels. A half-dozen or so eastern states concerned with haphazard development and loss of open space have adopted such programmes in recent years."[10]

LIMITING EXPLOITATION

The tactic of direct occupation, so successfully employed by movements in Brazil, has also been central to the struggle to reclaim other commons. In the Philippines, local fishing communities have reoccupied numerous coastal areas sequestrated by the political allies of former President Ferdinand Marcos. On Samar Island, 520 hectares of fishponds were successfully occupied by fisherfolk in 1989, with similar occupations taking place in Negros.[11] Organizations of small-scale fishers have mushroomed as fishing communities have joined forces to block the invasion of their fishing grounds by commercial fishing fleets and to prevent the degradation of waterways and coastal areas by pollution. In the Luzon area, CALARIZ, a confederation of local fishing organizations, have fought to prevent the enclosure of their fishing grounds in Laguna Lake by commercial fishpens. In the Visayas, illegal fish ponds in mangrove swamps have been dismantled and owners found operating without a licence have been arrested by members of local fisher organizations. In the Bicol region, fisherfolk have re-established their rights to a ten-kilometre strip of fishing grounds where they have banned modern commercial fishing gear: those operating trawls have found their nets confiscated or burned. In Bataan, protests by an alliance of fisherfolk have halted the construction of commercial fishponds: meanwhile, a former mangrove swamp, deforested under the Marcos regime, has been occupied and is now being reforested. In Bulacan, a paper mill which was causing severe pollution of a local river has been forced to close down until it installs anti-pollution devices. And in Manila Bay an alliance of groups are campaigning for a five-year "closed season" on fishing and a complete ban on all trawls. In March 1992, a "No Fish Day" was held, with fisherfolk conducting a variety of actions to dramatize their long-standing call for "economic relief and implementation of a comprehensive rehabilitation of the Bay."[12]

Local fishing communities have also taken up against deforestation, which causes their coral reefs and rivers to silt up, and to prevent mangroves from being cut down for fishponds. Tourist projects, too, have been opposed where they threaten livelihoods. In the San Pablo lakes region, for example, a powerful campaign has grown up to fight a tourism development plan that would enclose local fishing grounds. As Antonio Austria, President of the SPCMBY Fisherfolk Federation recalls, "We realized that if we did not group together to have a stronger voice, we could lose our means of livelihood. The proposed tourism plan called for dismantling the structures we use to gather fish for our living — floating fish cages, fish pens and guardhouses — to make way for the construction of hotels, restaurants, floating casinos and facilities for speedboat racing. We knew these activities would adversely affect the environmental quality of the lakes."[13]

SPCMBY, in common with many other groups, sees its priority as "working to bring about aquatic reform in the same way that there is agrarian reform." Central to that demand is that fishing communities should have a direct hand, through their own local organizations, in "the management and control of fisheries and aquatic resources." As one group has put it, "Fisherfolk believe that they themselves are the best people to protect the fishing grounds, these being their lifeblood."

In Kerala, a similar struggle is being waged to reclaim the marine commons. Faced with overfishing due to commercial trawling, artisanal fisherfolk joined together through the Kerala Independent Fishworkers Federation (KSMTF) to "demand measures to regulate the anarchic and destructive fishing of trawlers in coastal waters." The KSMTF's principal demand has been for a trawl ban in the monsoon months, during which many important fish species spawn in the coastal waters, and for measures to restore the coastal ecosystem. "A second demand was for effective enforcement of a trawler-free coastal fishing zone reserved exclusively for artisinal fishermen operating non-mechanized craft and for a total ban of purse-seiners from Kerala waters."[14]

In the coastal city of Calicut in Northern Kerala, a Hindu fisherman and a Catholic nun vowed to fast until death until the demands of the KSMTF were met; massive processions of fishworkers and their supporters have taken place in key cities; the main highway across the state was blocked with canoes; the railway tracks were picketed and the road to the airport in Trivandrum, the state capital, was blocked. Meanwhile, at the community level, fisherfolk began to take local action to rejuvenate the coastal commons. One response was the revival of such age-old practices as the creation of artificial fish sanctuaries or artificial reefs on the sea floor of the coastal waters, the reefs not only attracting fish but also deterring trawlers. The fisherfolk also saw the reefs as a means by which they could reaffirm the value and legitimacy of their own knowledge of the marine ecosystem:

> "Between 1985 and 1988, the resurgence of the idea gave rise to a rapid spreading of a movement to create people's artificial reefs (PARs) totally funded and erected by the fishermen — at times with the active collaboration of social activists and marine scientists sympathetic to their cause. PARs became the symbols of the attempts of the fisherfolk at 'greening their coastal commons'. Constructing PARs also provided an avenue for the creative use of their accumulated, transgenerational knowledge of the aquatic milieu and the behaviour of fish, which had been relegated with the coming of 'efficient' fishing gear which was without the ecological sophistication of traditional fishing methods. PARs also became appropriate physical structures for a fencing of their exclusive fishing zones against the incursion of trawlers."[15]

The PARs also helped ensure that decisions about stock management were made at local level, rather than by distant experts.

RECLAIMING VERNACULAR KNOWLEDGE

Like the fisherfolk of Kerala, numerous other communities are now looking towards their traditional practices for inspiration in restoring their commons. One reason is that such traditional ways are locale-specific and thus firmly grounded in the culture of the commons: another, more practical (and thus, perhaps, more important) is that they are known to work. As P. Sarmineto-

Resebal notes of Bontoc agriculture in the Philippines, "there is no need to reinvent the wheel to find environmentally sound, alternative approaches to the despoliation of land and resources that high technology farming often brings."[16]

In Ecuador, many farmers have learned through bitter experience that "improved" varieties of potatoes are not only ill-adapted to their needs but, because they require pesticides and fertilizers, are both costly and a major cause of environmental degradation. "The plots on which I use chemicals are dusty in the dry season, while the soil structure is retained in the plots where I don't," says one farmer from the village of Saquisili. As a result, many farmers no longer grow the modern varieties and, instead, have returned to growing a wide range of traditional varieties. To protect those local varieties and to ensure an independent seed supply system, a number of communities have set up seed banks. "The system is as simple as it is effective. Farmers get their seed potatoes from the local bank under the condition that, at harvest time, they replenish the seed bank with the same amount, plus an additional 20 per cent."[17] For the local community, the re-introduction and conservation of old varieties in the face of genetic erosion through the modernization of farming is part of a wider struggle to conserve and build upon their own cultural heritage. "Our Indian culture is not only our music or the dress our women wear, it is also the way we produce our food and the plants we and our fathers have developed for that."

In the mountains of northern Luzon in the Philippines, the Ikalahan people have also turned to their traditional farming practices to wean the land off chemicals, using organic techniques to increase the productivity of their traditional slash-and-burn agriculture. "As soon as the community was given control over its own land, its leaders decided to try to prevent the use of chemicals in the agricultural practices. . . They have discovered ways of improving food production with new varieties of sweet potato. They have also improved the fallow system by planting fertility-restoring plants that reduce the fallow period from 14 to 7 years. By integrating these methods into the ancient system, they can increase the carrying capacity of the area from 400 to 800 families while still allowing the forests to expand."[18]

In Thailand, some farmers, with support from progressive community hospitals and non-governmental organizations, are attempting to restore the traditional place of native medicinal herbs in village life, rebuilding local biodiversity (and the commons that secure it) which also allows villagers to reclaim control over their health. This particular move comes as a response to the growing awareness that dependence on the wider market for medicine has led to both financial insecurity and health risks. A decade ago, *Baan* Sok Khumpoon in Yasothorn province, which, together, with many such villages in the North-East, had been swiftly integrated into the cash economy in the 1960s and 1970s, was spending over US$500 a year on commercial drugs. These included pain-relievers which had led to the deaths of several residents from stomach ulcers. Now, however, following years of community efforts, medicinal herbs are flourishing around the village, the drug bill has been cut by three-quarters, the village is greener — and the health of local people is better.[19]

Indeed, throughout the South, villagers whose lives have been made insecure by overdependence on the market economy and whom experience has made wary of the monocultures demanded by modern agriculture are adopting strategies grounded in traditional practices as a means of restoring their environment and disengaging from the wider market economy. In the Segou region of Mali, for example, villagers have withheld co-operative labour from those who buy modern farm machinery, because it causes damage to the soil and undermines the tradition of shared labour that is crucial at certain seasons. Likewise, in Eastern Senegal, the Federation of Sarakiolle Villages — a peasant group — has "successfully resisted efforts by the state agriculture agency to impose irrigation systems, cropping patterns, uniform pricing policies and marketing restrictions."[20] The Federation, set up in the 1960s, has promoted crop production "primarily for food, secondarily for surplus distribution and only lastly for sales."

The response of local farmers to plantation-induced drought in

Maharastra, India, has similarly been to withdraw from cash-crop production. Sugar-cane has become the most important cash-crop in the region, but its high demand for water has deprived villagers of water for food crops. To prevent "the waste of scarce water resources through unjust and ecologically destructive cropping patterns", villagers have formed *Pani Panchayats* (water councils):

> "The central idea underlying the formation of the *Pani Panchayats* is that in a drought-prone area, no individual should be deprived of a rightful share of the limited water resources on which life and livelihood depend. To ensure equity, the *Pani Panchayats* treat water as a community resource, not as private property. Further, water rights are based on the number of family members, not on the size of landholdings. While members of the panchayat are free to decide how to use their water allocation, sugar-cane cultivation is completely banned as being inconsistent with the principles of responsible resource use. A suitable *Patkari* or water distributor, is appointed by the *Pani Panchayat* to assure fair day-to-day allocations of water to all its beneficiaries."[21]

RECLAIMING MARKETS

In the North, too, moves to reclaim the commons are often closely linked to attempts to disengage from the wider market, by networks of exchange over which a community or group has control. One example is to be found in the Community Supported Agriculture (CSA) movement, now taking root in Europe, the US and Japan. The special feature of CSA initiatives is that the community or a specific group of people from one local area agrees to share the risks and responsibilities of food production with the farmer. In some instances, a detailed budget for the farm is drawn up on an annual basis, which includes wages for those working on the land, and then the costs are shared by the community which the farm will support. Sometimes this is done on the basis of pledges made at a meeting at the beginning of the season, the amount pledged varying according to the ability to pay. One of the advantages for farmers is that they start to get paid as soon as the crops are planted, rather than having to wait until crops are harvested before they receive any return.

Once the costs have been agreed, and produce becomes available, families, depending upon the agreement, either get a share of the produce, or take according to need In the case of the Hudson-Mohawk community farm, some 20 miles north of Albany in New York State, for example, a single "share", costing $340 a year, provided enough vegetables to make four days' worth of meals a week.[22] Should a crop fail, however, then the 100 shareholders in the farm would bear the loss: indeed it is central to the philosophy of the community-supported farm movement that shareholders should share the risks that most farmers have to take alone. In 1986, when a thunderstorm over Indian Line Farm produced eight inches of rain in three hours, the winter storage/baking squash crop was badly affected. The shareholders experienced a loss of approximately $35 each, but under a conventional system the farm family would have lost $3,500, which might well have left them in serious financial trouble.[23]

Because farmers know that their income is guaranteed and they are growing produce for people and not for the market, they tend to grow a much wider variety of produce, and aim to provide what people want, instead of concentrating on the crops that give the highest returns. This diversity of crops creates conditions which are favourable for companion planting, and encourages the kind of integrated cropping practices which make crop failures less likely. The active involvement of shareholders in farm work is encouraged, a principle aim being to "reconnect" those whose primary activities lie outside farming with the land. This building up of a community sensitive to the vagaries of nature means that other related issues — such as land-ownership, conservation, recycling, and use of natural resources — become topics that are considered and discussed.[24] Moreover, the tying of production and consumption to a community level has the potential to create extra jobs in processing, local transport and retailing. These activities tend to put the heart back into a community, whereas the type of jobs which might be lost, such as long-distance truck driving, tend to take people and work out of the community.

In Switzerland, CSAs have existed for over 25 years and they are also to be found in Germany. In North America, community farms have been developing since 1985, with around 80 in existence in 1990, and nearly 150 by 1991. In Japan, very similar systems have developed since the 1970s, and now there are a variety of groups operating in different ways, all aiming to reconnect farmers with consumers, and concentrating on good quality food. The biggest of these groups, the Seikatsu club, has over 150,000 members, and operates as a form of buyers' co-op.[25]

Robyn Van En, who has given many talks on CSAs, says the concept "creates almost instant empowerment. People go home and join or start a project."[26] Trauger Groh, one of the pioneers of community-supported farming in the United States, has outlined some of the important aspects of community supported farms in a book called *Farms of Tomorrow*:

> "Some things are typical for all community-supported farms. In all of them there is a strong dedication to quality; most of them are organic or biodynamic farms, most of them show great diversification, most are integrated farm organisms having their own livestock and thus their own source of manure, or they are aiming in this direction. At all of them, far more people are working regularly per 100 acres than in conventionally run farms; and generally there are just many more people around participating in all of the dimensions of agricultural life: working, relaxing, storing, shopping, celebrating. This human element is of enormous importance. It shows that these farms have something to offer beyond good food. They embody educational and cultural elements that draw the interest of many people. Besides clean, healthy, life-giving food, and a strong contribution to an improved environment, the educational and cultural elements constitute the third great gift that farms of tomorrow have to offer."[27]

THE BALANCE OF POWER

If there is a common denominator to the initiatives and struggles described above, it is not that they share a uniform "vision" of the future, or adhere to a single "blueprint" for change, but rather that they are all, in their many and various ways, attempts by local people to reclaim the political process and to re-root it within the local community. The central demand made by group after group is for authority to be vested in the community — not in the state, local government, the market or the local landlord, but in those who rely on the local commons for their livelihood. As such, the struggle is for more than the mere recognition of rights over the physical commons: critically, it is also a struggle to restore or to defend the checks and balances that limit power *within* the local community.

As we have seen, enclosure fatally undermines the institutions and cultural patterns that prevent any one group within the commons from monopolizing power and imposing its will upon the community. The door has been opened to personal gain at the expense of the community's security, both social and environmental.

But the emergence of local élites does not mean that the commons has been shattered: the community often maintains features typically associated with the commons — networks of mutual aid, a limited market, production primarily for use rather than exchange, an emphasis on reciprocity and redistribution rather than accumulation, the extended family as the basic unit of socialization and production or an ideology that stresses harmonious relations with nature. And in numerous instances, local people have begun to evolve their own institutions, accountable to the community as a whole, to redress the imbalance in power and to reclaim control of the commons. For example, in Sarawak, where the indigenous élite very often sides with loggers against the local people, local communities have begun to evolve new "longhouse associations", run under much more democratic principles than the now discredited traditional institutions, to provide themselves with truly representative leadership.[28]

In India, the general failure of local *panchayats* (effectively, district councils) to reflect the will of the commons has led many communities to create alternative village-level institutions "that can work with a high order of democracy."[29] Only by so doing have villagers been able to regain the authority necessary to check and even reverse resource depletion. As Anil Agarwal and Sunita

Narain of the Delhi-based Centre for Science and Environment note of the old *panchayats*:

> "*Panchayats* tend to divide the community into factions and are themselves often dominated by the more powerful groups in the village which raises fears amongst the rest that the benefits will be expropriated by them. Being an elected body, the very birth of the *panchayat* takes place within an environment of village factionalism.

> ". . . *Panchayats* [are] too far removed from the 'grassroots' to be effective agents for good natural resource management. A village consists of several hamlets and a *panchayat* usually covers several villages . . . When people from one settlement decide to protect and rationally use the common natural resources around them, they run into conflict with people from other settlements. *Panchayats* are seldom able to resolve these conflicts, especially when these conflicts become caste conflicts as different settlements often consist of different castes. This makes the management of village natural resources by *panchayats* very difficult, if not impossible."[30]

Perhaps the best known example of villagers evolving alternatives to the *panchayats* is to be found in the Chipko movement. Having halted the logging of the watersheds in the Himalayas and secured control, though not ownership, of their hillsides, women's groups have mobilized effective tree planting programmes, an initiative that has now spread to many other parts of India. A key feature in the success of Chipko has been the development of new political associations which are open, accountable and, crucially, equitable.

Less well-known outside India are the *gramdam* villages inspired by Mahatma Gandhi. Such villages' executive and legal power is invested in the *gram sabha*, a body consisting of all the adults in the village. In Rajasthan, where villages can register under the Rajasthan Gramdam Act of 1971, the *gram sabha* has full control over all the land within the village boundary and lays down the rules for how the village commons should be used. It also has the power to judge, penalize and prosecute. Agarwal and Narain cite the village of Seed near Udaipur as "an excellent example of how the village ecosystem can be managed by an executive *gram sabha*":

> "The common land has been divided into two categories — one category consists of lands on which both grazing and leaf collection

is banned and the second category consists of lands on which grazing is permitted but leaf collection or harming trees is banned. The first category of land is lush green and full of grass which villagers can cut only once a year . . . Even during the unprecedented drought of 1987, Seed was able to harvest 80 bullock cartloads of grass from this patch. The grass was distributed equitably amongst all households.

"Seed's *gram sabha* does not even allow trees on private land to be cut. Prior permission from the *gram sabha* is required and it is granted only if the owner needs the wood for domestic reasons but not for sale. The *gram sabha* also has a system of penalties to enforce disciplined use of the village trees and grasslands."[31]

Seed only became a *gramdam* village some ten years ago, but in that time it has demonstrated how, once authority has been restored to the commons, the local environment can be defended, restored and improved for the benefit of the local community as a whole. Agarwal and Narain conclude:

"We are absolutely convinced . . . that there is no alternative to this concept. Increasingly we get convinced that the most sophisticated decision-making will begin only when people start sitting under banyan trees as a group to discuss their problems and find common solutions. Only this form of decentralized decision-making can match the enormous cultural and biological diversity of Indian villages. People sitting in closed rooms in distant Central and State capitals or even district headquarters can only produce monolithic nonsense which will have little relevance on the ground."[32]

ERODING POWER

That conclusion is also being drawn by other communities, both North and South. Across the world, grassroots movements are working to open up more space for the commons by denying that any single social whole — whether culture, language, livelihood, art, theory science, gender, race or class — has a right to assert privileged status over, and thus to enclose, all others of its type. They are creating space where, on the contrary, the local community has the right to decide its own future; the right to refuse to have to abide by an alien translation of its own words and practices; the right to its own culture.

Key to that struggle is the building up of open and accountable institutions that restore authority to commons regimes — a struggle which requires increasing the bargaining power of those who are currently excluded or marginalized from the political process and eroding the power of those who are currently able to impose their will on others. Only in this way — when all those who will have to live with a decision have a voice in making that decision — can the checks and balances on power that are so critical to the workings of the commons be ensured.

Achieving that political order requires promoting the virtues of receptivity, flexibility, patience, open-mindedness, non-defensiveness, humour, curiosity and respect for the opinions of others as a counterweight to the formulas, principles, translations or "limits" which trap people in single languages. It involves legitimizing a type of rational decision-making and self-correction which emphasizes not the application of predetermined methods, technical vocabularies, "objective" data and yardsticks — the machinery of enclosure — but the indispensability of open-ended conversation, a willingness to listen and learn, to change one's view and to work at achieving a consensus. As Sophie Pierre of the Ktunaxa/Kinbasket Tribal Council in British Columbia remarks of the decision-making process that still holds in her own community:

"My people have lived for thousands of years in that area of South-East British Columbia — from the Big Bend of the Columbia River in the North, to the Arrow Lakes in the West, to Missoula, Montana in the South, to the eastern slopes of the Rocky Mountains. That is my home. And in my homeland, consensus has worked for thousands of years.

" . . . By involving all the stakeholders, and using all of their good commonsense, one then expects responsibility and ownership for the decision that is made. The only way that you can accept that ownership is if you are part of it: you have to be involved . . . I grew up figuring that consensus meant that you chew on something long enough until everyone can swallow it easily and safely . . . Meetings would go on all day and all night if necessary — until everyone was heard, and then a decision was made. The problems, whatever they were, would be examined from all sides. Everyone who felt that a particular situation required their input, was heard. So consensus does take time and it does take patience. But it is the most effective way of making sure that everybody is responsible in the decision that is eventually made."[33]

For those who are used to imposing their will and languages on others, or who see the environmental threats facing humanity as so overwhelming that only centralized decision-making by cliques of experts can meet the task in hand, the call for community control is at best a threat to their power, at worst a recipe for indecision and muddling through to ecological disaster. But the evidence is overwhelming that local-level institutions in which power is limited and the common right to survival is the preoccupation of all, are the best means of repairing the damage done through enclosure. Equally overwhelming is the evidence that "non-local, state-management systems are both costly and often ineffective."[34]

All of which implies a reweaving of the current webs of power in a way which results in new forms of power resting with local people. Indeed, the struggle to retain, regain or create commons will always be a struggle to preserve one's community's backyard and independence. Increasingly, however, this involves helping to carve out a political space in which other communities' backyards can also be preserved. Thus in Thailand, peasant communities struggling to prevent dams from being built have called for a nationwide moratorium on dams, seeing this as being in their own local interest. Groups are calling not just for non-interference in their own evolution but are increasingly opposed to all "development" projects which forcibly threaten local ways against the wishes of local people. The receptivity and open-mindedness which any one commons regime needs to survive is needed by all. Only if there is a space for many commons will there be a space for one.

EVERYDAY COMMONS

It is a mistake to see acts of resistance and reclamation solely as the province of the politically active, or of those whose "backs are against the wall". On the contrary, resistance to enclosure takes place in countless everyday ways in both the South and the North. In Britain, for example, residents in public housing regularly refuse to abide by directives that all doors and windows should be a uniform colour, stamping their personalities on their homes by painting them whatever colour they choose. Acquiescent behaviour towards enclosers, and feigned ignorance or incompetence in their presence, allows individuals to retain their own sense of dignity by mocking the stereotypes that have been imposed upon them. As an Ethiopian proverb has it, "When the great lord passes, the wise peasant bows deeply and silently farts."[35] Feigned acquiescence and subservience, by relaxing enclosers' scrutiny, also makes it easier for ordinary people to find social and physical spaces where they can develop criticisms and alternatives to the dominant order.

When workers on a site politely acknowledge the pontifications of a visiting expert in his presence, but laughingly ignore them once he has gone, they are asserting the validity of their own practical knowledge. When someone discards non-essential pharmaceutical drugs or refuses unnecessary X-rays, they begin to reclaim power over their bodies. When someone opts for homoeopathic remedies, osteopathy or acupuncture to prevent and cure everyday health complaints, they gain further control, as do women when they reclaim their procreative powers by rejecting contraceptive methods which make them unhealthy. Even humble actions, such as deliberately choosing local produce, buying jumble and second-hand furniture or saving jam-jars for home produce stalls, are ways in which people express their dissatisfaction with the enclosed world of consumerism and reclaim an element of control.

These small-scale actions do not make headlines and may not even be noticed by the dominant groups within society; but they help empower individuals and communities and they create the confidence and vision to resist still further, whenever opportunities to do so present themselves. Indeed, as the structures of enclosure begin to falter and break down under the stress of economic recession, international debt, popular protest and every-day resistance to the anonymity of industrialization, new life is breathed into even the most seemingly dismal communities as people rediscover the value of coming together to resolve their problems. As Gustavo Esteva enthusiastically records for Mexico City:

"With falling oil prices, mounting debts, and the conversion of Mexico into a free trade zone, so that transnational capital can produce Volkswagen 'Beetles' in automated factories for export to Germany, the corruption of our politics and the degradation of Nature — always implicit in development — can finally be seen, touched and smelled by everyone. Now the poor are responding by creating their own moral economy. As Mexico's Rural Development Bank no longer has sufficient funds to force peasants to plant sorghum for animal feed, many have returned to the traditional intercropping of corn and beans, improving their diets, restoring some village solidarity and allowing available cash to reach further. In response to the decreasing purchasing power of the previously employed, thriving production co-operatives are springing up in the heart of Mexico City. Shops now exist in the slums that reconstruct electrical appliances; merchants prosper by imitating foreign trademarked goods and selling them as smuggled wares to tourists. Neighbourhoods have come back to life. Street stands and tiny markets have returned to corners from where they have disappeared long ago. Complex forms of non-formal organization have developed, though which the *barrio* (village) residents create protective barriers between themselves and intruding development bureaucracies, police and their officials; fight eviction and the confiscation of their assets; settle their own disputes and maintain public order."[36]

The erosion of the global economy, far from being a disaster, ushers in a new era of opportunities — the opportunity to live with dignity, the opportunity for communities to define their own priorities and identities, to restore what development has destroyed and to enjoy lives of increased variety and richness.

A CONCLUDING REMARK

It is customary to conclude a document such as this with policy recommendations. We are not going to do so. Our reasons are many but two of them have been expressed admirably (although in another context) by Philip Raikes in the introduction to his book *Modernising Hunger*:

> "It becomes increasingly difficult to say what are practical suggestions, when one's research tends to show that what is politically feasible is usually too minor to make any difference, while changes significant enough to be worthwhile are often unthinkable in practical political terms. In any case, genuine practicality in making policy suggestions requires detailed knowledge of a particular country or area; its history, culture, vegetation, existing situation, and much more besides. Lists of general 'policy conclusions' make it all too easy for the rigid-minded to apply them as general recipes, without thought, criticism or adjustment for circumstances."[1]

Like Raikes's book, our document is "full of implicit conclusions" and explicit demands, but to formulate them as "policy recommendations" would be to go against the case we have attempted to make. It would suggest that there is a single set of principles for change; and that today's policy-makers, whether in national governments or international institutions, are the best people to apply them. We reject that view.

A space for the commons cannot be created by economists, development planners, legislators, "empowerment" specialists or other paternalistic outsiders. To place the future in the hands of such individuals would be to maintain the webs of power that are currently stifling commons regimes. One cannot legislate the commons into existence; nor can the commons be reclaimed simply by adopting "green techniques" such as organic agriculture, alternative energy strategies or better public transport — necessary and desirable though such strategies often are. Rather,

196

commons regimes emerge through ordinary people's day-to-day resistance to enclosure, and through their efforts to regain the mutual support, responsibility and trust that sustain the commons.

That is not to say that one can ignore policy-makers or policy-making. The depredations of transnational corporations, international bureaucracies and national governments cannot be allowed to go unchallenged. But the environmental movement has a responsibility to ensure that in seeking solutions, it does not remove the initiative from those who are defending their commons or attempting to regenerate commons regimes. It is a responsibility it should take seriously.

REFERENCES

THE COMMONS: WHERE THE COMMUNITY HAS AUTHORITY

1. See, for example, "Traditions Resist Change" in Sanitsuda Ekachai, *Behind the Smile*: *Voices of Thailand*, Thai Development Support Committee, Bangkok, 1990, pp. 86–95.
2. Ostrom, E., *Governing the Commons: The Evolution of Institutions for Collective Action*, Cambridge University Press, Cambridge, 1991, p.27.
3. See, for example, Cruz, M.C.J., "Water as Common Property: The Case of Irrigation Water Rights in the Philippines" in Berkes, F. (ed.), *Common Property Resources: Ecology and Community-Based Sustainable Development*, Belhaven Press, London, 1989, pp.218–235.
4. See, for example, Acheson, J. M., "The Lobster Fiefs Revisited: Economic and Ecological Effects of Territoriality in Maine Lobster Fishing" in McCay, B. and Acheson, J.M. (eds.), *The Question of the Commons: The Culture and Ecology of Communal Resources*, University of Arizona, Tucson, 1987, pp.37–65.
5. Quoted in World Commission on Environment and Development, *Our Common Future*, Oxford University Press, Oxford, 1987, p.114.
6. Ostrom, E., op. cit. 2.
7. McCay, B. and Acheson, J.M., *The Question of the Commons*, University of Arizona, Tucson, 1987.
8. Fortmann, L. and Bruce, J. W., *Whose Trees? Proprietary Dimensions of Forestry*, Westview, Boulder, 1988.
9. McCay, B. and Acheson, J.M., op. cit. 7.
10. Norgaard, R., "The Rise of the Global Exchange Economy and the Loss of Biological Diversity" in Wilson, E.O. (ed.), *Biodiversity*, National Academy Press, Washington DC, 1988, pp. 206–211; Illich, I., *Gender*, Pantheon, New York, 1982.
11. Moench, M., "'Turf' and Forest Management in Garhwal Hill Village" in Fortmann, L. and Bruce, J.W., op. cit. 8, pp.127–136.
12. Cruz, M. C. J., op. cit. 3.
13. Bauer, D., "The Dynamics of Communal and Hereditary Land Tenure Among the Tigray of Ethiopia", in McCay, B. and Acheson, J.M., op. cit. 7, pp.217–232.
14. Illich, I., "Silence is a Commons", *CoEvolution Quarterly*, Winter 1983, pp.5–9.
15. World Bank, *World Development Report 1992: Development and the Environment*, Oxford University Press, New York, pp.15 and 83.
16. Hardin, G., "The Tragedy of the Commons", *Science*, 162, 13 December 1968, pp.1243–1248.
17. McEvoy, A., "Toward an Interactive Theory of Nature and Culture" in Worster, D. (ed.), *The Ends of the Earth: Perspectives on Modern Environmental History*, Cambridge University Press, Cambridge, 1990, p.226.
18. Chapeskie, A.J., *Indigenous Law, State Law and the Management of Natural Resources: Wild Rice and the Wabigoon Lake Ojibway Nation*, typescript, July 1988, p.18.
19. Ibid., p. 20.
20. Lane, C., *Barabaig Natural Resource Management: Sustainable Land Use under Threat*

References

of Destruction, Discussion Paper 12, UN Research Institute for Social Development, Geneva, 1990, p.7.

21. Ostrom, E., op. cit. 2, p.62.

22. Bromley, D.W., *Environment and Economy:Property Rights and Public Policy*, Blackwell, Oxford, 1991.

23. May, P.H., "A Tragedy of the Non-Commons: Recent Developments in the Babaçu palm-based industries in Maranhão, Brazil", *Forest Trees and People, Newsletter No. 11* (undated), Uppsala, Sweden, pp.23–27.

24. Khor, M., presentation at World Rainforest Movement meeting on land insecurity and tropical deforestation, 1 March 1992, New York.

25. O'Connor, R., "From Fertility to Order" in *Siam Society, Culture and Environment in Thailand*, Siam Society, Bangkok, 1989, pp.393–414.

26. Ostrom, E., "The Rudiments of a Revised Theory of the Origins, Survival and Performance of Institutions for Collective Action", Working Paper 32, *Workshop in Political Theory and Policy Analysis*, Indiana University, Bloomington, 1985.

27. Lane, C., op. cit. 20, p.8.

28. Altieri, M.A., "Traditional Farming in Latin America", *The Ecologist*, Vol.21, No.2, March/April 1991, p.93.

29. McCorkle, C. M. et al., *A Case Study on Farmer Innovations and Communication in Niger*, Academy for Educational Development, Washington DC, 1988, p.40. Cited in Rau, B., *From Feast to Famine: Official Cures and Grassroots Remedies to Africa's Food Crisis*, Zed Books Ltd, London and New Jersey, 1991, p.148.

30. Guha, R., "The Malign Encounter: The Chipko Movement and Competing Visions of Nature" in Banuri, T. and Apffel-Marglin, F. (eds.), *Who Will Save the Forests?*, Zed Books Ltd, London and New Jersey, 1993. See also Fortmann, L. and Bruce, J.W., op.cit 8.

31. Pinkerton, E., "Intercepting the State: Dramatic Processes in the Assertion of Local Comanagement Rights" in McCay, B.J. and Acheson, J.M., op. cit. 7, p.347.

32. McKean, M.A., *Management of Traditional Common Lands (Iriachi) in Japan*, Duke University. Cited in McCay, B.J. and Acheson, J.M., "Human Ecology of the Commons" in McCay, B.J. and Acheson, J.M., op. cit. 7, pp.1–33.

33. *Pakistan National Report to UNCED*, Islamabad, 1992, pp.74–75.

34. "The Lao Alternative", *Rain*, 14, 1, 1991, p.8.

35. Berkes, F. and Feeny, D., "Paradigms Lost: Changing Views on the Use of Common Property Resources", *Alternatives*, Vol. 17, No.2, 1990, p.50.

36. McCay, B.J. and Acheson, J.M., op. cit. 7.

37. Esteva, G., "The Right to Stop Development", *NGONET UNCED Feature*, 13 June 1992, Rio de Janeiro.

DEVELOPMENT AS ENCLOSURE

1. Lohmann, L., "Resisting Green Globalism" in Sachs, W. (ed.), *Global Ecology: Conflicts and Contradictions*, Zed Books Ltd, London and New Jersey, 1993.

2. Sadie, J.L., "The Social Anthropology of Economic Underdevelopment", *The Economic Journal*, No.70, 1960, p.302. Cited in Berthoud, G., "Market" in Sachs, W. (ed.), op. cit 1, pp.72–73.

3. Collings, J., *Land Reform*, Longmans, Green and Co., London, 1908, pp.87–88.

4. Ibid., pp.144–145.

5. Slater,G., "Historical Outline of Land Ownership in England", *The Land: The Report of the Land Enquiry Committee*, Hodder and Stoughton, London, 1913, p.lxxii.

6. Ibid.

7. Prebble, J., *The Highland Clearances*, Penguin, London, 1969.

8. Inglis, B., *Poverty and the Industrial Revolution*, Hodder and Stoughton, London, 1971, pp.87–91.

9. Cobbett,W., *Rural Rides, Vol. II*, Everyman, London, 1912, p.285.

10. Rackham,O., *The History of the Countryside*, Dent, London, 1986, pp.296–297.

11. Ibid., p.139.

12. Cobbett, W., *Selections from Cobbett's Political Registers*, 1813, Vol IV. Cited in Collings, op. cit. 3, p.77.

13. Trevelyan, G., *English Social History*, Longmans, London,1944, p.381.

14. Quoted in Roberts, P., "Rural Development and the Rural Economy in Niger, 1900–75", in Heyer, J., Roberts, P. and Williams, G. (eds.), *Rural Development in Tropical Africa*, St. Martin's Press, New York, 1981, p.195.

15. Cited in Dumont, R. and Cohen, N., *The Growth of Hunger*, Marion Boyars, London,1980.

16. Bodley, J.H., *Victims of Progress*, Mayfield Publishing Company, Palo Alto, 1982, p.97.

17. Ibid.

18. NRG, *The Agricultural Survey Commission Report, 1930–1932*, Government Printer, Livingstone, 1933. Quoted in Wood, A.P. and Shula, E.C.W., "The State and Agriculture in Zambia: A Review of the Evolution and Consequences of Food and Agriculture Policies in a Mining Economy" in Mkandawire, T. and Bourenane, N. (eds.), *The State and Agriculture in Africa*, CODESIRA, London, 1987, p.277.

19. Bodley, J.H., op. cit. 16, p.94. See also: Witte, J., "Deforestation in Zaire", *The Ecologist*, Vol. 22, No. 2, March/April, 1992, pp.58–64.

20. Bodley, J.H., op. cit. 16, p.30.

21. Ibid., p.9.

22. von Albertini, R., *European Colonial Rule, 1880–1940: The Impact of the West on India, Southeast Asia and Africa*, Greenwood Press, Westport, 1982, p.268. Cited in Bromley, D.W., *Environment and Economy: Property Rights and Public Policy*, Blackwell, Oxford, 1991, p.122.

23. *Rabaul Times*, 25 September 1936. Cited in Colchester, M., *Pirates, Squatters and Poachers: The Political Ecology of Dispossession of the Native Peoples of Sarawak*, Survival International/INSAN, London and Kuala Lumpur, 1989.

24. Colchester, M., "Guatemala: The Clamour for Land and the Fate of the Forests", *The Ecologist*, Vol.21, No.4, July/August 1991, pp.177–185.

25. Hopkins, A.G., *An Economic History of West Africa*, Longman, London, 1973, p.26.

26. Croder, M., *West Africa under Colonial Rule*, Hutchinson, London, 1968, pp.185–186. Cited in Franke, R.W. and and Chasin, B.H., *Seeds of Famine: Ecological Destruction and the Development Dilemma in the West African Sahel*, Landmark Studies, Allanheld, Osmun, New Jersey, 1980, p.72.

27. Franke, R.W. and Chasin, B.H., op. cit. 26, pp.71–72.

28. Ibid., p.72.

29. Buell, R., *The Native Problem in Africa*, Macmillan, New York, 1928, pp.937–1044. Cited in Bodley, J.H., op. cit . 16, p.128.

30. Bodley, J.H., op. cit. 16, p.128.

31. Bromley, D.W., op. cit. 22, p.121.

32. Ali, T. and O'Brien, J., "Land, Community and Protest in Sudanese Agriculture", in Barker, J. (ed.), *The Politics of Agriculture in Tropical Africa*, Sage Series on African Modernization and Development, SAGE series, Volume 9, Sage Publications, London, 1984, p.221.

33. Franke, R.W. and Chasin, B.H., op. cit. 26, p.71.

34. Colchester, M., op. cit. 23, p.13.

35. Ali, T. and O'Brien, J., op. cit. 32, pp.221–222.

36. Bromley, D.W., op. cit. 22, p.120.

37. von Albertini, R., op. cit. 22, p.163.

References

38. Ibid.

39. Bromley, D.W., op. cit. 22, p.118.

40. Mies, M., *Patriarchy and Accumulation on a World Scale: Women in the International Division of Labour*, Zed Books Ltd, London and New Jersey, 1986.

41. Ibid., p.98.

42. Hall, F., *A People at School*, cited in Mies, M. op. cit. 40. p. 93–94.

43. Holly, M., "Handsome Lake's Teachings: The Shift From Female to Male Agriculture in Iroquois Culture", *Agriculture and Human Values*, Voll. VII, No. 3 & 4, Summer–Fall, pp.80–94.

44. Merchant, C., *The Death of Nature: Women, Ecology and the Scientific Revolution*, Harper & Row, San Francisco, 1983, p.169.

45. Mies, M., Bennholdt-Thomssen, V. and von Werlhof, C., *Women: The Last Colony*, Zed Books Ltd, London and New Jersey, 1988, p.4, 103.

46. Gupta, A.K., *Agrarian Structure and Peasant Revolt in India*, Criterion Publications, New Delhi, 1986, pp.84–85. See also: Chandra, B., "The Rise and Growth of Economic Nationalism in India: Elements of Continuity and Change in Early Nationalist Activity", *Studies in History*, Vol. 1, No.1.

47. Cited in Shiva, V., *Ecology and the Politics of Survival: Conflicts over Natural Resources in India*, Sage/United Nations University, New Delhi, 1991, p.17.

48. Kilusang Magbubukid ng Pilipinas, *Sowing the Seed: Proceedings of the International Solidarity Conference for the Filipino Peasantry*, Manila, 1988, pp. 34 and 211.

49. Ibid., p.211.

50. Ibid., p.35.

51. Ibid., p.33.

52. Ibid., pp.212 and 41.

53. Hines, C. and Dinham, B., "Can Agribusiness feed Africa?", *The Ecologist*, Vol.14, No.2, 1984, p.65.

54. For an account of the project and resistance to it, see Beckman, B., "Peasants Versus State and Industry in Nigeria", in Goldsmith E. and Hildyard, N., *The Social and Environmental Effects of Large Dams*, Volume 2 (Case Studies), Wadebridge Ecological Centre, Wadebridge, Cornwall, 1986.

55. Halfani, M.S. and Baker, J., "Agribusiness and Agrarian Change" in Barker, J. (ed.), *The Politics of Agriculture in Tropical Africa*, Sage Series on African Modernization and Development, SAGE series, Volume 9, Sage Publications, London, 1984, p.48.

56. Gakou, M.L., *The Crisis in African Agriculture*, Zed Books Ltd/United Nations University, London, 1987, p.49.

57. Ibid.

58. MacDonald, N., *Brazil: A Mask Called Progress*, Oxfam, Oxford, 1991, p.32.

59. Ibid.

60. Ibid., p.49.

61. Bennet, J. and George, S., *The Hunger Machine*, Polity Press, Cambridge, 1987, p.144.

62. Ibid., p.144

63. MacDonald, N., op. cit. 58, p.48.

64. Hecht, S., "Landlessness, Land Speculation and Pasture-Led Deforestation in Brazil", *The Ecologist*, Vol. 19, No. 6, November/December, 1989.

65. Ibid.

66. "The Threat of Tourism", *Down to Earth*, May 1991, No.13, p.1.

67. Ibid., p.2.

68. Thrupp, L.A., "Inappropriate Incentives for Pesticide Use: Agricultural Credit Requirements in Developing Countries", *Agriculture and Human Values*, Vol.VII, Nos. 3 and 4, Summer-Fall, 1990, p.63–64.

69. Shiva, V., "The Green Revolution in the Punjab", *The Ecologist*, Vol.21, No.2, March/April 1991, p.60. Citing Gill. S.S, "Contradiction of Punjab Model of Growth and Search for

an Alternative", *Economic and Political Weekly*, 15 October 1988.

70. Dias, C., "Reaping the Whirlwind: Some Third World Perspectives on the Green Revolution and the 'Seed Revolution'", in *International Centre for Law in Development, The International Context of Rural Poverty in the Third World*, Council on International and Public Affairs, New York, 1986, p.58.

71. Kothari, M., *Forced Evictions and the United Nations*, undated paper.

72. Hallward, P., "The Urgent Need for a Campaign Against Forced Resettlement", *The Ecologist*, Vol.22, No.2, March/April 1992.

73. Kothari, M., op. cit. 71.

74. *Salisbury Journal*, 29 August and 19 September 1991.

75. Body, R., *Our Land, Our Food: Why contemporary farming practices must change*, Rider, London, 1991, p.4.

76. Belden, J.R., *Dirt Rich, Dirt Poor: America's Food and Farm Crisis*, Routledge and Kegan Paul, New York and London, 1986, p.3.

77. Edwards, R., "Scotland: Behind the Scenery", *Social Work Today*, 14(27), 1983, pp.10–14. See also: McLaughlin, B.R., "Rural Deprivation", *The Planner*, 67, 1981, pp.31–33; Newby, H., *A Green and Pleasant Land*, Hutchinson, London, 1979.

78. Lang, T., *Food Retailing Concentration: Its implications for consumers*, unpublished ms., 1991, p.12.

79. "Canada, Cargill and Free Trade", *Food Matters Worldwide* 10, 1991, p.10.

80. Erlichman, J., *Gluttons for Punishment*, Penguin, Harmondsworth, 1986, pp.68–69.

81. Heffernan, W.D., "Confidence and Courage in the Next 50 years", Presidential Address delivered at the Annual Meeting of the Rural Sociological Society, Athens, Georgia, August 1988, p.8.

82. Erhlichman, J., "Progress halves chickens' lifespan", *The Guardian*, 15 October 1991, p.4.

83. Fowler, C. and Mooney, P., *Shattering: Food, Politics and the Loss of Genetic Diversity*, University of Arizona Press, 1990, pp.118–139; Hobbelink, H., *Biotechnology and the Future of World Agriculture*, Zed Books Ltd, London and New Jersey, 1991.

84. Ibid., pp.123–124.

85. Ibid., p.124.

86. Shiva, V., *The Seed and the Spinning Wheel*, unpublished ms., 1991.

87. Ibid.

88. Ibid.

89. Hobbelink, H., op. cit. 83, Table 5.1, pp.55–58.

90. Fowler, C. and Mooney, P., op. cit. 83, p.132.

91. Hobbelink, H., op. cit. 83, p.99.

92. Rifkin, J., *Biosphere Politics*, Crown, New York, 1991.

THE ENCOMPASSING WEB

1. Illich, I., "Silence is a Commons", *The Coevolution Quarterly*, Winter 1983.

2. Illich, I., *Gender*, Pantheon, New York, 1982, p.111.

3. Ibid., p.18.

4. Shiva, V., "Resources" in Sachs, W. (ed.), *The Development Dictionary: A Guide to Knowledge as Power*, Zed Books Ltd, London and New Jersey, 1992, p.206.

5. Shiva, V., *Ecology and the Politics of Survival: Conflicts over Natural Resources in India*, Sage/ United Nations University, New Delhi, 1991.

6. Bandyopadhyay, J., "The Ecology of Drought and Water Scarcity", *The Ecologist*, Vol.18, No.2, 1988.

7. Illich, I., op. cit. 1, p.7.

8. Scott, J., *Domination and the Arts of Resistance*, Yale University Press, New Haven, 1990.

References

9. Berthoud, G., "Market" in Sachs, W. (ed.), op.cit. 4, p.83.

10. Rifkin, J., *Biosphere Politics*, Crown, New York, 1991.

11. Rau, B., *From Feast to Famine: Official Cures and Grassroots Remedies to Africa's Food Crisis*, Zed Books Ltd, London and New Jersey, 1991, pp.11 and 60.

12. Illich, I. , op. cit. 2.

13. Colchester, M., *Pirates, Squatters and Poachers: The Political Ecology of Dispossession of the Native Peoples of Sarawak*, Survival International/INSAN, London and Kuala Lumpur, 1989.

14. This example is taken from Chatchawan Tongdeelert and Lohmann, L., "The Muang Fai Irrigation System of Northern Thailand", *The Ecologist*, Vol.21, No.2, March/April 1991, pp.101–106.

15. Widstrand, C., "Conflicts over Water" in Widstrand, C. (ed.), *Water Conflicts and Research Priorities*, Pergamon, Oxford, 1980, p.142.

16. Ibid.

17. Banuri, T. and Apffel-Marglin, F. (eds.), *Who Will Save the Forests? Political Resistance, Systems of Knowledge and the Environmental Crisis*, Zed Press, London and New Jersey, 1993.

18. Illich, I., op.cit. 1.

19. Shiva, V., "The Seed and the Earth: Women, Ecology and Biotechnology", *The Ecologist*, Vol.22, No.1, January/February 1992, p.5.

20. Ibid.

21. Simmons, P., "Women in Development", *The Ecologist*, Vol.22, No.1, 1992, pp.16–21.

22. Tripp, A.M., *Defending the Right to Subsist: The State vs the Urban Informal Economy in Tanzania*, Wider Working Papers, World Institute for Development Economics Research of the United Nations University, 1989, pp.26–27.

23. Spender, D., *Man Made Language*, Pandora, London, 1980.

24. Scott, J.C., op.cit.8, p.127.

25. Caplan, P., "Development Policies in Tanzania: Some Implications for Women", in Dauber, R. and Cain, M. (eds.), *Women and Technological Change in Developing Countries*, American Association for the Advancement of Science, Washington DC,1981, p.107. Cited in Stamp, P., *Technology, Gender and Power in Africa*, International Development Research Centre, Ottawa, 1989, p.56.

26. Marglin, S. Farmers, *Seedmen and Scientists: Systems of Agriculture and Systems of Knowledge*, Harvard University, unpublished ms., March 1992, p.32.

POWER: THE CENTRAL ISSUE

1. Hobbelink, H., *Biotechnology and the Future of World Agriculture*, Zed Books Ltd, London and New Jersey, 1991, p.39.

2. Krebs, A.V., *The Corporate Reapers: The Book of Agribusiness*, Essential Books, Washington, DC, 1991, p.266.

3. Ibid., pp. 271–272.

4. For a full discussion of the role of FAO in promoting industrialized agriculture, see *The Ecologist*, Vol.21, No.2, March/April 1991.

5. Dinham, B., "FAO and Pesticides: Promotion or Proscription?", *The Ecologist*, Vol.21, No.2, March/April 1991, p.63.

6. Hobbelink, H., op. cit. 1, p.39.

7. Participants List, Codex Alimentarius Commission, Pesticides Residues Committee, 15–19 April 1991, Rome.

8. For comparisons between national pesticide residue standards and Codex standards, see

Ritchie, M., "GATT, Agriculture and the Environment", *The Ecologist*, Vol. 20, No. 6, November/December 1990, pp. 214–220; Lang, T., *Food fit for the world? How GATT food trade talks challenge public health*, the environment and the citizen, SAFE Alliance/Public Health Alliance, London, March 1992.

9. Cited in Clunies-Ross, T. and Hildyard, N., *The Politics of Industrial Agriculture*, Earthscan, London, 1992.

10. Kurien, J., *Ruining the Commons and Responses of the Commoners: Coastal Overfishing and Fishermen's Actions in Kerala State, India*, United Nations Research Institute for Social Development, Discussion Paper 23, Geneva, 1991.

11. Cited in Broad, R., *Unequal Alliance, 1979–1986: The World Bank, The International Monetary Fund, and the Philippines*, Ateneo de Manila University Press, Quezon City, Metro Manila, 1988, p.26.

12. Ibid., p.26.

13. Ibid., p.26.

14. Ibid., p.31.

15. MacDonald, N., *Brazil: A Mask Called Progress*, Oxfam, Oxford, 1991, p.52.

16. For a discussion of the impact of structural adjustment, see McAfee, K., *Storm Signals, Structural Adjustment and Development Alternatives in the Caribbean*, Zed Books Ltd, London and New Jersey, 1991; Onimode, B., *The IMF, The World Bank and the African Debt*, (Two Volumes), Zed Books Ltd, London and New Jersey, 1989.

17. Broad, R., op. cit. 11, pp.11–13.

18. Colchester, M., "Sacking Guyana", *Multinational Monitor*, September 1991, p.8.

19. Plant, R., "Background to Agrarian Reform", in Colchester, M. and Lohmann, L. (eds.), *The Struggle for Land and the Fate of the Forests*, World Rainforest Movement, Penang; Zed Books Ltd, London and New Jersey, 1993.

20. Rahnema, M., "Participation" in Sachs, W. (ed.), *The Development Dictionary*, Zed Books Ltd, London and New Jersey, 1992, p.120.

21. Khor, M., "Regulating Transnational Corporations: The Biggest Gap in UNCED's Agenda", *Third World Economics*, 16–30 April 1992, p.18.

22. Leggett, J. and Stevenson, P., "Fiddling while the World Burns", *Greenpeace* 16, Nov/Dec 1990.

23. Shiva, V., "US attempting to block biosafety regulations", *SUNS Monitor*, No.2803, 21 March 1992, pp.4–6.

MAINSTREAM SOLUTIONS

1. Rahnema, M., "Poverty" in Sachs, W. (ed.), *The Development Dictionary: A Guide to Knowledge as Power*, Zed Books Ltd, London and New Jersey, 1992, p.158.

2. Escobar, A., "Planning" in Sachs, W. (ed.), op. cit. 1, pp.136–7.

3. Ibid.

4. World Bank, *World Development Report 1992: Development and the Environment*, Oxford University Press, New York, 1992, pp.95–96.

5. Deutsch, K., quoted in Christodoulou, D., *The Unpromised Land: Agrarian Reform and Conflict Worldwide*, Zed Books Ltd, London and New Jersey, 1990.

6. Alvares, C., "Science, Colonialism and Violence: A Luddite View", in Nandy, A. (ed.), *Science, Hegemony and Violence*, Oxford University Press, Delhi, 1988, p.88.

7. Lohmann, L., "Who Defends Biodiversity? Conservation Strategies and the Case of Thailand", *The Ecologist*, Vol.21, No.1, January/February 1991, p.10, citing Montree Chanthawong, Paa choom chon, Bangkok, 1989.

8. World Commission on Environment and Development, *Our Common Future*, Oxford University Press, Oxford, 1987, p.33.

References

9. World Bank, op. cit. 4, p.11.

10. Myers, N., *The Primary Source: Tropical Forests and Our Future*, Norton, 1985.

11. Personal communication from Smitu Kothari. Others such as Sunil Roy put the figure even higher — at 20 million people. Since World War II, some 1,500 large dams have been built in India.

12. *Thai Development Newsletter*, No.19, 1991.

13. Pearce, F., "No Southern Comfort at Rio", *New Scientist*, 16 May 1992.

14. World Bank, op. cit. 4.

15. "Strands In The Web", an interview with Norberg–Hodge, H. by Gilman, R., *In Context*, No. 31, p.39–41. See also Norberg-Hodge, H., *Ancient Futures*, Sierra Club Books, San Francisco, 1991.

16. See Mies, M., *Patriarchy and Accumulation on a World Scale: Women in the International Division of Labour*, Zed Books Ltd, London and New Jersey, 1986; Fisher, E., *Women's Creation*, Anchor Press, Doubleday Garden City, New York, 1979; Hartmann, B., *Reproductive Rights and Wrongs, The Global Politics of Population Control and Contraceptive Choice*, Harper & Row, New York, 1987; Wichterich, C., "From the Struggle Against 'Overpopulation' to the Industrialization of Human Production", *Issues in Reproductive and Genetic Engineering*, Vol. 1, No. 1, 1988, pp.21–30.

17. Landes, D. S., *The Unbound Prometheus: Technological Change and Industrial Development in Western Europe from 1750 to the Present*, Cambridge University Press, Cambridge, 1969.

18. Shiva, V., "Population growth wrongly blamed for ecology problems," *Third World Resurgence*, No. 16, p.33.

19. Hartmann, B., op. cit. 16.

20. Lappé, F. M. and Schurman, R., *Taking Population Seriously*, Earthscan, London, 1989, p.20.

21. Hartmann, B., op. cit. 16. p.6.

22. Banuri, T., personal communication, 1992.

23. Duden, B., "Population", in *The Development Dictionary*, Sachs, W. (ed) Zed Books Ltd. London and New Jersey, 1992, pp.146–157.

24. Wichterich, C., op. cit. 16, p.24.

25. Lappé, F. M. and Schurman, R., op. cit. 20. p.27.

26. Wichterich, C., op. cit. 16, p.27.

27. Lappé, F. M. and Schurman, R., op. cit. 20.

28. World Bank, op. cit. 4, p.67.

29. "Gatt issues warning against environmental imperialism", *Financial Times*, 12 February 1992; Daly, H.E., *Review of International Policies to Accelerate Sustainable Development in Developing Countries and Related Domestic Policies (Section I, Chapter I of Agenda 21)*, Centre for Our Common Future, March 1992.

30. Daly, H.E., op. cit. 29.

31. International Monetary Fund, *World Economic Outlook*, Washington, 1988.

32. Norgaard, R.B., "The Rise of the Global Exchange Economy and the Loss of Biological Diversity", in Wilson, E.O. (ed.), *Biodiversity*, National Academy Press, Washington, 1988, pp.208–210.

33. Ibid.

34. World Bank, op. cit. 4, emphasis added.

35. Martinez-Alier, J., "Ecological Perceptions, Environmental Policy, and Distributional Conflicts: Some Lessons from History" in *Ecological Economics*, Columbia University Press, New York, 1991, p.134.

36. Robert, J., "Production" in Sachs, W. (ed.), op. cit. 1, p.188.

37. Helm, D. and Pearce, D., "Economic Policy Towards the Environment: An Overview" in Helm, D. (ed.), *Economic Policy Towards the Environment*, Croom Helm, London, 1991.

38. Bromley, D.W., *Environment and Economy, Property Rights and Public Policy*,

Blackwell, Oxford, 1991, p.61.

39. Daly, H.E., *On Thinking about Future Energy Requirements*, Department of Economics, Louisiana State University, Baton Rouge, 1976.

40. Perrings, C. et al., "The Ecology and Economics of Biodiversity Loss: The Research Agenda", *Ambio* 21,3, May 1992, p.204.

41. Pearce, D. (ed.), *Blueprint 2: Greening the World Economy*, Earthscan, London, 1991; World Bank, op. cit. 4; Winpenny, J.T., *Values for the Environment*, HMSO, London, 1991.

42. Daly, H.E. and Cobb, J., *For the Common Good*, Greenprint, London, 1990, pp.142–43.

43. Self, P., *Econocrats and the Policy Process*, Macmillan, London, 1970; Campen, J.T., *Benefit, Cost and Beyond*, Gunn, Cambridge, 1986; Paranjpye, V., *Evaluating the Tehri Dam*, INTACH, New Delhi, 1988.

44. Dowie, M., "American Environmentalism: A Movement Courting Irrelevance", *World Policy Review*, Winter 1991–1992, pp.67–92.

45. Aihwa Ong, *Spirits of Resistance and Capitalist Discipline*, SUNY Press, Albany, 1987, p.111.

46. Sachs, W., "The Gospel of Global Efficiency", *IFDA Dossier*, 68, November/December 1988, p.37.

47. Barde, J.-P. and Pearce, D. (eds.), *Valuing the Environment*, Earthscan, London, 1991, p.1.

48. Dowie, M., op. cit. 44, p.91.

49. Chris Blythe of Wisconsin's Citizen's Utility Board, quoted in "Selling Pollution", *Multinational Monitor*, June 1992, p.5.

50. Sagoff, M., *The Economy of the Earth*, Cambridge University Press, Cambridge, 1990, pp.81–88.

51. Helm, D. and Pearce, D. (eds.), op. cit. 37, p.3.

52. Turner, R.K., "Environment, Economics and Ethics", in Pearce, D. (ed.), op. cit. 41, p.220.

53. Rorty, R., *Philosophy and the Mirror of Nature*, Princeton, 1979; Apffel-Marglin, F. and Marglin, S.A., *Dominating Knowledge*, Oxford University Press, Oxford, 1991.

54. World Bank, op. cit. 1, p.71.

55. Esteva, G., "Development" in Sachs, W. (ed.), op, cit. 1, p.21.

56. Rorty, R., *Relativism, Objectivity and Truth*, Cambridge University Press, Cambridge,1991.

57. *Rocky Mountain Institute Newsletter*, Old Snowmass, Colorado, Fall/Winter 1990, pp.1–3; Bunyard, P., *Nuclear Power: Way Forward or Cul–de–Sac?*, Wadebridge Ecological Centre, Wadebridge, Cornwall, 1991, p.41.

58. *Rocky Mountain Institute Newsletter*, Old Snowmass, Colorado, 5, 3, Fall 1989.

59. Sagoff, M., op. cit. 50, p.88.

60. Escobar, A., op. cit. 2, pp.132–145.

61. Myers, N., "The World's Forests and Human Populations: The Environmental Interconnections", *Population and Development Review*, supp. to vol.16, 1990.

62. Weber, M., *The Theory of Social and Economic Organization*, (ed. and trans. by Talcott Parsons), Free Press, New York, 1964.

63. Ruckelshaus, W.D., "Toward a Sustainable World" in *Scientific American* (ed.), *Managing Planet Earth*, W.H. Freeman, New York, 1990, pp.125–135.

64. Orr, D.W., *Ecological Literacy and the Transition to a Postmodern World*, SUNY Press, Albany, 1992, p.36.

65. Berry, W., "Whose Head Is the Farmer Using? Whose Head Is Using the Farmer?" in Jackson, W. and Coleman, B. (eds.), *Meeting the Expectations of the Land: Essays in Sustainable Agriculture and Stewardship*, North Point Press, San Francisco, 1984.

66. Norgaard, R., "The Development of Tropical Rainforest Economics" in Head, S. and Heinzman, R.(eds.), *Lessons of the Rainforest*, Sierra Club Books, San Francisco, 1990, p.181.

References

67. Illich, I., "Silence is a Commons", *The CoEvolution Quarterly*, Winter 1983.

68. Enzensberger, H.M., "A Critique of Political Ecology" in *Dreamers of the Absolute*, Radius, London, 1988.

69. Simonis, U.E. et al., "The Crisis of Global Environment: Demands for Global Politics", *Interdependenz* 3, 1989, p.9.

70. Quoted in Prins, G. and Stamp, R., *Top Guns and Toxic Whales*, Earthscan, London, 1991, p.74.

71. Arney, W.R., *Experts in the Age of Systems*, University of New Mexico, Albuquerque, 1991.

72. Goldsmith, E., "Can We Control Pollution?", *The Ecologist*, Vol. 9, No. 8/9, November/December 1979, pp.273–290.

73. Barnaby, F., "The Environmental Impact of the Gulf War", *The Ecologist*, Vol. 21, No. 4, July/August 1991, pp.166–172.

74. *The Ecologist* special issue on transmigration, Vol. 16, No. 2/3, 1986.

75. Banuri, T. and Apffel-Marglin, F. (eds.), *Who Will Save the Forests?*, Zed Books Ltd, London and New Jersey, 1993, emphasis added.

76. Quoted in Prins, G. and Stamp, R.,op. cit. 70, p.56.

77. Ibid., p.56.

78. Illich, I., *Gender*, Pantheon, New York, 1982, p.19.

79. Escobar, op. cit. 2, p.144.

80. Bhasin K. and Agarwal B. (eds.), *Women and Media, Kali for Women*, New Delhi, 1984. Cited in Wichterich, C., "From the Struggle Against 'Overpopulation' to the Industrialization of Human Production", *Issues in Reproductive and Genetic Engineering*, Vol. 1, No. 1, 1988, pp.21–30.

81. Harrison, P., "Population" in Earth Summit special issue of *The Guardian*, 29 May 1992, p.29.

82. Duden, B., op. cit. 23.

83. Quoted in Kamm, H., "Indian State is Leader in Forced Sterilization," *New York Times*, 13 August 1976. Cited in Hartmann, B., op. cit. 16.

84. Hartmann, B., op. cit. 16. pp.237–238.

85. Wichterich, C., op. cit. 16.

86. Ada, G. L. and Griffin, P. D. (eds.), *Vaccines for fertility regulation: the assessment of their safety and their efficacy*, Cambridge University Press, Cambridge, 1991, p.239. Cited in Richter, J., "Research on Antifertility Vaccines – Priority or Problem?", *Vena Journal*, Vol. 3, No. 2., November 1991, pp.22–27.

87. Akhter, F., "New reasons to depopulate the Third World", *Third World Resurgence*, No. 16, pp.21–23.

88. For discussion on "fertility", see Mies, M., op. cit. 16, p. 72.

89. Hartmann, B., op. cit. 16, p.167.

90. Burfoot, A., "An Interview with Dr. Hugh Gorwill: Potential Risks to Women Exposed to Clomiphene Citrate", *Issues in Reproductive and Genetic Engineering*, Vol. 5, No. 1, 1992, pp.9–12.

91. Ericsson, R. J., quoted in Stokes, B., *Men and Family Planning*, Worldwatch Paper 41, Worldwatch Institute, Washington DC, December 1980, p.24. Cited in Hartmann, B., op. cit. 16, p.167.

92. "If the Cap Fits . . . " *Spare Rib*, Issue 57, April 1977, pp.45–47. Cited in Berkman, J. A., "Historical Styles of Contraceptive Advocacy", in. Holmes, H. B., Hoskins, B. B. and Gross, M. (eds.), *Birth Control and Controlling Birth: Women-Centred Perspectives*, Humana Press, 1980, pp.27–36.

93. Hartmann, B., op. cit.16, p.194.

94. Hartmann, B., op. cit.16, p.161.

95. Hartmann, B., op. cit.16, p.207.

96. Letter to Carlos Huezo, International Planned Parenthood Federation, from James D.

Shelton and Cynthia Calla, Office of Population, US Agency for International Development, 21 August 1991.

97. Wilson, J.R., quoted in Tietze, C. and Lewitt, S. (eds.), *Intrauterine Contraceptive Devices: Proceedings of the First Conference on the IUCD, April 30, 1962—May 1, 1962*, Excerpta Medica, Amsterdam, London, New York, 1962. Cited in Hartmann, B., op. cit.16. p.200.

98. Hartmann, B., op. cit.16, p.206.

99. Corea, G., quoted in Depo-Provera, *A Shot in the Dark*, Quebec Public Interest and Research Group, Montreal 1982, p.7. Cited in Hartmann, B., op. cit.16. p.188.

100. Berelson, B., "Beyond Family Planning", *Science*, Vol. 163, 7 February 1969, pp. 533–543.

101. Garcia, G. and Dacach, S., "Norplant® - 5 Years Later," WEMOS Women and Pharmaceuticals Project and Health Action International (HAI Europe), *A Question of Control: Women's Perspectives on the Development and Use of Contraceptive Technologies*, 1992, pp.29–33.

102. Scott, J. R., *Norplant: Its Impact on Poor Women and Women of Color*, National Black Women's Health Project, Washington DC. 1992.

103. Griffin, P.D. in Alexander, N.J. et al., (eds.), *Gamete Interaction: Prospects for Immunocontraception*, Proceedings of CONRAD-WHO International Workshop, San Carlos de Bariloche, Argentina, 27–29 November 1989, Wiley-Liss, New York, 1990, p.508.

104. Ada, G. L. and Griffin, P. D. (eds.), op. cit. 86.

105. Richter, J., op. cit. 86.

106. Akhter, F., "The Eugenic and Racist Premise of Reproductive Rights and Population Control", *Issues in Reproductive and Genetic Engineering*, Vol. 5. No. 1, 1992, p.1–8. See also "The State of Contraceptive Technology in Bangladesh", *Issues in Reproductive and Genetic Engineering*, Vol 1., No. 2, 1988, pp.153–158 and *Depopulating Strategy, Theory and Practice: A View from Bangladesh*, UBINIG, Bangladesh, 1986.

107. Wichterich, C., op. cit. 1. p.26.

108. Ibid.

109. Lappé. F. M. and Schurman, R., op. cit. 20.

110. Wichterich, C., op. cit.16, p.27.

111. Wichterich, C., op. cit.16, p.29.

112. Wichterich, C., op. cit.16, p.26.

113. World Bank, op. cit. 4, p.85.

114. Ibid., p.65.

115. Page, S. and Page, H., "Western Hegemony over African Agriculture in Southern Rhodesia and its Continuing Threat to Food security in Independent Rhodesia", *Agriculture and Human Values*, Vol. 8, No. 4, Fall 1991, p.5.

116. Rau, B., *From Feast to Famine: Official Cures and Grassroots Remedies to Africa's Food Crisis*, Zed Books Ltd, London and New Jersey,1991, p.145.

117. Pereira, W., *The Other Side of History*, Centre for Holistic Studies, Bombay, 1990, p.27.

118. Kerridge, E. , *The Agricultural Revolution*, Allen and Unwin, London, 1967.

119. Pereira, W., *From Western Technology to Liberation Technology, Centre for Holistic Studies*, Bombay, 1990, pp.21–24.

120. Richards, P., *Indigenous African Revolution*, Hutchinson, London, 1985, p.64.

121. Jodha, N., "Intercropping in Traditional Farming Systems", *Proceedings of the International Workshop on Intercropping, 10–13 January 1979*, ICRISAT, Hyderabad, 1981. Cited in Marglin, S., *Farmers, Seedsmen and Scientists: Systems of Agriculture and Systems of Knowledge*, unpublished manuscript, Harvard, 1992.

122. Richards, P., op. cit. 120, p.70.

123. Ibid., p.64.

124. Goldsmith, E. and Hildyard, N., *The Social and Environmental Effects of Large Dams*, Sierra Club, San Francisco, 1984, pp.277–279.

References

125. Ibid., p.305.

126. Ibid., p.307 ff.

127. Rau, B., op. cit. 116, p.153

128. Ibid., p.23

129. Andrae, A. G. and Beckman, B., *The Wheat Trap*, Zed Books Ltd, London and New Jersey, 1985, p.95.

130. Stamp, P., *Technology, Gender and Power in Africa*, International Development Research Centre, Ottawa, 1989, p.68.

131. Ibid., p.70.

132. Andrae, A.G. and Beckman, B., op. cit. 129, p.140.

133. Pearce, F., "British Aid: A Hindrance as much as a Help", *New Scientist*, London, 23 May 1992, p.12.

134. UN Food and Agriculture Organization, *Technological Options and Requirements for Sustainable Agriculture and Rural Development*, Main Document 2, S'Hertogenbosch, 1991, p.5.

135. Norwegian Water Resources and Energy Administration, *Hydropower — Its potential and environmental properties in a global context: A report from an international symposium*, (Draft), Oslo, Norway, October 1991.

136. World Bank, op. cit. 4, p.93.

137. UN Food and Agriculture Organization, *Sustainable Crop Production and Protection: Background Document*, S'Hertogenbosch, 1991, p.2.

138. United Nations Conference on Environment and Development, *Science for Sustainable Development, Chapter 35 of Agenda 21: Technology Transfer*, Geneva, 1992, passim.

139. McCully, P., "The Case Against Climate Aid", *The Ecologist*, Vol. 21 No. 6, November/December 1991, p.248.

140. National Research Council, *Alternative Agriculture*, National Academy Press, 1989.

141. Kloppenburg, J. Jr., "Social Theory and the De/Reconstruction of Agricultural Science: Local Knowledge for an Alternative Agriculture", *Rural Sociology*, Vol. 56, No.4 , 1991, p.523.

142. World Bank, op. cit. 4, p.20.

143. Norman, D., "Rationalising Mixed Cropping Under Indigenous Conditions: The Example of Modern Nigeria", *Journal of Development Studies*, Vol.11, No.1, p.17. Cited in Marglin, S., op. cit. 121, p.31.

144. Burch, D., "Appropriate Technology for the Third World: Why the Will is Lacking", *The Ecologist*, Vol.12, No.2, March/ April 1982, p.56.

145. Southern Networks for Development (SONED), *SONED on UNCED: A Southern Perspective on the Environment and Development Crisis*, SONED, Geneva and Nairobi, 1991, pp.30–31.

146. Payer, C., *Lent and Lost: Foreign Credit and Third World Development*, Zed Books Ltd, London and New Jersey, 1991. p.117.

147. Forrest, R. A., "Japanese Aid and the Environment", *The Ecologist*, Vol.21, No.1, January/February 1991, p.26.

148. Payer, C., op. cit. 146, p.117.

149. Ibid., pp.115 and 116.

150. Ibid., p.124

151. Ibid., p.109.

152. Ibid., p.116.

RECLAIMING THE COMMONS

1. Silton, T., *Environmental Justice: Ideas for the Future*, unpublished ms., 1992, pp.13–14.
2. Scott, J. C., *Weapons of the Weak: Everyday forms of Peasant Resistance*, Yale University Press, New Haven and London, in collaboration with Department of Publications, University of Malaya, Kuala Lumpur, 1985.
3. Colchester, M., "Land Security and Sustainable Resource Use" in Colchester, M. and Lohmann, L. (eds.), *The Struggle for Land and the Fate of the Forests*, World Rainforest Movement, Penang/Zed Books Ltd, London and New Jersey (forthcoming).
4. Reyes, C., "Triumph of a Take-Over", *Panoscope*, May 1991, pp.18–19.
5. Comissão Pastoral da Terra, Conselho Indigenista Missionário, Central Unica dos Trabalhadores, Movimento dos Trabalhadores Rurais sem Terra, *Democracy: Heritage and Defense of Life and Nature*, Goiania, 1992.
6. Reyes, C., op. cit. 4.
7. Ekins, P., personal communication, July 1991.
8. Comissão Pastoral da Terra, Conselho Indigenista Missionário, Central Unica dos Trabalhadores, Movimento Sem–Terra, op. cit. 5.
9. Strange, M., *Family Farming: A New Economic Vision*, University of Nebraska Press and Institute of Food and Development Policy, London and San Fransisco, 1988, p.276.
10. Ibid., p.277.
11. Briefing prepared by Pambansang Lakas ng Kilusang Mamamalayakaya ng Pilipinas, P.O.Box 10223, Broadway Centrum, Quezon City, Philippines.
12. Philippine Rural Reconstruction Movement, *Bataan: A Case on Ecosystem Approach to Sustainable Development in the Philippines*, Quezon City, 1992, pp.55–70.
13. Austria, A. M., "Fishing for a Voice: Grassroots Organizing among Small Fisherfolk" in Meyer, C. and Moonsang, F.,(eds.), *Living with the Land: Communities Restoring the Earth*, The New Catalyst Bioregional Series, Philadelphia and Gabriola Island, 1992, p.121.
14. Kurien, J., "Ruining the Commons and Responses of the Commoners: Coastal Overfishing and Fishermen's Actions in Kerala State, India", *UNRISD Discussion Paper 23*, United Nations Research Institute for Social Development, May 1991, p.19.
15. Ibid., pp.26–27.
16. Sarmiento-Resebal, P., "Tribal Filipinos Practice Ecologically-Sound Farming", *Third World Network Feature*, 391/89.
17. Hobbelink, H., "Saving Potatoes in the Andes", *Seedling*, Vol. 8, No.1, February 1991, pp.8–11.
18. Rice, D., "Land Security, Self-Sufficiency and Cultural Integrity in the Philippines" in Friends of the Earth, *Rainforest Harvest*, Friends of the Earth, London, 1992.
19. Lohmann, L., "Who Defends Biological Diversity? Conservation Strategies and the Case of Thailand", *The Ecologist*, Vol.21, No.1, January/February 1991, p.10.
20. Rau, B., *From Feast to Famine: Official Cures and Grassroots Remedies to Africa's Food Crisis*, Zed Books Ltd, London and New Jersey, 1991, p.156.
21. Shiva, V., *Ecology and the Politics of Survival: Conflicts over Natural Resources in India*, Sage/United Nations University, New Delhi, 1991, pp. 269–270.
22. Cook, J., "Farm Fresh", *Harrowsmith Country Life*, May/June 1990, pp.53–57.
23. Personal communication from Robyn Van En, Indian Lines Farm, Mass., USA, September 1991.
24. Ibid.
25. *The Sieikatsu Club*, The Seikatsu Club Consumers Cooperative, Tokyo, 1988/1989.
26. Robyn Van En, op. cit., 23.
27. Groh, T. M. and MacFadden, S.H., *Farms of Tomorrow: Community supported farms, farm supported communities*, Bio-Dynamic Farming and Gardening Association, Kimberton, 1990, pp.6–7.
28. Colchester, M., op.cit. 3.

References

29. Agarwal, A. and Narain, S., *Towards Green Villages: A Strategy for Environmentally-sound and Participatory Rural Development*, Centre for Science and Environment, New Delhi, 1989, p.23.

30. Ibid., p.21.

31. Ibid., p.25.

32. Ibid., p.26.

33. Pierre, S., "Consensus Decision Making in Aboriginal Communities", *Forest Planning Canada*, Vol.8, No.3, May/June 1992, pp.5–6.

34. Freman, M., "Graphs and Gaffs: A Cautionary Tale in the Common-Property Resource Debate" in Berkes, F. (ed.), *Common Property Resources: Ecology and Community-Based Sustainable Development*, Belhaven Press, London, 1989, pp.92–109.

35. Scott, J.C., *Domination and the Arts of Resistance*, Yale University Press, New Haven, 1990.

36. Esteva, G., "Development: The Modernization of Poverty", *Panoscope*, November 1991, p.28.

A CONCLUDING REMARK

1. Raikes, P., *Modernizing Hunger*, Catholic Institute for International Relations, London, 1988, p.v.

INDEX

212

Index

greenhouse gases 105
Greenpeace USA 78
grilagem 44
Groh, Trauger 188
Guatemala 32, 136, 161
Gulf War 133
Guyana 84

Hainault Forest 26
Hall, Fielding 37
Harare 161
Hardin, Garrett 12, 13
Harrison, Paul 141
Harsud 176
Hecht, Susannah 45
Helm, Dieter 117, 125, 126
Higaonon resistance 178
high-income countries 104
Himalayas 18, 105, 172, 190
Hindustan Lever 55
Hobbelink, Henk 75
Hoechst 55, 75
human resources development 103
Human Resources Deployment Act
  (1983) 70
Hungary 110
hydropower systems 128, 129, 159,
  168, 176

ICP 76–7
ignorance 151–2, 159
Igorot peoples 42
Ikalahan people 184
Illich, Ivan 11, 60, 61, 68, 132, 140
IMF 21, 82, 83, 84, 167, 169
imports 26, 37
  liberalization 167; tariffs 84
'improvement' 23, 51
in vitro fertilization 69
income 104
  distribution 121, 165; guaranteed
  187
INCRA 178
India 26, 30–1, 55, 103, 104
  British rule in 21, 107; Centre for
  Science and Environment 190;
  contraception 148, 149; *gramdam*
  villages 190–91; industrialization
  38–9; Institute of Technology
  161; introduction of British
  contract law 35; *khadi* workshops
  28; local power 9; National
  Campaign for Housing Rights 49;
  nava dhanmyam (nine grains)
  practice 154; *panchayats* 186,
  189–90; population control
  programme 141–2; rice
  cultivation 99; water supply 61
  see also Bombay; Calcutta;
  Chipko movement; East India
  Company; Karnataka; Kerala;
  Ladakh; Maharashtra; Punjab;
  Rajasthan; Seed; Tehri
Indians
  Cherokee 27; Iroquois 37–8;
  subjugation of 32; Xavante 172–3
indigenous people 31, 32, 42
Indonesia 42, 45, 49, 77, 147, 167
  Transmigration Programme 134
industrialization 36, 38, 109, 110,

195
  commitment to 39; export-
  orientated 82; protest against the
  ravages of 86; waste products of
  89
infrastructure 86
  decline 53; improved 45;
  international aid for 84
institutions 78, 79, 134
intercropping 153–4, 157
interest groups 74, 80, 84
interests 39
  agrochemical 74–8, 85;
  commercial and industrial 87;
  industrial, research and training
  dominated by 76; private,
  intellectual property of 60; vested
  2, 79, 81
intermediate technology 162–3
international development agencies
  76
International Tropical Timber
  Organization 176
intervention 26, 34, 96, 116, 133
Iran 86, 154, 155
iriaichi 18
irrigation 66, 67, 124, 129, 155,
  156–8
  communal societies 10; local
  traditional system 100; *shadoof*
  157
IUDs 145, 147, 149

Jaakko Pöyry Oy 136
Japan 18, 42, 47, 167, 186, 188
Java 7, 45, 49, 134
Jodha, N S 154

Kalimantan 42, 49
Kalinga people 177
kampong 123
Kano River Irrigation Project 156–7
Karnataka State 176–7
Kenya 30–1, 50, 79, 143
Kenyatta, Jomo 50
Kerala 80, 81, 182–3
Kloppenburg, Jack 164
knowledge
  bureaucratization and enclosure of
  68; global, global management
  needs 130–2; local 68, 164;
  practical 193; systematic
  colonization of 166; traditional, of
  contraceptives 106; vernacular
  72–3, 155; reclaiming 183–6;
  women's 69
Kothari, Miloon 49–51
Krenak people 7
KSMTF 182, 183

Ladakh 105, 106
Lancashire 21, 28
land
  access to 14, 107; arable 8, 23;
  collectively owned 31; common
  24; conflicts 43–4; cultivated 31;
  degradation 16; demand to restore
  to the commons 85; disembedded
  59; enclosure 27–8, 61, 103;
  escalating prices 44; export

agricultural 40; expropriation 33,
  40; farm, idle 104; grazing 14–15,
  30; legal title to 30; ownership of
  31, 38, 40, 43, 54; prime
  agricultural 40; redefining, as
  property 23; reform 50, 85, 178;
  rights to 14, 30, 31, 35, 50;
  speculation 44–5; taken out of
  production 89; tenure 11, 24, 35,
  36; uncultivated 30; values 45
landgrabbing 40, 41, 43, 44
landless people 48–50, 70, 82, 103–
  4, 171
landowners 24, 25, 36, 44
language
  enclosure 71–3; imposition 193;
  local 126; religious 7; taught in
  state schools 7; *see also* dialects
Laos 7, 8, 19
large-scale investors 16
Latin America 85, 107
LDC (less developed countries) 82
Lepanto Mining 42
Levine, Dennis 79
livelihoods 6, 17, 29, 71, 80, 171
  dependence on corporations for
  43; deprived of 34; long-term 18;
  sustainable 2; threatened 182;
  undermining 38, 111
lobbying groups 76–7, 90
logging operations 2, 30, 89, 103,
  178
  concessions 59; illegal 172;
  sustainable 176
London 32, 58
Los Angeles 115, 175
Lovins, Amory 127
low-income countries 104, 110
Lubrizol 75
Luzon 182, 184

machinery 52
McNamara, Robert 103
Maharashtra 55, 186
Malaysia 8, 31, 123, 135
male dominance 36–8
Mali 43, 185
Malthus, T 105, 136
Manila 101
Manila Bay 180
Manila Paper Mills Inc 41
Maputo 28
Marcos regime 40, 41, 177, 180
Marglin, Stephen 72–3
markets 33–4, 38, 127–8
  absence of 117; control of 46, 80;
  distant 103; domestic 47, 167;
  enclosed 28, 54; encroachment of
  29, 55; export 47; external,
  demand for goods and services
  10; global, unstable 43; growing,
  of the North 111–12; local 54–5;
  only mode of social communication 63; reclaiming 186–8; timber,
  expanding 45; wool export 24
Marques Goulart, João 82
marriage
  and inheritance laws 37;
  monogamous, Christian 109;
  polygynous 106

Index